The Role of the Church
in New France

THE FRONTENAC LIBRARY
GENERAL EDITOR — Geoffrey Milburn
Althouse College of Education
University of Western Ontario

THE ROLE OF THE CHURCH IN NEW FRANCE

Cornelius J. Jaenen

McGRAW-HILL RYERSON LIMITED

Toronto   Montreal   New York   London   Sydney
Johannesburg   Mexico   Panama   Düsseldorf
Singapore   São Paulo   Kuala Lumpur   New Delhi   Auckland

Dedicated to my family
whose patience is limitless

THE ROLE OF THE CHURCH IN NEW FRANCE

Cover photo courtesy of L'Office du Film de la Province de Québec.

ISBN 0-07-082258-1

1 2 3 4 5 6 7 8 9 0 AP 5 4 3 2 1 0 9 8 7 6

Printed and bound in Canada

Contents

Foreword

In *The Role of the Church in New France* Dr. Jaenen assesses the two principal functions of that influential institution: the conversion of the Amerindians, and the maintenance of the Catholic faith in the French colony. The questions he puts to his evidence are important, and the answers he gives are clearly stated, perceptive and enlightening. He notes the interrelationship of religious and commercial forces in the Amerindian missions and comments on the effects of intercultural contacts on the development of the Church. He examines the part played by the Church in the political, social and economic life of the colony and explains how religious ideals were tempered by the realities of a frontier society. His assessments, based upon a detailed knowledge of the available primary sources, may do much to dispel some of the myths that have attached themselves to this period of history in both French- and English-speaking Canada.

Dr. Jaenen's book is also a fascinating example of the way in which a single study may throw light not only on a particular period in our past, but also, perhaps in an indirect fashion, upon our own time. Certain concerns such as the role of religious ideals in public decision-making, for example, or the means of coming to terms with different cultural groups within society, play as significant a part in our life, as they did on the banks of the St. Lawrence two hundred years ago. If we are to learn from our own experience, or even consult our memory, the historical record is our principal source. *The Role of the Church in New France*, therefore, may encourage us to reflect not only on an important aspect of Canadian history, but also on a number of persisting issues in our own society.

G. MILBURN
1 JUNE 1975

Introduction

Nowadays, the church is commonly regarded as a voluntary association of people corporately organized for the worship of God and the pursuit of religious objectives. In New France, a comprehensive term for the French area of colonization and exploration in North America which encompassed such regional units as Canada and Acadia, the Catholic Church was the exclusive institutional expression, at least after 1627, of the religious and spiritual life and activities of the colonial population.

In France, there was a historic bond between church and state dating from the first Capetian kings, if not earlier; so, in New France, conceived by some as a transplant of the metropolis, there developed as part of the seemingly natural evolution of an organized French colonial society a "state church" on the model common to all Western European societies, whether Protestant or Catholic, in the seventeenth century and, in many cases, throughout the eighteenth century. The pattern of social organization in religious matters which imposed itself in French North America, therefore, was approved and nourished both by the French hierarchy and Assembly of the Clergy, or the "church", and by the King, his Court and royal administration, or the "state". At the level of more immediate interventions by the Gallican Church, this metropolitan direction and support manifested itself in the activities of several religious institutes (e.g. Recollets, Jesuits, Capuchins, Ursulines, Hospitallers), of the seminaries of the secular clergy of the Foreign Missions at Quebec and the Sulpicians in Montreal, and of the semi-secret *dévot* network of the Company of the Holy Sacrament. The Vicariate Apostolic, created in 1659, was elevated to a diocese in 1674 with its Ordinary stationed at Quebec. At the level of immediate state control, responsibility was vested, after 1669, in the Ministry of Marine, to which the administrators of the *pays d'élection* of New France, centred in Quebec, reported. This was the rationalized framework within which spiritual development and religious expression operated.

For purposes of convenience, two parallel roles may be distinguished in the North American context. Firstly, there was a missionary church, which directed slight attention, initially, to visiting
fishermen and fur traders and to the native peoples with whom
they established contacts in the New World. However, as more
permanent commercial centres developed, the missionary clergy,
conscious of the vast possibilities for the conversion of aboriginal
peoples (the example of Spain before them) and conscious of a
Huguenot presence within the French Atlantic commercial expan-
sion, became more zealous in ministering to the needs of the relatively few Frenchmen who settled permanently in North America.
Even more attractive were the outlets for a new wave of religious
activism which characterized the French church in the early decades of the seventeenth century. Hopes of conversion of the
Amerindians offered possibilities for self-sacrifice, suffering and
even martyrdom to religious enthusiasts, not only among the militant Jesuits but also among the secular priests (who belonged to no
religious order or institute) and among religious women. The
growth of small towns and the slow development of agricultural
settlement, mostly along the St. Lawrence river line, gave rise to a
second role for the church — the transplanted institutional church
or the colonists' church. This colonial church, unlike the missionary church which operated simultaneously in the largely unorganized territory and stressed conversion to Catholicism, was intended to reproduce in New France the attitudes and activities
connected with civic and domestic life in Old France. These two
distinct roles, although pursued simultaneously by the one state
church, with which the King of France identified himself and his
administration, can conveniently be considered separately.

The church in New France was the creation of the metropolitan
Gallican Church, but never became its creature. During the first
half of the seventeenth century, the religious institutes were established in the New World on the basis of French bequests, nourished
by the generosity of pious men and women, especially wealthy
widows. The formal structures, including schools, hospitals,
poorhouses, seminaries, a cathedral chapter, an ecclesiastical court
and even a college, were all in place and functioning before the end
of the seventeenth century, and little was added in the ensuing
century. The missions to both the Amerindians and the unchurched *habitants* continued to be sustained by the religious congregations and seminaries of seculars who undertook them, while
the diocesan and parochial institutional church came to rely less on

wealthy benefactors while continuing to require substantial financial support from the Crown and royal administration. The secular clergy distinguished themselves from the regular clergy in the eighteenth century by an increasingly Canadian membership and by a growing dependence on internal or colonial revenues.

Francis Parkman set the pattern of interpretation of this period of history for several generations of historians, including surprisingly enough, a good proportion of present-day history students. The political role of the church and the influence of the bishop and of his clergy have been grossly exaggerated. Parkman concluded in his documented studies that a servile and superstitiously devout people were liberated by the British Conquest, that the "power of Rome" was at least limited, if not broken completely, and that a new climate favouring individualism and democratic liberty was henceforth obtained. Conversely, Parkman paid high tribute to the heroism and relative success of the Jesuit missionaries, to the cohesiveness of the over-extended aggressive French colony, and to the deep-seated loyalty and sense of identity of its people.

More recent writers on the role of the church in New France have obscured social and political realities by emphasizing the Jansenist and Quietist influences, by overplaying the struggles and misunderstandings between members of the clergy and state officials, by magnifying the possessions and supposed power of the religious estate, and by underestimating the independence, assertiveness and ingenuity of the Canadian *habitant*. The questions of political influence, economic strength, cultural conditioning, social service, and religious uniformity can readily be documented and defined. There remains, nevertheless, the less manageable and thus the more fascinating and perhaps more instructive area of religiosity with which to grapple. It is in examining indices of religious attitudes and beliefs, in analyzing behavioural patterns, in assessing the manners and morals of the colonial population, that a clearer picture emerges of the role of the church in New France.

In the light of these considerations, just as outmoded and unsound as the long-prevalent view of Papist domination and royal absolutist oppression propounded by Protestant-oriented writers are the equally long-prevalent views of French-Canadian Catholic writers. The latter have tended to see New France as a heroic age of virtuous patriotism, a Golden Age for the church which laid the foundations for national group survival following conquest at the hands of alien Protestants. In their frustrations with the present they have often tended to read their history backwards and to idealize their past. Unfortunately, these apologists were no closer to discerning the quality of religious life in the colony than were the partisans of the Parkman school. Reassuring themselves of their providential mission in the New World, they wrote primarily in a hagiographical context, often to promote causes of beatification and canonization of heroes and heroines of a romanticized age.

The time is ripe, therefore, for a more penetrating and constructive overview of the role of the Catholic Church during the French régime. This study cannot within the confines of the present series pretend to accomplish more than the outlining of the nature and directions of religious organization, belief, and practices. It is not intended to defend either of the polarized views in the spectrum of historical interpretations of this subject, nor is it intended to limit itself to a critique of these approaches.

CORNELIUS J. JAENEN
Ottawa, 1975

Part One:

The Missionary Church

Chapter I

Missionary Origins: 1541–1659

The French discoverers and explorers of the New World did not believe that their adventures were accidental or without previous Divine design. If France was given a share in the exploitation of the Americas, it was probably because there was an eternal and immutable purpose that the Amerindians should be brought the light of the Gospel. Jacques Cartier urged Francis I to patronize missionary enterprises designed to win the newly discovered "savage peoples living without a knowledge of God and the use of reason" to the Catholic Church. André Thévet was among the first to suggest that the natural primitiveness of the American aborigines augured well for missionary activity and that the church should undertake a dual mission of civilizing and Christianizing the natives. He wrote in 1555:

> America is inhabited by marvellously strange and savage people without faith, without laws, without religion, without any civilities, but living like unreasoning beasts as nature has produced them, eating roots, men as well as women remaining ever naked, until perhaps such time as they will little by little learn to put off this brutishness to put on more civil and humane ways.[1]

Antoine Biet, Claude d'Abbeville and Samuel de Champlain by their writings at the beginning of the following century would perpetuate this initial belief that the brutish savages had "neither faith nor any shadow of religion", therefore their social organization was defective, yet receptive to Catholicism which they ignored but did not oppose.

The first missionaries to the natives were chaplains who accompanied the fishing and fur trading vessels from the French Atlantic ports. They requested letters of provision, or faculties, from the Ordinaries of the ports from which they sailed in order to give themselves some legitimate authority. Members of religious orders or institutes found it easier to undertake missionary work in new regions than did the secular clergy because the Generals of their orders usually had authority from the Holy See to engage in such activity. The chaplains, for example, who accompanied the Cartier expedition of 1535, Dom Guillaume Le Breton and Dom Anthoine, were likely Benedictines. Although the Pope held universal jurisdiction, and heathen lands fell under his direct charge, no institution existed in Rome prior to the creation of the *Propaganda Fide* in 1622 to control and coordinate foreign missions in unorganized areas such as New France. When Fathers Pierre Biard and Ennemond Massé sailed for Port Royal in 1611, they went under the general authorization of the mission powers granted by the Pope to the Jesuit General. In 1615 Champlain obtained four Recollet missionaries for the St. Lawrence valley region of Canada. The two priests from the Province of Aquitaine, which he and the controller-general of the salt works at Brouage had requested, were opposed by their Recollet brethren from the province of Paris and were replaced. The rivalry between the two Recollet provinces was temporarily resolved "in this country of Canada" by the letters-patent granted by Louis XIII on June 14, 1618, which stipulated that "no other Recollet religious may go, unless it be through the obedience granted them by the said provincial or of the said province of Saint-Denis in France."[2]

In June 1620 the Recollets laid the foundations of their monastery at Notre-Dame des Anges, near Quebec. At the first general assembly of the clergy held in Canada, at which Champlain and six other laymen were present, a four-point program was adopted for the missionary church. This program called for: French-type village settlements, agricultural resettlement of select Amerindian bands, construction of a "seminary" for the education of Amerindian youth, and exclusion of all Huguenots from the colony.[3] During the fifteen years of initial missionary work, the Recollets sent ten priests and eight lay brothers to the colony. It soon became evident to them that the slow pace of progress would not bring about the millenial kingdom in the New World which they had dreamed of creating among the sedentary Huron tribes. Their mission among the Montagnais was even less encouraging. Speculations that the Amerindians were descendants of the Ten Lost Tribes of Israel, that the discovery of the New World heralded the advent of the Third Age of the Holy Ghost spoken of by the mystics since the twelfth century, and that the rapid conversion of the Amerindians would result in the restoration of the church to its

Apostolic purity preceding the end of the world, and of the Parousia, or second advent of Christ, were severely shaken.

In 1625 the Jesuits joined the Recollets in Canada. The latter soon had some misgivings about sharing their apostolic labours with a competing religious institute and the merchants, especially the Huguenots, openly opposed the disciples of Loyola. The raids of the five Kirke brothers and the English occupation of Quebec from 1629 to 1632 forced the abandonment of the missions.

Fortunes were no better in Acadia. Four Recollets from the province of Aquitaine had come to Acadia in 1619 at the invitation of merchants from Bordeaux and provided with letters of authority from the Archbishop of Bordeaux. Their mission was a failure for a number of unrelated reasons: Father Sebastien Bernardin perished while on a missionary journey; the association of Bordeaux merchants which had sustained their enterprise was dissolved in 1623; and Acadia fell into Scottish hands in 1624. The three surviving Recollets from Aquitaine fled by the overland route to Quebec to join their brethren from Paris, but they were disappointed and were forced to return to France the following year.[4]

In 1630 the Company of New France (One Hundred Associates), created by Cardinal Richelieu for the commercial exploitation, civil administration, settlement and evangelization of New France, sent two more Recollets of the province of Aquitaine with the supply fleet of a Captain Bertrand Marot to take charge of spiritual affairs at Cape Sable in Acadia, which Charles de La Tour was still holding for France. They were the only missionaries left in the whole of New France — both Canada and Acadia — when the colony was officially restored to France in 1632. Be that as it may, Cardinal Richelieu did not intend to grant them any special privileges because his influential confessor, Father Joseph Leclerc du Tremblay, better known as the "grey eminence", convinced him to assign the restored colony to the Capuchins, another branch of the Franciscans, as their mission field. This plan had the support of the Propaganda in Rome which wished to withdraw as much as possible the foreign missions from the jurisdiction and control of the Superiors of the exempt religious orders. In this case, the Propaganda had assigned wide prerogatives to Father Joseph as prefect of missions rather than assigning the jurisdictional powers to the superior of the Capuchins. But Richelieu's decision was not enforced because the Recollets already in Acadia refused to leave and the Jesuits, armed with provisions from their General, immediately returned to Canada at the restoration. In this way the

Recollet–Capuchin rivalry and the Jesuit–Capuchin confrontation took on the quality of a struggle between missionaries commissioned by the Propaganda in Rome and missionaries commissioned by exempt religious orders. The Recollets could have pushed political intrigues to their advantage had they known at the time that the Capuchin letters of provision were extensions of faculties granted by the Propaganda for missionary work in New England.[5]

The Capuchin mission had an encouraging beginning. Six religious accompanied Governor de Razilly to Port Royal and within a few years mission stations were established at Port Royal, Rivière St. Jean, Canseau, St. Pierre, Nipisiguit, Kennebec, and Pentagouet. The distinguished humanist, Nicolas de Peiresc, who carried on an extensive correspondence with members of the order, reported on the apparent success of the enterprise:

> I experienced a great consolation upon hearing of the favourable success of the new missions of Canada where they have acquired so much credence and I look forward to much fruit there with God's blessing.[6]

Reverses, however, began to plague them in 1635. First they lost three missionaries bound from La Rochelle to Acadia. Then, the death of their protector, the Governor Claude de Razilly, resulted in a prolonged struggle for power between Charles d'Aulnay and Charles de La Tour. This so disturbed the political scene that the missionaries had reason to complain that La Tour connived with the New England corsairs to ruin their missions. The situation became so unsettled that Father Côme de Mantes returned to France to attempt to obtain a firmer basis of support for the Capuchin mission. Then, in 1638, Father Joseph, their prefect and chief advocate in the Court circles, died. The Propaganda sought to retain a distinction between missionary authority and religious authority within the order but the Capuchin superior resisted the attempt to diminish his powers. The acrimonious quarrel which resulted was adjudicated by Louis XIII who asked the Propaganda to assign the prefecture of missions in each case to the Provincials in order to avoid jurisdictional disputes.

The rivalry between d'Aulnay and La Tour grew into armed conflict and the Capuchins reported that both were supported by Protestant suppliers, the former by Emmanuel Le Borgne, an ambitious Huguenot entrepreneur from La Rochelle, and the latter by Bostonians. All eight remaining missionaries had asked to be repatriated, but in 1643 four were recalled to France for unspecified misdemeanours. In the following year, d'Aulnay with support from Le Borgne sent a secret emissary known only as Sieur Marie, widely believed to have been a Capuchin in disguise, to Boston to protest against the assistance being offered to La Tour. At this juncture, the two Recollets at Fort St. Jean, who had been protected by La Tour, found him unbearable. They excommunicated him, then fled to join their Capuchin rivals at Port Royal. They returned to France the same year, thus bringing to a close the mission of the Recollets of Aquitaine to Acadia.

In 1650 d'Aulnay died and the Capuchins buried their syndic with great pomp in their chapel at Port Royal, pondering no doubt on their uncertain future. Two years later Le Borgne reappeared on the scene to worry them — indeed, two priests were ordered back to France, the others took to the woods to live with the Amerindians, and Father Léonard de Chartres stayed at Port Royal to protect their property. In 1653 he presided at the wedding of d'Aulnay's widow to Charles de La Tour, a union which terminated the long and bitter rivalry between the two political factions. But disaster struck again in 1654 when Puritan merchant Robert Sedgwick overran the Acadian posts. De Chartres countersigned the articles of capitulation of Port Royal in which he succeeded in having included a guarantee of complete religious freedom for the missionaries.[7] Nevertheless, the Capuchins were all forced to leave by 1655, except de Chartres who was apparently murdered shortly afterwards by Cromwellian soldiers. Nicolas Denys, who held a royal charter for the exploitation of the Gulf of St. Lawrence region, had replaced the three last Capuchins there by "three Jesuits and a secular" in 1658.[8] Father Ignace de Paris made valiant efforts to interest the French court in a renewal of the mission, but even the Propaganda ruled out the possibility and considered instead sending out two Oratorian priests. Thus terminated the first mission authorized by the Propaganda in New France; its religious had not fared well at the hands of the economic exploiters who sought to establish their administrative authority.

Although Richelieu had assigned Canada to the Capuchins in 1632, he had accepted the rapid return to Quebec of the Jesuits as a *fait accompli*. Not only were the Jesuits highly recommended by the "sanctimonious clique" of the Company of the Holy Sacrament, a secret society of *dévots* with cells throughout the realm who were organized to promote high religious ideals in public and private life alike, but they were supported by Jean de Lauzon of the Company of New France, which held the charter rights of the colony. Although the Propaganda officially approved resumption by the Recollets of their former mission in Canada in 1635, the trade monopolists and the Jesuits were agreed on excluding them for the moment. The Jesuits, in fact, were installed in the former Recollet monastery near Quebec. They enjoyed all the temporal assistance that was directed to the Canadian missions, they were able to influence the civil officers to punish harshly such misdemeanors as blasphemy and drunkenness, and they acquired choice lands around Quebec, Trois-Rivières, Tadoussac, and near Montreal. They were on friendly terms with a number of the chief *habitants*, an emerging "aristocracy of the beaver", whose power was institutionalized in the Community of Habitants in 1645, a monopoly which the Jesuits supported at Court. Thus were laid foundations of their enduring missionary enterprise.

Their position in New France was further consolidated when they established themselves as the chief teachers of the boys — this representing a departure from their usual pattern of offering only secondary and advanced level studies in France. Both the Ursulines and the Hospital Nuns sought their spiritual advisors among the Jesuits. Furthermore, several of the first parishes in the colony — notably Montreal before the arrival of the Sulpician seculars — were served by Jesuits. They were a disciplined and cohesive group whose members were carefully selected and rigorously trained to be a spiritual elite in the church. There is record of only one person, an obscure Jean François Elie who, in 1667, left the Society of Jesus and hastened away, almost secretly, after casting off his priestly habits.[9] In their Huron missions patterned after a successful Paraguayan model, they expected to receive free lodgings and food but they soon found that the natives demanded payment for work done, and generous gifts were required to keep their hearers attentive to their message. Their most ardent supporter was Bishop Laval, himself the product of a Jesuit college. They were able to extend their missionary activity rapidly to Cape Breton, the Gulf of St. Lawrence, the Iroquois country, the Tadoussac and Lake St. Jean area, the Abenakis country, and the Far West including Lake Superior and the Illinois country. Finally, they penetrated into the Hudson Bay region where they encountered the English.

In 1642 Jérôme de la Dauversière, the Baron de Faucamp and the *Abbé* J. J. Olier were instrumental in founding the Society of Notre-Dame for the colonization of the island of Montreal and the evangelization of the Amerindians. Olier, who was an influential member of the semi-secret Company of the Holy Sacrament, whose network he employed to bring together individuals who were willing to support colonization and missionary work in Canada, also brought together a number of secular priests into a seminary in Paris. In 1657 the first Sulpician clergy came to the colony to establish their apostolic labours; since they were not an exempt order or institute they could not receive faculties or provisions from their Superior, therefore they turned to the Archbishop of Rouen for the necessary authorization. The archbishop was quite anxious to give them their letters of authority because it tended to confirm his claims that New France fell under his jurisdiction, paralleling the rather vague concept at that time that the colony came under the jurisdiction in civil matters of the Parlement of Normandy. Montreal did not prove to be a useful mission station for those interested in the conversion of the natives, so in 1663 the seigneury of the island passed to the Sulpicians who shortly thereafter established missions in the western interior and organized a reservation near the town.

Both the Jesuits and Sulpicians were greatly assisted in their evangelical labours by communities of religious women. One of the outstanding characteristics of the Canadian experience was that women's communities were given an opportunity to play a significant role on the mission field. Although there was never any question of the cloistered nuns establishing themselves in the native villages or encampments, they were on the "frontier" in the two major towns and exercised their ministry of teaching and healing among the aborigines and colonists. The first contacts of the Ursulines with New France came as a result of the mystical experiences of Mother Marie de l'Incarnation, a cloistered nun at the Tours convent, who in 1633 and in 1635 had prophetic visions of an apostolate in the New World. While Marie de l'Incarnation was pressing the unprecedented case of women labourers or assistants in the foreign mission field, the Ursulines at Tours received their first Acadian novice, the daughter of Saint-Etienne de La Tour and his native wife, brought to France by Razilly. The following year, her younger sister was received at the abbey of Beaumont-les-Tours.[10] Following upon the reading of the Jesuit *Relations* (the great propaganda pieces of the day), correspondence with Father Paul Le Jeune of the Canadian mission, conversations with other missionaries, and a close spiritual fellowship with her spiritual director who was interested in the foreign missions, she planned the founding of a convent at Quebec.

The Ursulines were officially welcomed at Quebec in 1639 by Governor Montmagny, who also examined their letters of authority from the Archbishop of Tours. Not until the spring of 1641 were they able to lay the cornerstone on land granted to them by the Company of New France for a monastery which Mme. de la Peltrie, their benefactress, had built for them. In Quebec they decided to offer both the elitist education for daughters of the upper classes and the primary education which they gave to the children of the poor. Within one week of their arrival they had six Amerindian girls to educate but no facilities to operate a school. Mother Marie de l'Incarnation summed up their needs and aspirations:

> If the poor of France sometimes bring tears to one's eyes, I can assure you that the sight of our poor Savages would make your heart bleed, if you could see them as we do, in need of instruction for their souls and of everything else for the maintenance of their lives.[11]

The basic problem facing the Ursulines was inadequate financial resources for the execution of the work envisaged. At the very time that the fires of religious revivalism burned lower in Old France and charitable donations dwindled, in New France hundreds of persecuted Amerindian refugees, some ridden with disease and infections introduced by the French, came seeking relief.

On the other hand, in spite of their precarious financial situation during the early decades of their work in Canada, their numbers increased steadily. In 1640 two Ursulines from Paris had joined the first contingent, in 1641 five more from Ploermel, Dieppe and Tours, and in 1671 the last contingent from France consisting of two nuns from Paris and two from Bourges arrived. To these eighteen nuns from four different houses in France, each of which had its own distinctive constitution to which the sisters were much attached, were soon added two candidates from the colony, in 1646 and 1648 respectively. Hopes of attracting Amerindian novices proved ephemeral, however; two young girls raised with such a design died at a young age.[12]

In 1639 a hospital was founded at Quebec by three sisters of the Hospital Nuns of Dieppe. Their benefactress, a niece of Cardinal Richelieu, was the Duchess d'Aiguillon, whose philanthropic contributions had improved the lots of condemned Frenchmen, converted African slaves and Chinese beggars. She had been influenced to support this new enterprise by the Jesuit missionary Paul

Le Jeune and a Carmelite nun whose uncle, Brulart de Sillery, financed the first "reservation" in Canada. Another niece of Cardinal Richelieu, Mme. Claude de Bullion, widowed in 1640 and bequeathed an immense fortune, provided important revenues for the establishment of the hospital. The Hospital Nuns had letters of authority from the Archbishop of Rouen, and upon arrival at Quebec were almost immediately at work because an epidemic was raging in the colony.

They agreed to open their first hospital at the "reservation" at Sillery, not in the town of Quebec. This reserve had been created in 1637 as a segregated re-settlement project for Amerindians, with the specific objective of promoting both their evangelization and their assimilation. Two more recruits arrived from France in 1640, at which time they decided to expand their work to include a school for Amerindian girls and a few French girls at Sillery. They soon found the costs of operating the school and hospital extremely high, and concluded that they were not fulfilling their religious vocation in the colony by remaining outside the chief town; they decided in 1646 — in spite of Jesuit protests — to establish themselves in Quebec, where their hospital would serve as a military and naval hospital, and the pay of the officers and soldiers treated there would help defray expenses. In 1646 they received their first Canadian novice, a gain which was somewhat offset in 1649 by the return to Dieppe of two dissatisfied nuns. Their work received a brief encouragement in 1656 when a young Huron girl, Geneviève Skannd'haron, was received into their community and two days later, just prior to her death, was permitted to pronounce her final vows.

Montreal also had its hospital. In 1641, Jeanne Mance heard of the mission work in Canada from members of the Company of the Holy Sacrament. She sailed to Quebec, spent the winter at the reservation at Sillery with Mme. de la Peltrie and Maisonneuve, then went on to Montreal the following spring to open a small hospital near the fort. Following an injury in 1657, she contemplated closing her clinic in order to seek medical treatment in France. The *Abbé* de Queylus brought two of the Hospital Nuns from Quebec to manage the small dispensary during her absence. Jeanne Mance returned in 1659, miraculously healed of her infirmity through the supposed intervention of Monsieur Olier, founder of the Sulpicians, and accompanied by three Hospital Nuns of La Flèche. Bishop Laval would have preferred to see all the hospitals operated by one order of religious but the Hospitallers of St.

Joseph (La Flèche) held out against pressures to turn their work over to the Hospital Nuns of Dieppe and were strongly supported by the pious founders of Montreal and the Company of New France.

Not all the women's communities were regularly constituted religous orders. The Ursulines and both communities of Hospital Nuns had all begun as secular communities of devout laywomen. In 1653 a secular association of devout women, known commonly as the Sisters of the Congregation, undertook a ministry of teaching in Montreal under the guidance of Marguerite Bourgeoys. They soon patterned themselves on the Sisters of Charity, a movement initiated by St. Vincent de Paul to encourage simple, frugal, tough "country girls" to dedicate themselves to the service of the unfortunate and to go from village to village in France teaching the poorest children the little they themselves knew. She described the humble beginnings of her work in these words:

> ... four years after my arrival Monsieur de Maisonneuve wanted to give me a stone stable to make a house to lodge those who would teach school. I had a chimney built and what was necessary in order to lodge the children there.[13]

This project became involved with caring for the needy, a kindergarten and a nursery school, and a study circle for adolescent brides. The task was soon too great for Jeanne Mance and her part-time assistant, Marguerite Picard, so she went to France to recruit young women to assist in her missionary enterprise. Three of the young women she recruited were of middle-class background and prepared to take charge of a *petite école* there in 1670. Their work was highly appreciated, and popular requests for *petites écoles* in the developing parishes resulted in the formal authentication by the Bishop of their congregation for service restricted to New France. Already the missionary church had given birth to its first religious congregation.

The greatest threat to the missionary beginnings seemed to be the presence of Huguenots in New France. One of the persistent myths about French colonization is the belief that if Protestants had been afforded the opportunity to settle in the Americas, they would have helped resolve the problem of religious diversity in France and would have established industries and commerce in New France which would assure the prosperity of both the metropolis and the colony. Actually, the Huguenots were involved in abortive colonization schemes in Canada in 1541, in Brazil in 1555 and in the

Carolinas in 1562. This disappointing experience only increased their reluctance to emigrate and confirmed their inclination to restrict their colonial involvement to trade, shipping, investment, insurance and supplying.

The Huguenots continued to be involved in the exploitation of the Newfoundland fisheries and the development of a Canadian fur trade. These did not require any extensive immigration. The letters-patent of Henry III to Jacques Cartier's nephews, Jacques Noël and Etienne Chaton, in 1588 did stipulate that only the Catholic religion was to be implanted in Canada where they received a trade monopoly. In 1599 Huguenot participation in the exploitation of New France was considerably enhanced by Pierre de Chauvin de Tonnetuit who obtained a trade monopoly from Henry IV for the entrance of the St. Lawrence River, an area in which he had been involved in both the fur trade and fishery for at least three years. In 1600 he left Honfleur where he had been an officer in the important Huguenot garrison, came to New France, accompanied by Pierre Du Gua de Monts, another Protestant officer of the same garrison, and founded a trading post at Tadoussac. Champlain later complained that Henry IV, by giving a trade monopoly to "a man of contrary religion", had compromised the proper propagation of Catholicism among the natives who came to Tadoussac because the Huguenots held Catholicism "in horror and abomination".

De Monts brought two Catholic missionaries to Acadia, according to the terms imposed on him by his charter, but he also brought a Protestant pastor, and a large proportion of his crews were Huguenots. The Edict of Nantes of 1598 did not specifically extend toleration to the colony, but nevertheless, the maritime practice of making sea captains responsible for the spiritual care of their crews enabled Huguenots to provide themselves with Protestant chaplains who held religious services on board their vessels. Champlain, who accompanied De Mont's 1604 expedition, was not impressed by the joint Huguenot-Catholic ventures. He wrote:

> . . . two religions are never a great fruit for the glory of God. I saw the minister and our priest fight each other with their fists about religious differences: I do not know which was the better fighter; but I know that the minister complained sometimes about having been beaten, for so they settled their points of controversy. I leave it to you to decide if that was edifying to witness. The savages are sometimes on one side,

then on the other side, and the French became involved according to their own beliefs.[14]

Champlain credited De Monts with attempting to keep harmony in the expedition and not favouring those of his own religious persuasion. When an epidemic carried off both the Catholic priest and Protestant pastor, the irreverent sailors buried them in a common grave, allegedly "to see if in death they would remain at peace, since during their lifetime they had been unable to agree."[15] Skepticism and lack of respect for religion disturbed men like Champlain and evoked bitter criticism from the Recollet missionaries.

An anonymous memorandum was sent to the Court requesting the establishment of Catholic missions entrusted to a religious institute which could assure a regular supply of missionaries and could underwrite the financial obligations of such a program. The main arguments for the proposal were fourfold: firstly, since the lieutenant-general was a Huguenot, it was not to be expected that he would actively promote Catholic missionary activity; secondly, New France would have a supply of Protestant pastors who would supplant the Catholic priests; thirdly, there would be rivalry between the two religious confessions in the colony and the Catholics might suffer most from such confrontations overseas; fourthly, there would be a variety of obstructions posed to Catholic practices if the Huguenots continued to exercise paramount influence.

> For a Catholic, were he the stronger, would not wish to tolerate the exercise of Huguenotism, so much less would a Huguenot endure the free exercise of the Catholic religion, seeing himself lord and sovereign of the place, not bothering much about the King's will, were it not favourable to him . . .[16]

A few Catholics were inclined to be somewhat more tolerant than the aforementioned petitioner. Marc Lescarbot, for example, did not believe Protestant preaching was without merit, especially because it was difficult "for mortals to lead all men into the same opinion", and he found that Huguenots were not without interest in evangelizing the Amerindians. He informed his compatriots:

> I will say that it is a shame to our religion that the Protestant Ministers of La Rochelle pray to God daily in their meetings for the conversion of these poor savage tribes, and also for our own safety, and that our Churchmen do not the like.[17]

On the other hand, the Protestants could on occasion be aggressive too. They opposed the transporting of the first Jesuit missionaries to Acadia, forcing the wealthy Marquise de Guercheville to buy a controlling interest in a vessel and enter into a commercial pact with the Jesuits, in order to secure their passage to the New World. In 1615 the Huguenots at both Honfleur and Tadoussac sought to dissuade the Recollet missionaries bound for Canada from continuing on their mission. To add to their feeling of being unwanted, the seamen sang their "songs of Marot" very loudly whenever the priests tried to say mass. Each year from 1616 to 1621 Recollet missionaries returned to France to lay complaints against the Protestant merchants and seamen.

Eventually, on August 18, 1621, an assembly was held at the Recollet headquarters at Notre-Dame-des-Anges to discuss ways and means "to conserve the Catholic Apostolic and Roman religion in its entirety, the authority of King inviolate, and also the obedience due to the said lord, the Viceroy". Three weeks later, Father Le Baillif sailed for France with a formal petition to Louis XIII, with whom he obtained two audiences, for the purpose of expounding his views on the proper conduct of commerce and colonization in New France. Le Baillif presented nine requests to the King, among them the following: assurance against attack from foreign powers; construction of a fort at Quebec; prohibition of Huguenots' furnishing arms to the Amerindians; settlement of the rivalry between two groups of merchants interested in the fur trade of the colony; establishment of firmer policing in the colony; founding of a "seminary" near Quebec for native children; and, an increase in the powers and emoluments of Champlain. This strong demand for the exclusion of the Huguenots and the breaking up of joint Catholic-Protestant enterprises came at a period when such commercial ventures were causing many quarrels and legal battles in France.[18]

The Jesuits added their voices to the Recollet complaints after 1625 when the anti-Jesuit pamphlet, the *Anti-Coton*, was reportedly "circulated from chamber to chamber". The following year, Father Philibert Noyrot was sent to France to inform the Court that no effective colonization or evangelization would be accomplished "so long as the control of the trade remains in the hands of Calvinists". He told the Court that these "fanatical heretics" blocked all the efforts of their traditional enemies the Jesuits, that they "distilled into the minds of the savages no respect for the sacred mysteries", that they opposed colonization as supposedly ruinous for their fur trade, and that quarrelling and dissension were rife among them.[19]

Cardinal Richelieu became a member of the Council of State in 1624, and in 1627 he became the superintendent of the navy and began to move to suppress the Protestant participation in the development of New France. He moved against La Rochelle itself, one of the chief sources of Protestant backing for commercial activities in New France (One Hundred Associates), and he restricted settlement to "natural-born French Catholics" thus eliminating both Protestants and naturalized foreigners. This move reflected a growing concern at the close co-operation between the Huguenots and the Dutch commercialists on the one hand, and the increasingly significant group of Huguenots and Walloon Protestants settling in New England and in New Netherland.

The restoration of Quebec to France in 1632, following a brief English occupation, included no recognition of Huguenotism in the colony. Therefore, the fact that Protestants possessed no schools, no literature, no pastors, no public exercise of their religion, no immigration to reinforce their ranks, and no support from state authorities, seemed to mean their eventual absorption by the Catholic majority. In France, the Company of the Holy Sacrament mounted an effective campaign against the dissentients. Throughout the 1640s and 1650s in Canada the Huguenots and Dutch maintained their commercial activities, while the missionaries, notably the Jesuits, ably assisted in time by the Hospital Nuns, sought out suspected and known Huguenots and attempted to obtain formal abjurations of heresy from them. The numbers who converted, also known Protestants who were confirmed by the Bishop when he arrived in 1659, indicated the appreciable role they had played in early colonization. There were Huguenots who resisted pressures to convert or who succeeded so effectively in "living as Catholics without causing scandal" that they escaped detection. Among the suspects ferreted out was an apostate Benedictine monk, "who had converted at La Rochelle", and who in New France had "pretended to wish to become a heretic again". In Acadia the Protestant merchant Emmanuel Le Borgne drove some of the Catholic missionaries out of the colony, but at Quebec, Dutch and Huguenot merchant firms continued to supply both the Community of Habitants and the Jesuit missions. All in all, by 1659 any Protestant threat to Catholic ascendancy had been eliminated; there were no indications that much toleration would be accorded the Huguenot minority.

Although the French Court was concerned about the Protestant problem in the colony, the Roman Curia was more concerned about the jurisdictional problems involved in the transatlantic activities of the French clergy. Technically, so long as the North American missions were without a bishopric the missionary church came under the direct jurisdiction of the Holy See, and, after 1622, more specifically under the jurisdiction of the Sacred Congregation for the Propagation of the Faith. The problem was to assert this jurisdiction in the face of strong Gallican sentiments, or how to integrate a missionary region into the Gallican Church. Presumably, if a bishopric were created in the New World, dependent upon a French archbishopric, then the colony would be integrated effectively into the Gallican fold, or so it appeared.

The need on the part of the clergy for authority could give rise to an inordinate overseas extension of the jurisdiction of the French dioceses. In 1649, according to Marie de l'Incarnation, the first incumbent of the newly created diocese of La Rochelle, Jacques de la Guiborgère, claimed jurisdiction over New France.

> M. de La Rochelle, uncle of Mother Saint-Joseph, told her that he is our bishop because according to law lands newly converted pertain to the nearest bishop. We were told that in Rome they wanted to grant him the responsibility for this nascent church in the erection of his new bishopric, but that he did not want to accept it for fear that he be obliged to visit it. Time will tell what God has preordained.[20]

The obvious alternative to the extension of port authority was the creation of a Canadian diocese.

The solution was first suggested by the Secretary of the Propaganda in 1631. Ingoli recommended the appointment of one of the Recollet missionaries as bishop "who living without ceremony among his comrades would subsist on alms while awaiting a pension from the King, or a simple benefice" befitting the Ordinary of a missionary diocese. The Recollets were not interested at the time in such a plan. In 1634, the Propaganda again suggested the creation of a diocese in New France and suggested a Recollet of the province of Aquitaine as first incumbent, but the Recollets of Paris who had laboured in Canada opposed the plan. The arrival of the Montreal colony in 1642, many of whose members were closely associated with the movement for spiritual renewal in France, added new strength to the demand for a bishopric. In 1643, the Montreal associates wrote to the Holy See suggesting Father Thomas LeGauffre as a suitable candidate because he was intimately associated with the activities of the Company of the Holy Sacrament in France and was acceptable to the Jesuits who were now responsible for Amerindian missionary work in Canada. Cardinal Mazarin and the Assembly of the French Clergy were prepared to submit LeGauffre's name to the King for his formal nomination, according to the long-standing customs of the realm whereby the King nominated the bishops. However, the plan foundered again when the Jesuits began to have second thoughts about the proposal, and then LeGauffre died suddenly. Marie de l'Incarnation wrote her son in 1646:

> They speak of giving us a bishop in Canada; I do not know if you know how this went in France. Last year, M. LeGauffre, person of eminent piety, gave in alms the sum of thirty thousand pounds for the founding of the bishopric. Those into whose hands he gave this amount believed there was no one more worthy of this dignity than he . . . this great servant of God suspected nothing for he was an extraordinarily humble man; also he would not agree to the proposal which was made to him except after a retreat to prepare him to ascertain God's will and to ask his director's advice. During this time of preparation he was seized by apoplexy which carried him off in three days; thus the will of God was made known and the plan disrupted. As for me, my sentiment is that God does not want a bishop in Canada, the country is not sufficiently developed, and our Reverent Fathers having planted Christianity here, it seems necessary that they should cultivate it for some time to come without anyone contradicting them in their views.[21]

Yet it was precisely because the Jesuits exercised a virtual monopoly in Canada, that it seemed necessary to have a clear definition of jurisdiction.

Ironically, it was also the establishment of Ursulines in the colony that raised questions of ecclesiastical jurisdiction. There was some uncertainty whether the Jesuits could receive their professions and there was some uncertainty about the validity of marriages performed in the colony. Therefore, in addition to the provisions granted by the General, they sought faculties from the Propaganda, and made overtures to the Archbishop of Rouen, who was regarded in many quarters as exercising ecclesiastical jurisdiction over New France.

Father Vimont having consulted Rome, the leading Fathers of our Company at the *maison-professe* and the college, the consensus was that it was necessary to apply to and attach ourselves to M. de Rouen. Father Vimont spoke to Father Pingeolot then rector of the college at Rouen by whose favour and assistance he obtained from the Archbishop of Rouen, the elder, letters of grand vicars; which they brought here with the letters and resolutions of all our fathers confirming the matters aforementioned, we proceeded with assurance to receive the professions of the religious. We did not judge it expedient nevertheless to make much issue beyond this.[22]

The Jesuits, intent on upholding the privileges of an exempt order, did not divulge their double game until 1653.

They were not without interest in having one of their own society named to the episcopal see. In 1639, Father Charles Lalement, who favoured a diocese suffragan to Paris, wrote of the need for a bishop to administer confirmation and ordain clergy if the church of the New World were to grow to full stature. The names of Charles Lalemant, Paul Le Jeune and Paul Ragueneau were presented for consideration to the appropriate intermediaries in Paris and Rome, but the Company of New France, which exercised political jurisdiction over the colony, recommended only Lalemant to the King. The Company of New France claimed that the colony required a bishop to oversee the spiritual welfare of an estimated 20,000 converted natives and about 3,000 French colonists, and to supervise the labours of an estimated 50 Jesuits, 10 Capuchins and 4 secular priests. Their statistics were inflated, of course, but more realistic in view of growing Amerindian hostility in Canada, was the suggestion that the episcopal see be located at Quebec "where is located the fortress in which the Bishop could take refuge in times of persecution". This proposal ran into two roadblocks. Firstly, the General of the society in Rome informed the directors of the Company of New France that a Jesuit was prohibited by the special vows he took from assuming the episcopal dignity. Secondly, the Montreal community, which had not been consulted, countered with a suggestion that the bishopric be established in Montreal, not in Quebec.

The Montreal community was anxious to have the Sulpicians assume the charge of their spiritual care, the seigneurial rights of the island, and the development of Amerindian missions. Since the secular clergy of St. Sulpice were concerned about the validity of their provisions it would be a distinct advantage to have one of their own community named to the episcopal chair. Eventually, two candidates were proposed in France; the *Abbé* Gabriel Queylus, who was supported by the Montreal community and Cardinal Mazarin, and the *Abbé* Francois de Laval, backed by the Queen Mother, the Jesuits and the clergy associated with the Hermitage of Caen, a cell of the Company of the Holy Sacrament. Early in 1657, Louis XIV communicated with Pope Alexander VII nominating Laval to the bishopric to be created in New France. Negotiations in Rome extended over many months and finally it was decided to organize New France into a Vicariate Apostolic with Laval as titular bishop of a diocese in Arabia which had fallen to Islam, postponing the creation of a North American diocese until such time as "the country will show itself capable of maintaining one". Louis XIV was willing to accept this arrangement provided the incumbent would exercise his episcopal functions "without prejudice to the ordinary jurisdiction" until the erection of a diocese suffragan to the metropolitan see of Rouen.

New France being among the first Vicariates created in the history of the Catholic Church, there were no precendents to guide canonists. Did Laval exercise the full rights and privileges of an Ordinary? Was New France part of the Gallican church? Some believed the jurisdiction of the Archbishop of Rouen in the colony had been terminated. Laval would govern his territory as a titular bishop under the immediate jurisdiction of the Propaganda and as a representative of the Holy See, but this did not necessarily exclude integration of this missionary church into the French national church. The Archbishop of Rouen circulated a protest among his colleagues in the French hierarchy claiming that the Holy See had intruded upon the jurisdiction of a see of the Gallican Church and demanding that Laval present himself before the Assembly of the French Clergy to justify his "surreptitious means of obtaining letters of expedition". Members of the French hierarchy declined to consecrate Laval, and the outcry was even greater when the nominee was consecrated by the papal nuncio in Paris in the church of St. Germain-des-Prés, a church which was exempt from the jurisdiction of any of the Gallican bishops. The Parlement of Paris prepared a strongly-worded censure, but eventually Louis XIV, influenced by members at Court who supported the missions in New France and were convinced of the need for formal institutional structures in the colony, issued letters-patent requiring that Bishop Laval "be recognized by all our subjects in the said province to carry out his episcopal functions throughout the breadth of New France without prejudice to the ordinary jurisdictions". Also, there was inserted a clause which proved objectionable to the nuncio and the "Romanists" because it invited the Archbishop of Rouen to reassert his claims when a colonial diocese was created:

> We have accepted and do accept the disposition of the Holy Father while awaiting the creation of a bishopric, it being agreed that the bishop of such a diocese shall be suffragan of the archbishop of Rouen.[23]

Laval, the Bishop of Petraea, took the customary oath of fidelity to the King before sailing from La Rochelle for the colony, where he took care to have the royal orders posted and proclaimed in every church. The missionary church had come of age.

Chapter II

Amerindian Missions

Amerindians (both captives and visitors) had been brought to St. Malo, Rouen, Dieppe, Paris, Bordeaux, La Rochelle and Troyes in the sixteenth century as a result of fishing contacts with the New World, voyages of exploration, and the two principal Huguenot colonization schemes in the Americas. By the beginning of the seventeenth century, when the Recollets and Jesuits began intensive missionary work among the natives of New France, Frenchmen were aware of Montaigne's warning against hastening the ruin and decline of the New World, John Major's arguments for the subjugation of the aborigines, Gilbert Genebrard's speculative theories regarding Amerindian origins, Etienne Pasquier's hypothesis that they were really new peoples resembling the ancient ancestors of the Europeans, and Jean Bodin's environmentalist conclusions drawn from the discoveries in North America. Sufficient information was circulating in French literary circles to lend support to myths of noble savages and an earthly paradise. The bull *Sublimus Deus* of Pope Paul III reassured Catholics that the American natives were "true men" who should not "in any way be enslaved" and who were "capable of understanding the Catholic faith". By happy coincidence, the period of economic exploitation of New France in the early seventeenth century corresponded with a resurgence of spirituality and mysticism in religious circles in France. Thus the stage was set for missionary activity in the New World.

From the outset, evangelization was closely linked with policies of assimilation, economic exploitation and imperialism. Holders of commercial monopolies for exploitation of the colony's fur trade and fishery were enjoined to transport missionaries to the New World, to support these men and use their influence to bring the natives into obedience of the faith. The monopolists were more interested in the protected profit their charters promised than in promoting missionary work; nevertheless, the Crown, in granting monopolies, invariably attached obligations to evangelize the Amerindians. When De Monts' charter was reviewed, for example, the royal confessor, Father Coton, persuaded the king to send some Jesuit missionaries to Acadia. In order to forestall Coton's plan, the Huguenot merchants in 1610 took with them a secular priest, the *Abbé* Jessé Fléché of Langres, and after only three weeks of missionary work he baptized twenty-one converts, most of them members of a tribal chieftain's family. One year of missionary labour in Acadia resulted in a total of one hundred and forty-one converts, a very remarkable achievement given the facts that the natives had had little previous knowledge of Catholicism and that the missionary spoke none of the native languages.[1]

When the first Jesuit missionaries did succeed in obtaining passage to Acadia, they resolved not to baptize any adults unless they were well catechized, and to devote much of their time initially to language study and the compilation of vocabularies and grammars. Although they built on the contacts already established by Fléché, they did indicate that rapid and numerous conversions were unlikely. Champlain seconded the missionary observation that the mercantile interests were not sufficiently committed to religious objectives to leave the support of missionary work in their care. He did believe there could be a beneficial relationship between religious activities and commercial exploitation, however, and that close association between French and Amerindians would result in the assimilation of the natives, in their civilization and conversion, and in commercial and cultural advantages for the French. Champlain expressed his concern for the conversion of the Amerindians and asserted his belief in the joint responsibility of the French state and Gallican church in these terms:

> You will perceive that they are not savages to such an extent that they could not, in course of time and through association with others . . . become civilized . . . with the French language they may also acquire a French heart and spirit . . .
> It is a great wrong to let so many men be lost and see them perish at our door, without rendering them the succour . . . which can only be given through the help of princes, and ecclesiastics, who alone have the power to do this.[2]

It did not occur to him that the Amerindians might resist assimilation and conceive their own culture to be superior, or that the French in transplanting their institutions and culture, might modify these in the New World.

Champlain was instrumental in having Recollets engage in missionary work among the Montagnais near Tadoussac, and among the Hurons near Georgian Bay far in the interior. The Recollets decided to establish their chief mission among the Iroquoian Hurons, an agricultural-hunting confederacy, to attach them more firmly to a sedentary life, and to "francisize" them. These conclusions were founded on two convictions which most Frenchmen held throughout the colonial period: firstly, that peoples who lived by hunting and fishing and led a nomadic life were idlers and vagabonds — like the beggars and wandering unemployed of French towns and cities; secondly, that conversion required sedentary settlement so that the natives might come under regular religious instruction, so that schools and religious institutions could be established among them, and so that eventually a parochial system could be organized among them to serve their spiritual needs. Whatever hopes the Recollets may have entertained of establishing the millenial kingdom in Huronia were soon shaken.

Tensions between missionaries and the young interpreters and traders sent among the natives soon made themselves felt. These *coureurs de bois* took too readily to aboriginal life-styles for missionary tastes, and even the Hurons noted disparities between the moral and ethical code of the Recollets and the Jesuits who joined them in 1625, and the practices of these young bush-rovers. The economic demands of the fur trade had introduced into the subsistence Algonkian cultures a new motive for hunting, in addition to new tools and weapons. But it had also introduced the pernicious brandy traffic which had the slow but unrelenting effect of undermining the traditional values and pattern of life of the northern tribes. At first, neither the missionaries nor the tribesmen were aware of the far-reaching consequences of this dubious European contribution. The Jesuits quickly realized that the quality of French immigration would be a crucial factor in the contact experience with the Amerindians. One missionary wrote:

> It is to be feared that in the multiplication of our French, in these countries, peace, happiness, and good feeling may not increase in the same ratio as do the inhabitants of New France. It is much easier to control a few men than whole multitudes.[3]

Selective immigration would have to be combined with special evangelical techniques to ensure absorption of a converted native population into a French colonial population which realized the high ideals expected of it by the pious patrons in France.

The Recollets, realizing the difficulties in weaning independent and self-reliant natives from their traditional culture and religious belief system, decided to emphasize the education of the young in the hope of rearing up a generation in the Catholic religion and in French manners and customs. For the achievement of their objective they organized a "seminary" at Notre-Dame-des-Anges, near Quebec, hoping thereby eventually to gain more influence over the adults, as well as to decisively influence the succeeding generation through an educated leadership. The permissiveness of native child-rearing, and the complete integration of educational processes in the every-day life and routine of Amerindian communities, militated against the success of the rigid, formal and spartan schooling which the French sought to impose on Amerindian boys. The entire educational program had been predicated on the desirability of assimilation of the native population into a French way of life. The Amerindian boys found French-style education irrelevant to their mode of life and irreconcilable with their previous upbringing. Eventually all the boys left the "seminary". Even a youth sent to college at Calleville in France reverted to his ancestral ways when he returned to the colony.[4]

Cardinal Richelieu, in the charter terms granted the "one hundred associates" of the Company of New France, which assumed the administrative responsibility over New France in 1627, granted equal citizenship rights to Amerindians "who shall be brought to the knowledge of the Faith and make profession thereof" as "natural-born Frenchmen" with the citizens of metropolitan France. The exercise of these rights to "acquire, bequeath, inherit and accept gifts and legacies as do the native-born Frenchmen, without being required to take letters of declaration or naturalization" was limited, however, to their taking up residence in France.[5] This remarkable policy of official equality, which had no counterpart in other colonial societies, had few consequential results.

In 1632 the Jesuits became the sole successors of the Recollets in Canada, even taking over their monastery, and perpetuated their missionary policy of sending a few select students to France, of gathering native children for the "seminary" to be exposed to French ways of living, and of pursuing evangelical labours in select villages and encampments.

Their "seminary" for Amerindian boys, with which it was originally planned to associate a college for French boys and select native students, began in 1636 with the instruction of 6 Huron boys sent to Quebec by Father Brébeuf. By 1640 the plan had been virtually abandoned at Notre-Dame-des-Anges, although a fire at the house in Quebec which the Jesuits rented from the Company of One Hundred Associates forced them to move their school to Sillery, where they were joined briefly by the Hospital Nuns who took charge of a few native students too.

The Jesuits continued their own linguistic studies and compiled translations of essential texts in the native tongues. Although they fashioned their curriculum on the *Ratio Studiorum*, even for Amerindian pupils, they did adapt to the new environment by concerning themselves with elementary schooling and by permitting co-education, at least in the initial years. By 1673 the few Amerindian boys who came to the Jesuits, or who were virtually forced to attend school as part of exchange agreements between the tribes and the French, reacted to the Jesuit educational curriculum, the strict discipline and the tedious application to incomprehensible subjects like "wild asses' colts" and they all ran away.[6] Although Father Paul Le Jeune's educational program saw no notable success, it continued to be applied with short-term successes throughout the seventeenth and eighteenth centuries. Invariably, no great influence was exercised thereby on Amerindian society, and the long-range results of attempts to assimilate the natives or to raise them to the cultured level of Frenchmen were always negligible. The rigidity of learning experience, the new concepts of time and order, the punishments for misdemeanours, the loneliness of boarding-school life, the competitiveness and advantages of the French boys, and the irrelevance of the curriculum were factors which militated against the success of the Jesuit educational program.

Father Paul Le Jeune, after a missionary tour among the Algonkian tribes during the winter of 1633-34, concluded that the *reducciones* of Mexico and Paraguay provided a suitable model for the formation of "reservations" where native peoples could be segregated from their former pagan life and from the evil influences of the French towns and the fur trade, to be raised as model Christian communities. This reserves policy did not initially receive any royal support. The resettlement of families at Sillery and Trois-Rivières was undertaken as a religious experiment with the financial assistance of wealthy patrons in France. Noël Brulart de Sillery provided 32,000 livres to launch the reserve near Quebec in 1637.

The Amerindians themselves organized a segregated community at Tadoussac in an effort to isolate themselves from the evils of the brandy traffic. By 1645 there were no less than 167 domiciled and converted Amerindians living at Sillery who were such models of piety and industry that they were commonly referred to as "the true believers". Significantly perhaps, these natives were regarded as children, unable to manage their own affairs, and therefore, like minors, were controlled by appointed tutors and guardians. The lands that were conceded for the reservations were always held in trust for the natives by the missionaries, and the Governor Jean de Lauzon went so far as to forbid domiciled Amerindians from leaving the reserves without the permission of their missionaries.

In 1642 another element was added to the evangelization campaign through the efforts of pious persons in France, mostly members of the Company of the Holy Sacrament. The Society of Notre-Dame for the colonization of the island of Montreal chose the site of their activities with an eye to agricultural development of a communications centre with the northern and western hinterlands and with the English and Dutch colonies to the south. The *Véritables Motifs* placed the Amerindian missionary impulse high amongst its priorities:

> Thus God, the great saver of men's souls, who possesses not only the wisdom of the ages but also places convenient for the welfare of his creatures, seems to have chosen this site of Montreal as agreeable and useful, not only for the subsistence of Quebec, on which it depends, but in its own right to assemble a people made up of French and Indians who will be converted so as to render them sedentary, to train them to practice the mechanical arts and farming, to unite them under a common discipline in the exercise of the Christian life, each according to his strength, inclinations and industry, and to have celebrated the praises of God in the desert . . . and if once reason obtains the advantage over their old customs, with the example of the French which they esteem and respect, inciting them to work, it seems that they will set themselves straight, withdrawing from a life so full of poverty and afflication, and that they will take their places beside the Frenchmen or Christian Savages.[8]

The pious founders had no doubt about the French way of life being based on right reason and right religion; they were grossly mistaken in their assumptions about native evaluation of European life and standards, however.

In 1639 teaching nuns and nursing sisters arrived in the colony to assist in the program of evangelization. The Hospital Nuns conducted a hospital or clinic for ailing Amerindians at Sillery for a couple of years before consolidating all their nursing services at their principal residence in the town of Quebec. Within a year, the Ursulines had eighteen Amerindian girls in their "seminary", besides a number of French girls in their distinct day school. Marie de l'Incarnation, our principal source of information about Ursuline activities in these pioneer years, soon began to write about native resistance and counter-innovative techniques developing among the Hurons. Then came the news of the terrible onslaught of the Iroquois against the Hurons, the total destruction of the Jesuit missions in Huronia, and finally the arrival of Huron refugees at Trois-Rivières and Quebec. The reserves now took on a second characteristic — they became refugee camps for persecuted converts and for refugees from inter-tribal wars. In May 1654 a Mohawk expedition attacked the main body of refugees on the island of Orleans, carrying off five or six hundred into captivity before the eyes of the powerless French. During the next decade the colony fought for its survival, and there were a number of times when it seemed that the missions would have to close completely and the religious communities in the principal town might have to return to France.

Another means of encouraging integration of the two cultural communities was miscegenation. Champlain had told the Hurons that the French traders would go to live among them and marry their daughters; the settlers of Montreal in 1642 had as one of their objectives inter-marriage with the natives as a means of effecting large-scale conversions, increasing the French population, and developing agriculture. What these plans ignored was the experience French fishermen and sailors had with the Micmacs of Acadia with whom casual liaisons had been very common. The offspring of such liaisons, being raised in the native environment by their Amerindian mothers, were gains for the native population and losses for the French, as far as assimilationist aspirations were concerned. Although the Company of New France had thought such alliances would make up the deficiencies in French population — correcting also the male preponderance in French colonial society and the female preponderance in Amerindian society — the natives had to be reproved in 1635 for marrying only within their tribe and for avoiding alliances with Frenchmen.[9]

Mixed marriages, although supposedly encouraged in the early seventeenth century, were always subject to careful scrutiny. The first sacramental marriage between a Frenchman and an Amerindian woman took place on November 3, 1644, when Martin Prévost married Marie Manitouabewich. In 1648 the Jesuit missionaries attempted to obtain a papal dispensation permitting the marriage of native women, who were receiving Catholic instruction, but were not as yet baptized, to Frenchmen, but without success. That same year, a trader named Chastillon wanted to marry a Amerindian girl who had spent four years at the Ursuline school, and left the religious a substantial sum of money as a pledge but the maiden "did not want him at all, and preferred a savage and to follow the wishes of her parents". Of six other marriages, performed before 1663 without special permission, between Frenchmen and Hurons and Algonkians, none is better known that that of Pierre Boucher, sometime governor of Trois-Rivières, and Marie Chrestienne.[10] Laurent Duboc was given 500 livres in 1662 when he married a native girl, and a week later Jean Durand was given 260 livres when he married a Huron girl. During the next decade there is record of five such marriages, and over the next twenty-five years, that is until 1700, of only four more mixed marriages. Thus by beginning of the eighteenth century the practice was quite opposed by the missionaries and the bishop. The missionary Albanel, for example, was moved from his mission at Tadoussac with a reprimand for having performed a marriage between a trader named Nicolas Pelletier and a converted Montagnais woman in June 1677 "without the publication of banns, or advice given beforehand to the relatives, to Mons. the Bishop, nor Mons. the Governor."[11] The suggestion that such a marriage, apart from the publications of banns, required the express approval of the bishop and of the governor and the consent of the parents indicates that intermarriage was not generally recommended or approved. As it turned out, Nicolas Pelletier and his wife were often hosts to visiting missionaries and both were supporters of the church at Tadoussac. Their good example did nothing to change the general prejudice against such marriages.

The Hurons were from the beginning regarded with great hope for the foundation of a native church because they were sedentary agricultural tribes. The Recollets were the first to indicate that they might also become the great suppliers and middlemen in pursuit of the fur trade. Sagard, commenting on his Huron hosts, remarked:

> ... we exerted ourselves to receive and treat them so kindly
> and courteously that we won them over, and they seemed to
> vie in courtesy in receiving Frenchmen in their lodge when
> the needs of business put the latter at the mercy of these
> savages. Our experience with them showed that they were
> useful to those who had traded with them, while we hope by
> this means to make our way towards our main purpose, their
> conversion, the only motive for so long and distressing a
> journey.[12]

The Jesuits, who succeeded the Recollets in this mission, arrived at
a critical decision in 1639 in their missionary work. They decided to
establish a permanent centre in Huron territory which would not
only be a missionary headquarters, but would also become a centre
of a model Amerindian Catholic community, a commercial and
administrative centre, an experimental farm and perhaps even a
fortress. By 1648 Paul Ragueneau could report a network of ten
mission stations in Huronia with Ossossané the "most fruitful of all,
as regards both numbers of Christians and their zeal". This pre-
dominantly pro-French Bear community was organized into a
model Catholic village under converted chieftains who refused to
tolerate pagan festivals and observances and who appointed a
Jesuit as the chief headman with authority to act as censor of public
morals. A growing division made itself felt throughout the Huron
confederacy as the Deer and Rock tribes resisted conversion and
the Bear and Cord tribes were more receptive, though still inter-
nally divided. One missionary said it was difficult to be a good
Christian and good Huron at the same time; one convert said that
"I am more attached to the church than to my country or relatives".
A plot on the part of the non-Christians to drive out the missionaries and their staunchest converts failed as the Christianized
leaders were able to gain the upper hand and "carried even the
majority of the infidels with them; so that it was publicly decided
that reparations should be made to us in the name of the whole
country".[13] The missionaries had come very close to being murdered and their work completely obliterated by the pagan resisters
in Huronia.

What the unconverted in Huronia failed to do the Iroquois invaders accomplished within the space of five weeks. An immediate
consequence of the collapse of the Huron mission was that Jesuit

missionary attention was forced to concentrate more on the far west and the north, and also to investigate the possibility of taking the gospel boldly to the Iroquois, who now appeared as the chief opponents to the Catholic religion. A split in the traditional cohesion of the Iroquois Confederacy in 1654 seemed to offer the Jesuits the opportunity they were seeking. The Jesuits sounded out the Onondagas and sent Father Le Moyne to New Netherland to determine their disposition. The French succeeded in consolidating friendly relations with the Onondagas and the Senecas, but the Mohawks secured Dutch assistance on a scale that convinced the tribes friendly to the French that they should make common cause with the Mohawks. By 1658 the French had given up any hope of a rapid and massive conversion of the Iroquois.

When Bishop Laval arrived in the colony in 1659 as its Vicar Apostolic, he demonstrated great enthusiasm for the Amerindian missions, and he seized every public occasion to proclaim his zeal for the conversion of the natives and the creation of an Amerindian church which would be a model among the Catholic communities. Before long, however, he was convinced by those who had more experience in the colony that the Iroquois were "a scourge" which ought to be annihilated in the interests of the progress of the missions and of settlement. This remarkable change from one of interest and sympathy to one of open hostility did not pass unnoticed. Marie de l'Incarnation attempted to explain the bishop's change of heart to her son in France, who had also embraced a religious life and followed developments in the Canadian missions with uncommon interest:

> You are astonished by this resolution, and you say that it is repugnant to the spirit of the Gospel and the Apostles who risked their lives to save the infidels, even those who caused them sufferings. Monseigneur our Prelate was of your opinion, he even had Monsieur de Bernières learn their language to go to instruct them . . . after so much useless effort, and so many experiences of the perfidy of those infidels, Monseigneur changed his views, and he fell into accord with all the wise persons of the country, either that we have them exterminated, if it can be done, or that all Christians and the Christianity of Canada perish. When there is no longer any Christianity or any missionaries what hope will there be for their salvation? Only God by a very extraordinary miracle can put them on the way to Heaven.[14]

Both laymen and clergy pressed the French royal administration for military aid and for a more stable colonial administration.

The result was that Colbert was quite convinced that the Iroquois were to be "subdued", that they were barbarians and "infidels" as Laval called them, and that military assistance was absolutely essential. The anti-Iroquois policy pursued by Courcelles was continued by Frontenac, La Barre and Denonville, with varying degrees of success. Denonville's scheme to enslave a number of Iroquois warriors and use them in the galley fleets of the Mediterranean was a particularly unsuccessful episode in this prolonged hostility. In 1684, towards the end of his episcopacy, Laval wrote to Louis XIV that "we have every reason to believe that God reserved to Your Most Christian Majesty, eldest son of the church, the destruction of these peoples who are such a powerful obstacle in the growth of Christianity".[15] Not until 1701, however, did the Iroquois accept conditions of peace at Montreal. By that time, from the minority in their villages who accepted the message of the determined Jesuit missionaries, there were persecuted refugees who came to seek a quieter life in the few reserves near Montreal. They, in turn, became valuable intermediaries between the French community and the Iroquois and the English to the south interested in trade with Montreal and the upper country.

State officials, both Governors and Intendants, demonstrated a great interest in the progress of missionary efforts, pressed by the Gallican and mercantilist views of the Ministry of Marine. The mission of the Sulpician seculars at the Bay of Quinté received special assistance and was often compared favourably with the Jesuit missions. By 1677, however, the natives were deserting the mission station for the more attractive environs of Fort Frontenac, the agricultural efforts were proving disappointing, the missionaries were discouraged and the financial costs were exorbitant. The Sulpicians tried to console themselves, and to appease the state officials, with optimistic forecasts for their reservation near Montreal.

In 1698 Bishop Saint-Vallier granted permission to the secular priests of the seminary of Quebec to engage in missionary work in the interior. Three priests, armed with passports issued by Governor Frontenac, were soon on their way into the Illinois country where they admired the piety of the Amerindian girls married to French settlers.[16] By 1718 they were thinking of abandoning this mission having run into difficulties with both the Jesuits and the civil officers in Louisiana. They made urgent appeals to France for financial assistance but obtained little more than sympathetic letters from Maurepas, the Minister of Marine. The Bishop of Quebec decided in 1721 to divide the Mississippi field, and within a few years the Seminary of Quebec retained only its missions at Cahokia and Tamaroa, the rest of the area being assigned to the Jesuits and the Capuchins. On learning of the British conquest in 1763, the incumbent superior of this mission sold the properties at a ridiculously low price and ran off. The seminary of Quebec never recouped these losses nor did it re-establish its mission.

Bishop Saint-Vallier also succeeded in having a few Sulpicians establish a mission in Acadia, although both Tronson and Leschassier as superiors in Paris did not favour this assumption of responsibilities in Acadia. Louis Geofferoy, Claude Trouvé and Jean Beaudoin served both Acadians and Micmacs before the British occupation; Jean Beaudoin also accompanied Saint-Castin's sortie into New England in 1692 and Iberville's expedition against Newfoundland in 1696. Although there were no Sulpicians in Acadia between 1704 and 1720, a few missionaries did return there during the British period (which commenced in 1713). They had been preceded by Recollets from the Province of Paris, but following the Treaty of Utrecht these missionaries withdrew in favour of their brethren from the Province of Brittany, who were soon left with the chief responsibility for Louisbourg and after 1724 for Isle St.-Jean.

The ecclesiastics from the Seminary of Quebec were encouraged by Bishop Laval to enter the Acadian field. In 1676 he named the *Abbé* Petit, stationed at Port Royal, his Vicar General for Acadia. Bishop Saint-Vallier had the *Abbés* Gaulin, Rageot, Giray and Maudoux posted to the Amerindian missions of Acadia, and named Louis-Pierre Thury, who laboured among the natives of Miramichi Bay, his Grand Vicar. When the area fell under British jurisdiction in 1713, the secular priests supplied by the Seminary of Foreign Missions in Paris continued to supply missionaries to the Amerindians, notably to the Micmacs and Abenakis. Saint-Rouey, Maufils, Manach, Le Loutre, Courtin and Maillard were active in the region not only in keeping Catholicism alive and flourishing, but also in keeping the natives to their French allegiance.

The *Abbé* Maillard is among the better-known missionary workers of this period. It was he who perfected the Micmac syllabic alphabet which the Recollet missionary Chrestien LeClercq had developed, and he defended it against suggestions that the Roman alphabet ought to have been employed by pointing out that in this manner the missionaries could exercise a complete censorship over the Micmacs. It was necessary to keep them under control, to maintain them in some position of inferiority and dependency, and what better segregationist device than a separate alphabet. The missionaries were quite successful in stirring up the Micmacs and Abenakis against the English and in pursuing frontier raiding throughout much of the eighteenth century; however, the missionaries were not so successful in controlling the cruelty associated with these expeditions, and were quite unable to uproot the brandy traffic which played havoc with their missions and undermined Amerindian society. The Jesuit missionary de Rasle, among the Abenakis, the *Abbé* Maillard who wielded great influence over the Micmacs, and the *Abbé* Le Loutre (commonly referred to as "General Le Loutre"), who was stationed at Beaubassin — the nerve centre of Micmac resistance to British rule in 1749 — all wrote in the same vein. They were successful in holding the Amerindians of Acadia to their identification with Catholicism and with France, but they had serious doubts about the depth of their religious convictions and about the French missionaries' ability to control them. That the missionaries were not able to establish their absolute authority over their converts is not surprising when it is recalled that neither Micmacs nor Abenakis ever permitted their chieftains to exercise absolute authority over them. The most the missionaries could hope for was to become esteemed as chieftains among them. So far as the British discerned, they were successful in this role. The clergy of the Foreign Missions in Paris were proud of the achievements of their community in Acadia, although French officers at Louisbourg and Beauséjour were sometimes jealous of the prestige and influence of the missionaries in the area.

As already indicated, an important aspect of the policy for assimilating the Amerindians was the creation of reservations. These reserves of land were designed initially to induce the tribesmen to adopt a sedentary agricultural way of life, to become integrated into the seigneurial pattern of colonial life. The seigneury of Sillery was granted directly to the domiciled converts through the Jesuit missionaries who were to hold it for them in *franc alleu* and not in seigneurial tenure, and such lands as had already been granted within the seigneury to French settlers were reserved but the rents were transferred to the Jesuits for and as the property of the Amerindians. Governor de Lauzon soon declared the "nations and savage peoples of New France" to be like children, unable to manage their commercial and legal affairs, therefore necessarily subject to the Jesuits as "tutors and mentors". The Jesuits soon took charge of the lands granted them, and in 1656 the Governor forbade them to leave the lands reserved for them without the permission and consent of the Jesuit superior. By 1656 the refusal to recognize any native title to land was standard practice.[17]

Not all the reservations, however, operated in the same manner as did Sillery. At Prairie de la Madeleine and at Sault St. Louis (Caughnawaga) the Jesuits were given the title to land, but it was clearly stipulated that this concession was for the settlement and maintenance of the Amerindians and that when the lands were abandoned by the latter the title would revert to the Crown. Already it was recognized that the converts did not take readily to agriculture. However, the reservation had also taken on the characteristics of a "refuge" from persecutions and wars. The grant for the Abenakis in 1697 was made to the missionaries who held the land for settlement and occupation by what were essentially refugees. In 1671 the Sulpicians had started a mission known as La Montagne, near Montreal, for Hurons, Algonkins, Pawnees, Sioux, Fox and Iroquois. Soon this was moved to Sault-au-Recollet, still on the island of Montreal but farther removed from the French settlements. Soon there were reports of drunkenness and disorders here, culminating in 1680 in charges of witchcraft.[18] In 1714 the Sulpician superior in Paris asked to have the mission for the Iroquois, Algonkins and Hurons moved to Lac de Deux Montagnes. In 1717 a concession was granted to the Sulpicians for a seigneury to which they could remove the Amerindians, and where they were required to erect a church and a stone fort at their own expense for the security of their wards. In 1733 this concession was enlarged and the obligation to build a fort was allowed to lapse. The Sulpicians were not required to grant land to their charges, and the French administration recognized no Amerindian title to land. The only obligation on the part of the missionaries was to maintain a mission "for the instruction and spiritual care of the Algonkians and Iroquois". This contrasted markedly with the original Sillery concession, which Ruette d'Auteuil insisted the Jesuits ought not to retain in 1703 because it had been granted originally for the Algonkians and none had been resident at Sillery for more than thirty years. The position of the native peoples never improved so far as proprietary rights were concerned during the French régime. After the British conquerors came, the Catholic bishop concluded that the missionary movement, on the whole and especially taking into account the reservations policy, had been unsuccessful:

> The savage missions which in the past were numerous are today reduced to six or seven to which we take care to send missionaries. In general there is little that can be done for the salvation of these barbarians whose immoderate use of intoxicants each day exposes them to committing great crimes. I was myself a missionary among them for several years and I saw how little one can expect from them.[19]

The British concern that the Catholic missionaries had attached the native tribes firmly to the French cause in North America was closer to reality than the belief that they had also succeeded in thoroughly converting them.

Part Two:

The Colonial Church

Chapter III

The Church and Political Life

When we speak of the church in New France we are dealing with a missionary enterprise to which was added, and upon which was superimposed, an overseas extension of the French institutionalized church. For example, in France there were no national councils and only a few provincial councils; legislative activity was concentrated in diocesan synods (presided over by the bishop), which concerned themselves with local administrative matters. Likewise in Canada, Bishop Saint-Vallier convoked four diocesan synods and established ecclesiastical conferences. Towards the end of the French régime, Bishop Pontbriand did all in his power to centralize ecclesiastical power. He personally supervised the training of his clergy and through conferences and retreats sought to impose a uniform practice among the clergy. He hoped that by adhering strictly to the diocesan *Rituel* and the censures and declarations of the assembly of the French clergy, his pastors and confessors would everywhere act and speak in identical fashion. In France there was great literary and polemical activity dealing with virtually every aspect of canon law, doctrine, church–state relations and dissent, and all these discussions found an echo in Canada.

Important to the functioning of the metropolitan church were such institutions as the *Officialités*, the seminaries, the *fabriques* or parish councils, and the various fraternities and sodalities. Similarly, the activities of these institutions constituted the functioning of the church in the colony. The religious were a conspicious element of the population through their wearing of religious habit and through the buildings constructed for their use. However, there were fissures in the wall of religious conformity, as state officials and clergy vied for power and influence, as regulars and seculars mistrusted each other to a certain extent, and as religious orders or institutes openly competed. The church in New France was an extension of the Gallican Church; in the transfer of institutions and intuitions local problems and projects asserted themselves together with old-world controversies and concerns which continued to find expression in a new environment.

Foremost among factors in the development of French political and ecclesiastical life, when the structures of New France were being laid, were three important institutional changes enhancing the role of the centralized monarchy without requiring simultaneous constitutional changes. The dismissal of the Estates-General on March 24, 1615, and the failure to call another representative assembly of the realm (although preliminary moves were undertaken in 1649), marked an important gain for royal absolutism. It should not be overlooked that it was the clergy, nobility and commoners quarrelling among themselves in 1614–15 which had necessitated an appeal to royal supremacy and had led to the request for monarchical intervention and authoritarian arbitration.

The third Estate, sensing itself a majority, took advantage of the contemporary European controversy regarding pontificial power over monarchs to strike a blow at the clergy in general, and the Jesuits in particular, by placing at the head of its general *cahier* the following article:

> The King shall be supplicated to have decreed in assembly of the Estates, as a fundamental law of the realm, inviolable and binding on all, that, as he is recognized Sovereign of his State, holding his Crown from God alone, there is no power on earth, whether spiritual or temporal, which has any authority of his kingdom to deprive the sacred persons of our Kings nor to dispense or absolve their subjects of the fealty and obedience which they owe them for whatever cause or pretext whatsoever.[1]

The traditional royal doctrine in France was that since earliest Capetian times the King received his crown directly from God and not from the people nor from any ecclesiastical authority. Although the early Capetian kings were elected, the concept of a delegation of powers never took root in France. The Protestant party sought to reintroduce the concept in the sixteenth century, to justify its actions, but its efforts only served to discredit completely in France this alternative concept of the source of authority and legitimacy. If the King held his authority by divine right it followed that his power was absolute and that he was sovereign. Parallel to this traditional royalism had evolved the religious concept of His Most Christian Majesty as "the eldest son of the church". The divine quality of kingship was recognized by the coronation ceremony, assured by his anointing, and manifested to the people by the power of healing which was imparted to the royal person.[2]

Furthermore, the Third Estate refused in 1614 to adopt a motion requesting the adhesion of the realm to the decrees of the Council of Trent. To have published the decrees of Trent would have been tantamount to having them become a part of the common law and fundamental law of the kingdom; in other words, the particular customs observed by the French church would no longer be considered privileges. This the commons found "contrary to the maxims of our State, which are that the liberties of the Gallican Church are truly common law, so long and so stoutly maintained in France", and they affirmed their intention to retain inviolate these rights and privileges. The clergy hoped the King would have them published and observed without the formal assent of the Estates-General, but this hope proved vain. All that could be salvaged was for the Assembly of the Clergy to accept the discipline of Trent, not to be confounded with the decrees of the Council, individually in their dioceses.[3]

Another institutional change which enhanced royal power was the firm establishment of the Intendants in all the provinces of the realm. Also, the mature development of the seigneurial system aided both royal authority and royal revenues. All of New France was to be divided into seigneuries, on the premise, however, that the King was the universal seigneur in whom all titles and property were originally vested. These substantial gains for royal authority must also have been seen in the context of the king as a spiritual person and the monarchy as a divine institution. The effectiveness of Catholicism as another vehicle for the exercise of royal authority and for social control may be questioned in overseas territories. One French traveller observed that metropolitan controls "lost their strength with distance, just as an arrow falls short of the target which is too far from the archer's arm". Gallicanism found its ultimate expression in the Four Articles of 1682, which, along with the formal condemnations of Jansenism, were never formally registered in Canda by the Sovereign Council. Gallicanism so far as the colony was concerned was best defined by the first Minister of the Marine, Colbert, when he remarked, "when the Pope is our friend, he will be infallible, when he is not our friend, he will be heretical".[4]

Of paramount importance to the church was the establishment of a bishopric in New France which would give institutional form and political presence to the ecclesiastical estate. Rouen, St. Malo,

La Rochelle, Paris and Rome all extended their jurisdiction at one time or another to the colony, and not until 1631 did the Secretary of the Propaganda in Rome advocate the erection of a bishopric in New France with one of the Franciscan missionaries as its Ordinary. In 1643 the pious founders of Montreal advocated the creation of a diocese in the colony and proposed another Franciscan candidate for the see. Then, the French Jesuits who had opposed the proposal for a Franciscan bishop whose see might be in Montreal, advanced their own candidates much to the chagrin of their General. The French Court had become interested in the proposal by this time but two rival candidates were mentioned: *Abbé* Gabriel Queylus, a Sulpician, who was supported by the Montreal associates and Cardinal Mazarin, and *Abbé* François de Laval, who was sponsored by the Queen Mother, the Jesuits, and many of the *dévots* of the secret Company of the Holy Sacrament. In 1657, young Louis XIV chose Laval for bishop, but it was not until two years later, after protracted negotiations between Paris and Rome, that it was finally settled that New France would be erected into a Vicariate Apostolic under the immediate jurisdiction of the Propaganda and that Laval, who was consecrated Bishop of Petraea, would be a prelate enjoying all the rights and privileges of his Gallican colleagues. There ensued even more intensive negotiations between the two courts as the Gallicans sought to have a diocese suffragan of Rouen erected and the Romanists sought to retain the jurisdiction of the Propaganda in New France. In 1674, when Laval was consecrated Bishop of Quebec, Rome succeeded in keeping the diocese independent of any French metropolitan see. Although the diocese became part of the Gallican establishment, Laval having received his nomination from Paris and being required to swear fealty to Louis XIV, its Ordinary remained aloof from the activities of his Gallican colleagues and he had neither seat nor voice in the Assembly of the French clergy.

To what extent was the church directly involved in the political life of the colony? It is necessary to distinguish between power and influence, also between direct and exclusive exercise of jurisdiction and participatory and consultative roles in government. In the initial stages of commercial exploitation both in Acadia and Canada, and by virtue of the good will of the King's representatives and the cooperation of the entrepreneurs interested in exploiting the colony, the missionary clergy wielded great influence without holding political office. An evident share in administrative power was accorded them in 1647 when Pierre Le Gardeur de Repentigny returned from France with orders for the creation of a council whose composition was delineated as follows:

> To wit, there shall be established a Council composed of the Governor of the said country, and until there is a bishop named, of the Superior of the house of the Jesuits, which will be at Quebec, together with the local governor of the island of Montreal; and in the absence of the Governor of the said country and of the local governor of the said Montreal, of their Lieutenants; which Council will be held in the communal House where is established the Magazine of Quebec.[5]

This council exercised both specific and general powers in the realm of commerce, police and war. In this manner the Jesuits, sole representatives in government of the first estate, were closely identified with the commercial elite, the three "classes" of the Community of Habitants who held the trade monopoly.

The following year, as a result of demands for greater local representation and complaints from dissatisfied colonists carried directly to France, a commission of investigation was appointed to report to the Crown on Canadian affairs. The report of Laisné, Mesme and Morangis, all members of the Montreal association and *dévots*, resulted in a reorganization of the Council in March, 1648. Henceforth, the Council would consist of the Governor, the Superior of the Jesuits *ad interim*, any former Governor still resident in Canada, and two inhabitants of the colony elected for three-year terms by the full Council, including the non-voting syndics of Quebec, Trois-Rivières and Montreal who sat as observers.

That political office also accorded political influence and power is suggested by the fact that in 1648 the Jesuits succeeded in reversing a death sentence imposed by Maisonneuve on the drummer of the Montreal garrison for an unspecified "detestable crime". Moreover, it was Father Druillettes who was sent by the Council to Boston in the spring of 1650 to negotiate a treaty of commerce and mutual assistance with Governor Dudley, and it was Father Jérôme Lalemant who was entrusted with a mission in France of enlisting assistance for a colony threatened by Iroquois invaders and French creditors. Just as significant was the fact that Jean-Paul Godefroy, Admiral of New France, and Jacques Maheux, syndic of Quebec, who were also in Paris in 1651, invited the Recollets to return to Canada because some colonists were disturbed at having "to deal with the same people in temporal and spiritual matters".[6] Jean de

Lauzon, who had already received his commission as Governor of the colony, succeeded in having the decision in this matter referred back to the Council at Quebec, where he and the Jesuit Superior employed their influence to sabotage the protest movement.

The Jesuits began to see threats to the success of their primary goal of evangelization of the native peoples as the fur trade declined, and they were closely associated in many circles with those traders who, suspected of fraud and graft, profited from the trade at the expense of the less favoured colonists. Accordingly, in 1656 they appealed to the home government to be relieved of their administrative responsibilities (that is, of their seat on Council), in order to pursue without distraction their missionary activities. The Company of New France asked Louis XIV to reorganize the administration of the colony. The Council of Quebec, which was more managerial than governmental, consisted, after March 7, 1657, of the Governor appointed by the Crown, a director of the monopoly trade of the Community of Habitants appointed by the Company of New France, and four elected councillors, each representing approximately four hundred inhabitants. Neither the Superior of the Jesuits, nor the Grand Vicar of the Archbishop of Rouen, nor the Vicar Apostolic was given a seat on this reconstituted Council.[7]

The clergy, however, were not without a hand in political affairs. Bishop Laval, who had arrived at Quebec as Vicar Apostolic of New France in 1659, was a party to the recall of Governor Argenson in 1661. Also that year, the new Governor, Avaugour, a trusted friend of the Jesuits and a known *dévot*, took the unusual step of insisting that Father Paul Ragueneau, who already had a reputation among some of his colleagues for "meddling too much in government affairs about which he has no idea at all", take his place "at the head of a general council for the service of the King and the welfare of the country". The measure, ostensibly in recognition of the evangelical labours of the Jesuits "who have worked more than any others for this country," was even more incomprehensible in view of the fact that a brevet from the Council of State issued four months earlier had ordered that the Bishop be given a seat and a vote in the colonial Council.[8] In the circumstances, it was not surprising that the investigator, Jean Peronne Dumesnil, who acted on behalf of the Company of New France, should have recommended that an independent judiciary be named by the colonists in order that "governors, Bishop, and Jesuits cannot intervene and insert themselves at all", and also that the Bishop be restricted to "spiritual affairs and matters relating to the Church".

By this time Governor and Bishop were quarrelling over a number of matters, to the point that in 1662 Governor Avaugour suddenly dismissed the councillors and appointed ten new members, five of whom were to serve for four months and then the other five would succeed them. The Governor himself was dismissed shortly thereafter, some said on the advice of Bishop Laval. Others attributed it to the influence of the Jesuits at Court, and still others said it was because he had alienated "the most influential men in the country" and had isolated himself from those traders who could have acted as his advisors. Early in 1663, the colony reverted to the Crown, the monopoly company having surrendered its proprietary rights, and largely on the advice of Bishop Laval, a Sovereign Council was created, with a trusted *dévot* — Saffray de Mézy — as Governor of the royal province. Louis Gaudais-Dupont was sent out to investigate and report on the general state of the colony, and was also given secret instructions to inform himself about the recent quarrels between the previous governors and the Jesuits and the Bishop, also to check on Laval's conduct "relative to the spiritual direction of the church, also relative to the business in the country and the families which he visits".[9]

The inauguration of royal government in the autumn of 1663 has sometimes been seen as the high period of ecclesiastical influence in political affairs in the colony. Bishop Laval, in conjunction with Governor Mézy, was to nominate the first slate of sovereign councillors who would assist in the administration of the province and who would sit as the highest overseas court. This gave the Bishop tremendous leverage because he knew the colonial oligarchs from his several years' residence in the colony, whereas the Governor, who was a convert from debauchery and a former colleague of Laval at the Hermitage of Caen, relied on him. Not surprisingly, the nominees were all leading members of the first class of habitant traders, the "aristocracy of the beaver", who were being accused by investigator Dumesnil of fraud and embezzlement. For a few months, the King's representative and the chief ecclesiastic jointly and harmoniously made appointments, established courts, settled questions of proprietary rights, and expedited routine administrative matters. Laval seemed to be achieving the objective he had set for himself and the clergy in going to France to petition for a new administration, namely a guarantee to the first estate of a significant role in political affairs.

A storm erupted in February 1664, when Governor Mézy wished to put an end to the practice of the Bishop and councillors privately hearing, and adjudicating cases, and ordered that henceforth all petitions should be addressed to the Sovereign Council through him. The Sovereign Council split evenly in the dispute between Governor and Bishop, and Mézy proceeded to expel two members of the so-called "Bishop's cabal". The acrimonious quarrel continued for months and was soon confused with another dispute over the election of a syndic for the town of Quebec. Laval had had himself replaced on Council by his vicar general, *Abbé* de Lauzon-Charny, but the latter took a somewhat too vigorous stand in expressing popular resentment of the Governor's and Council's managed elections. In the end the Governor repented on his deathbed and was reconciled to the Bishop, but the metropolitan authorities had been given ample grounds to suspect clerical intervention in state affairs. For his part, the Bishop never again had a lesser cleric replace him on Council when he could not be present himself, although the royal edicts clearly gave him this privilege. Paradoxically, the clerical victory over Mézy marked an end to the "joint rule" concept.

The arrival of the Marquis Prouville de Tracy from the West Indies in June 1665 initiated a new era in colonial administration because Laval, who had been given to understand that the Lieutenant-General would rely heavily upon him for advice, discovered that Tracy was quite independent in arriving at his own conclusions. Moreover, the appointment and arrival of an Intendant greatly reduced the legislative function of the Sovereign Council and injected into the local administration an officer who rapidly established himself as the kingbolt in the governmental structure. Colbert's instructions to Jean Talon constituted one of the clearest statements of official Gallican policy ever despatched to the colony. One section read:

> It is absolutely necessary to hold in just balance the temporal authority, which resides in the person of the King and in those who represent him, and the spiritual authority, which resides in the persons of the said Bishop and the Jesuits, in such a manner, nevertheless, that the latter be inferior to the former. The first thing which the Sieur Talon will have to observe well, and about which it is good for him to have fixed ideas before leaving France, is to know perfectly the state in

which these two powers are at present in the colony, and the state in which they naturally ought to be.[10]

In a communication addressed to the Vicar Apostolic, on the other hand, Colbert announced an increase in the subsidy alloted to the church and urged continued progress in seeing the sacraments administered in the most remote settlements and in having the children of the colonists suitably educated. There was no contradiction between these instructions. Gallican officials desired the church to fulfil its role and mission as a dutiful agency of social order. According to this view, no state agencies other than the Catholic Church could bring salvation and a proper understanding of and reverence for the established order of the realm. The state must support and protect the church in proportion to the efforts made by the ecclesiastical community to sustain the political and social establishment.

Disputes about precedence, imposition of the tithe, reservation of the sacraments, assimilation of the native peoples, jurisdiction of church courts, and control of the brandy traffic resulted in repeated warnings to colonial officials from the Ministry of Marine, which in 1669 assumed responsibility for the colonies, to limit clerical power, to restrict the Bishop and the Jesuits in their political activities, and to report any suspected encroachment by the first estate in areas outside the purely spiritual domain. Governor Courcelles, for example, was advised to "act with great prudence and circumspection," so that the clergy would not suspect they were being closely watched — even spied upon — and was informed that the prevalent opinion in official circles in France was that when the population of New France increased "assuredly the Royal authority will surpass the Ecclesiastical and will resume the correct proportion it ought to enjoy".[11] In other words, political imbalance was a consequence of colonial disorganization, retardation of development and isolation.

It should not be imagined that the church resented or resisted the role which the French state assigned to it. When Governor Frontenac decided in 1672 to organize the population into four estates for an impressive and pompous public swearing of fealty, as the Marquis de Tracy had done in 1665 in Martinique, the clergy raised no objections to the self-styled "High and Mighty Lord". The only alteration suggested by the Grand Vicar was that seculars and regulars should not be placed together in the procession; the

Jesuits graciously offered their new church for the ceremonies and decorated it appropriately for the occasion. The oath administered to the clergy, as a corps or estate, raised no protests but was considered quite "normal":

> You swear and promise before God to labour with all your strength for the maintenance of the Catholic, Apostolic and Roman Religion, to promote it as best you can through your example and care by the purity of your doctrine and the proclamation of the Gospel, and to be faithful to the King as required under the authority of the charge with which he has honoured you in this province. You promise, in addition, that if a matter comes to your knowledge which is contrary to His Majesty's service you will advise us thereof, and in case it were not remedied by us, you will inform His Majesty thereof.[12]

The mild reprimand from France that Frontenac should never again convoke such a colonial "Estates-General" was wide of the mark and demonstrated both ignorance of events overseas and corresponding concern about any popular manifestations or suggestions of representative government.

Colbert, Seignelay, Pontchartrain and Maurepas seemed to have assumed that the Marine officials in France would constantly have to guard against ecclesiastical encroachments in the political sphere. The greatest danger, from their point of view, was when a civil officer acquiesced in the natural tendency of the ecclesiastical estate to overreach its proper bounds. Thus, Intendant Duchesneau was reprimanded for being too complacent and trusting; he was told that the King wished him to read several authors who had written about the Gallican liberties and the relations between church and state. The Baron de Lahontan suggested that the Sovereign Councillors, who after 1675 were nominated for life by the King and given royal commissions, were too often the tools of the clergy:

> When they have nice points under their consideration they usually consult the priests or Jesuits: And if any case comes before 'em, in which these good Fathers are interst'd they are sure not to be cast, unless it be so very black, that the cunningest Lawyer can't give it a plausible turn . . . [13]

Even more distressing to Gallican officials was the fluctuating influence which royal confessors and mistresses held over the King himself. Father La Chaise's influence over Louis XIV or Madame de Pompadour's influence over Louis XV could have direct consequences for religious policy.

The two-power orientation of juridical thought required the establishment of a church court parallel to the royal courts. The Archdiocese of Rouen seemed to have the strongest claims to jurisdictional rights in the colony and it is almost certain that *Abbé* Queylus established an *Officialité* in the colony. In 1659, Laval, the Vicar Apostolic, formally constituted such a court, which he reorganized and expanded in 1675 after being named Bishop of Quebec. This ecclesiastical court was formally recognized by the state in 1684. It sat only in Quebec and appeals from it went to the Sovereign Council. It did not exercise the right of high justice; nevertheless it did maintain a prison for women at the General Hospital of Quebec where inmates were appropriately under the care of a mistress of discipline.

That the Canadian church exercised its distinctive ecclesiastical rights and privileges is abundantly documented. Very early in the development of the riparian colony, monitories, or ecclesiastical censures designed to enforce compliance with canon and civil laws, were read from the pulpits demanding revelation of all knowledge of infractions or crimes on pain of excommunication for the withholding of information. But this form of judicial pressure had more symbolic value in establishing the union of church and state than in procuring actual convictions. Joint action between the church court and the civil officers resulted in the return to France, in 1659, of the parish priest at Beauport, *Abbé* Guillaume Vaillant, about whom the parishioners had complained. On the other hand, the civil power upset Bishop Laval's arbitrary action of removing a young girl from the home of her employer and placing her in the Ursuline convent for further education.

In 1675 the *Abbé* Thomas Morel was arrested for refusing to comply with an order of the Sovereign Council regarding precedence. The church court claimed jurisdiction and eventually the Sovereign Council backed down. Similar procedural wrangles were avoided in future by an edict of 1678 requiring that all criminal charges against the clergy be proceeded with jointly by church and royal judges. The arrest of the *Abbé* François de Salignac de Fénelon (a half-brother of the illustrious Bishop of Cambrai), for preaching an Easter sermon attacking Frontenac's abuse of power in Montreal created much more stir in the colony. The Sulpician was pursued for seditious libel and the case turned on the respective jurisdictions of the *Officialité* and the royal justice. Eventually, following appeal to the King, a non-decision was handed down which satisfied none of the parties and left the separation of powers as ill-defined as before. The royal verdict said in part:

> I have reproved the conduct of the abbé de Fénelon and I have ordered him not to return to Canada, but I also must inform you [Governor] that it was troublesome to institute criminal charges against him or to oblige the priests of the Seminary of St. Sulpice at Montreal to make depositions against him. It was mandatory to send him back to the bishop or grand vicar to have him punished by the ecclesiastical power, or else to arrest him and have him sent back to France by the first vessels.[14]

In fact, the secular power had intervened in a case which clearly belonged to the *Officialité*. At about the same time, the attempt to have a case involving pursuit of a notorious brandy trafficker at Lachine brought into the church court rather than the Sovereign Council was successfully quashed.

Quarrels over precedence were more than mere strife for priority of place, or superiority of rank, in the conventional system of arranging the order of dignitaries in public ceremonies, and in intercourse in private life. Louis XIV himself insisted that these matters were more than questions of etiquette and honour because his subjects, not fully understanding the affairs of state and of the Court, usually judged external appearances and it was "according to rank and precedence that they set their respect and submission".[15] The question seems to have been raised for the first time in the small town of Quebec in 1645 when the Jesuit Superior failed to observe the custom of giving communion first to the Governor. Thereafter, there were innumerable incidents, some culminating in judicial pursuit, throughout the French régime and beyond into the period of British military occupation. When officers of the Marine troops quarrelled with the churchwardens about their pretended honours and privileges, Louis XIV found it necessary to issue a regulation (March 2, 1668) assigning precedence to the Governor-General or the local Governor, then the justices, followed by the churchwardens "without the officers of the troops who are, or hereafter shall be, in the said country presuming any rank in the said processions or other public ceremonies". People at all social ranks and in most parishes engaged in debates about who should receive what honours, civilities and special recognition in solemn processions, in receiving the blessed bread, candles, palms, communion and incense.

Quarrelling and backbiting indicated a need for strong leadership in the colonial church. Unfortunately, the diocese was so extensive that none of the bishops visited it in its entirety. Laval only touched briefly at Gaspé, although Saint-Vallier managed to visit Acadia on two occasions — in 1686 he spent three months visiting the French posts preaching, hearing confessions and administering the sacraments, also visiting the Amerindian missions at Miramichi, Richbouctou, Shediac, Chedabouctou, Beaubassin, Minas and Port Royal, and in 1686 he visited Placentia in Newfoundland, the islands of St. Pierre and Miquelon, and Port Royal in Acadia. None of the succeeding bishops ever ventured beyond the St. Lawrence valley; indeed, Bishop Mornay never came to his diocese but remained in France. The upper country of Canada, the Illinois-Mississippi region and Louisiana received no episcopal visit during the entire French régime.

Bishop Saint-Vallier had published a very optimistic account of the colonial church following his visit in 1685. He became Bishop of Quebec in 1688, after the usual procedures of royal nomination and papal confirmation which proceeded without any delays in spite of the quarrels over regalian rights and the papal censure of the French hierarchy for having promulgated the Four Articles of 1682. After only a few months more intimate acquaintance with his bishopric he withdrew the optimistic comments published in his *Estat présent de l'Eglise et de la Colonie*. The flock of 12,000 souls, he intimated, was threatened not only by the English and the Iroquois, but by such internal enemies as drunkenness, immorality, luxury and gossiping.[16] In 1694 he again expounded on the need for better social control, and indicated that the earlier view of the apocalyptical church of the final triumphant age had been dissipated. Six years later he again noted "much relaxation in ecclesiastical discipline", and by 1712 he despaired of any decent moral standards being maintained among the French settlements of the Mississippi valley. Studies of social conditions at the end of the seventeenth century would seem to confirm Saint-Vallier's conviction that "the Church is only two finger lengths away from complete ruin". It was a low period spiritually and intellectually, giving cause for concern about the future in addition to creating complete despair of attaining the high ideals and utopian vison of the nascent Canadian church.

The political implications of such a spiritual and moral crisis were understood by the Bishop. Saint-Vallier upheld the special role of the monarchy in protecting religion and virtue, while the English were always pictured collectively as the "heretical enemy". Thus the church upheld the sacred monarchy, enjoined prayers for the royal family, and expected in return the aid of the secular arm in repressing vice and evil and imposing a Christian social order.

This did not prevent Saint-Vallier from placing certain spiritual prerogatives above national and political considerations. He stubbornly attacked the practice of army officers withholding soldiers' pay and the indiscriminate sale of alcoholic beverages to the Amerindians, despite official sensitivity on these points. He successfully resisted court efforts to have him resign, and obtained the support of the University of Paris in his struggle against the profiteers and traffickers; the Bishop, by obtaining a Sorbonne decision, officially bound the King, and placed himself above civil action for refusing absolution to those considered to be willful sinners and transgressors.

The prestige of the episcopacy was not enhanced by all Saint-Vallier's actions, however. In 1692-94 he managed to quarrel with almost everyone in the colony. First, he attempted to reform the Seminary of Quebec and to undo Laval's centralized plan. In 1689 he had left the Seminary to establish his own residence and had then requested the return of his library and the modest fund he had given the Seminary; the secular community of priests refused to return these, and a bitter quarrel ensued. Laval was living in retirement at the Seminary and he came to the defence of his centralized Seminary plan, but to no avail, for the French Court stood behind Saint-Vallier. The reorganization did enable the Seminary to become more intellectual and even a little less austere. The Bishop claimed the Church of Notre-Dame in Quebec as his cathedral church; however, the chapter looked upon it as the canonical church, while the rector and churchwardens regarded it as the parish church of the town. The precise relationship between these roles was never satisfactorily defined or delimited during the French régime. In 1693 there were bitter quarrels between the Bishop and the cathedral chapter and the canons had recourse to the Sovereign Council in an attempt to forestall the Bishop's appointments.

Laval had instituted a cathedral chapter in 1684, ten years after the creation of the diocese, which theoretically should have served as his ecclesiastical council. He joined it to the Seminary of Quebec in conformity with his original centralizing plan for the latter institution. But Bishop Saint-Vallier soon made of the chapter a distinct and autonomous body enjoying the revenues of the French abbeys of Maubec and Lestrées which had originally (in 1674) been given to Laval for the support of the diocese. The chapter accepted a subsidy of 8,000 livres in return for the King's right to nominate the dean and precentor. It is not an exaggeration to say that, for most of its existence, the chapter was important only for the quarrels which it generated among the various ecclesiastical and secular officials. It served no vital function, although it provided some interim administration, in the colonial church until 1760. In the face of British military occupation, it rallied and gave the Canadian church necessary leadership and worked out with the new political masters the election of an Ordinary.

Moreover, Governor Frontenac took great exception to Saint-Vallier's intervention in prohibiting the staging of Molière's *Tartuffe* and especially to the arrest of Mareuil, "the great organizer", his trial before the Sovereign Council and his forced return to France. In 1694 there was a notoriously scandalous outburst between the Bishop and local Governor of Montreal about the placement of their respective *prie-Dieu*'s in the Recollet church which finally involved the Recollets in acrimonious debate with the Ordinary. There were widespread complaints from the clergy about the large number of reserved cases and about episcopal interference with internal rules and customs of regular and secular communities. The result of these developments was the recall of Saint-Vallier to France for "consultations".[17]

Saint-Vallier met with hostility from a number of the leading clerical advisors on Canadian affairs in Paris, and his interviews with Louis XIV and Pontchartrain, the Minister of Marine, were brief and rather cool. Like a good politician and military leader, Saint-Vallier took the initiative. He drew up a memorandum on the Recollet interdict, asked the Sorbonne to pass judgment on his action in forbidding officers to retain a soldier's pay, left to the Sulpician superior Tronson the revision of the constitutions of the Sisters of the Congregation, and wrote conciliatory letters to his cathedral chapter, the Jesuit missionaries, and Bishop Laval. In June 1695 the Council of State found that Saint-Vallier had been legally correct in all his quarrels but it nevertheless deplored many of his actions. It was hoped in many quarters that he would resign; the King thus deferred giving any decision. Soon the Sulpician clergy came to his support, and the influential Bishops Bossuet and Fénelon opined that he could not be forced to resign his bishopric. In 1697 the King authorized him to return to Quebec. The colonial Bishop had successfully weathered the resignation crisis.

He was not long back in his diocese when a series of quarrels erupted with the Jesuits. Saint-Vallier had permitted the secular clergy of the Seminary at Quebec to set up a mission station among the Tamaroas, a small tribe which, the Jesuits claimed, was in their Illinois missionary territory. Actually, the Jesuits saw in this move a political manoeuvre to expel them gradually from their North American missions just as the clergy of the Foreign Missions, of which the Quebec Seminary was a part, were seeking to drive them out of the Far Eastern missions over the "Chinese rites" controversy. Saint-Vallier went to Paris and obtained the full support of the Court. During his stay in Paris, the Jesuits requested that they be given a clearly demarcated district in the colony of Louisiana and that their Superior there be named one of the Bishop's vicars-general. Saint-Vallier refused them this cooperation, so that only the clergy of the Foreign Missions remained in Louisiana.

Then the Jesuits attempted to settle scores with the Bishop in the political sphere. Father Samuel Martin Bouvart, Superior of the Jesuits in Canada from 1698 to 1704, attacked the orthodoxy of Saint-Vallier's three publications — the catechism, the *Rituel* and the compilation of ordinances — intimating that they were inspired by Jansenism and would lead the colonial church into error and schism. Jansenism, so named after its chief exponent, Cornelius Jansen who was Bishop of Ypres, was a revival in an acute form of austere religiosity, of Augustinian theology, of simple pietistic appeals directly to God, and sometimes resulted in a neglect of the sacraments and of the mediatory role of the priesthood. Although several members of the secret Company of the Holy Sacrament and of the pious association formed to found Montreal in 1642 were Jansenists, there does not appear to have been a direct Jansenist immigration into Canada. One of the Hospital Nuns was suspected in 1651 of being "tainted with Jansenism which is causing great trouble in France," but after a prolonged probation she was re-examined and permitted to take her final vows as nothing was discovered "that seemed heretical".[18] The Papacy condemned the Jansenist rigourism and theology, and the Jesuits assumed the leadership of a movement for dead-centre orthodoxy in France.

The issue became more political than theological. Jansenists were associated with leaders of the revolutionary *Fronde*, particularly with the exiled Cardinal de Retz. Papal bulls issued by Innocent X and Alexander VII condemned the alleged "five propositions" of Jansen, and a formulary was drafted by the national assembly of the French clergy. Louis XIV came to distrust the Jansenists for several reasons: first of all, he feared the political influence which they might exert; secondly, as head of the Gallican church, he regarded any rebellion in religion as equivalent to treason; thirdly, he disliked their doctrine, their other-worldly ecstasy and asceticism which stood in great contrast to his licentious convention-ridden Court; lastly, he disliked any manifestation of individualism, whether religious or political. Six weeks after the death of Cardinal Mazarin, Louis XIV demanded adherence to the formulary of the national clergy, and in April 1665, issued an edict condemning Jansenism and restricting the dissemination of Jansenist doctrines. It said:

> The design we have of seeing all our subjects reunited in the same belief in matters of faith and of religion, obliges us to watch incessantly to prevent the progress of all new ideas which might trouble the repose of consciences, and the peace of the church and the state, there being no precaution that we have not taken to have all contentions cease and to arrest the course of errors that could alter the purity of the faith which we have received from our ancestors. In this design we have supported with our authority the decisions of the Popes, as accepted by the church, for the destruction of the new sect which has arisen by reason of the doctrine of Jansenius . . . [19]

The attack on the Jansenists must be seen not so much as a triumph for the Jesuits as it was for the monarchy and royal Gallicanism. In the following decade, relations between Rome and Paris were very strained, in part because the Papacy had over-emphasized its own authority and jurisdiction. By the 1670s the French clergy was objecting to papal "interference in Gallican affairs" in dealing with recalcitrant Jansenist bishops. The Declaration of the Rights of the French Clergy, issued in 1682, regarded as the key document in the evolution of Gallican rights and liberties, marked a definite triumph for the theory of the divine right of kings, but did little for the divine right of the episcopacy, its immediate jurisdiction from Christ, and its succession from the apostles.

Had the Jesuits been able to make charges of Jansenism stick, they would have undermined Saint-Vallier. He took his case directly to the Sorbonne, which in 1704 cleared him of all taint of Janenism and declared all his publications to be perfectly orthodox.[20] Saint-Vallier took the precaution to have all papal and royal documents relating to the schismatic movement publicized in the colony and took speedy action against a defrocked Benedictine monk accused of Jansenism in 1718. The rigourism or "puritanism" of the Canadian church sprang from the French Counter-Reformation input in the formative years of missionary activity and development of the diocese, not from the indirect influences of Jansenism that may have been perpetuated in New France by virtue of Saint-Vallier basing some of his *Rituel* or catechism on French models which were accused of being Jansenist-inspired. The issue was important in the sense that it strengthened the political status of the church as orthodox Gallican in constitution and doctrine.

From 1704 to 1708 Saint-Vallier was a prisoner-of-war in a little village outside London; when he returned to France in 1708 he asked permission to return immediately to his diocese which was reported to be in spiritual decline and want, but he was retained for a variety of reasons until 1713. The long absence of the Bishop inevitably encouraged civil officials to take advantage of the situation. Governor Beauharnois, apparently severe in dealing with those who "lacked respect for ecclesiastics", actively protected the interests of the Seminary of Quebec, arbitrated disputes between the clergy and seigneurs over the obligation to construct parish churches of stone, but opposed any imposition of tithing at the original rate of 1/13th. Saint-Vallier was told concerning the Governor: "He was Bishop in your absence, and Bishop of the Jesuits. He was an apostate for his mother and his family were Jansenists, this said in jest".[21] The warning, nevertheless, was important because protracted vacancy of the episcopal see could result in an erosion of ecclesiastical influence.

The years of the Bishop's absence were years of crisis for the colony. In the first place, in 1704 the colony suffered a shortage of salt, essential for preserving meat and fish, following the capture by the English of the annual supply vessel from France. Governor Beauharnois in response to a popular demonstration, undertook to sell the salt from the King's stores at fixed prices, but in Montreal some two or three hundred people clamoured at the town gates until *Abbé* Belmont, superior of the Sulpicians in that city, placated them. Thus, a riot was averted by a sympathetic secular priest who promised to intervene on behalf of the common people. Governor

Ramezay of Montreal, in fact, did agree to the "suggestion" transmitted by Belmont, who took the additional precaution of protecting himself and assuring the common people the concessions he had obtained for them by publishing a *mandement* confirming the terms agreed upon. Then, an epidemic of smallpox struck the colony, carrying off between 1000 and 1200 people. The Seminary of Quebec burned down in the midst of these calamities. Complaints increased about the poor quality of religious services available in the rural areas. There was a report that not only were the ranks of the clergy being thinned through death, but also new ordinations were impossible since the death of Laval and the absence of Saint-Vallier. The situation in 1707 seemed to be that about 80 per cent of the clergy were concentrated in the towns having 26.5 per cent of the total population, while the remaining 20 per cent of the clergy were expected to serve the needs of 73.5 per cent of the people outside the chief towns. Disorder and vice were rampant; one cleric described Quebec as "an open bordello".

During Saint-Vallier's captivity in England, it had been arranged that the diocese of Quebec should be administered by the Grand Vicars Maizerets and Glandelet at Quebec and Belmont at Montreal with Bishop Laval, who lived in retirement at the Seminary of Quebec until his death in 1708, officiating at important functions when invited by the Grand Vicars to do so. Saint-Vallier sent several proposals to the King and to members of the French hierarchy asking that a coadjutor be appointed to assist him, but the royal disposition was rather to obtain his resignation and to appoint a successor. Saint-Vallier would not accept the compromise that if he be permitted to return to New France for a brief visit, accompanied by a coadjutor, he should resign the see upon his return to France.

On June 22, 1713, the King named Father Louis-François de Mornay, a Capuchin, coadjutor with the right of succession. Saint-Vallier had returned alone to Quebec where he was soon immersed in quarrels with the Seminary of Quebec regarding the composition of the cathedral chapter. Governor Vaudreuil and Intendant Bégon added their voices to the Bishop's urgent request that the coadjutor be sent to the colony to assist him. Mornay was consecrated Bishop of Eumenia and affirmed that he would proceed to New France in 1715. Saint-Vallier counted heavily on him to represent him in Louisiana, but Mornay informed the Court he could do nothing for the spiritual welfare of that remote region of the diocese unless he had more material resources "to subsist and with which to assist the poor and the savages". So the poor

Capuchin who had given up his monk's cowl for a bishop's robe, secured from the French Court, which had already paid for his bulls and his ornaments, a raise in annual pension.

Mornay was quite decided not to go to the colony and he emphasized Saint-Vallier's desire that he occupy himself principally with affairs in Louisiana. He did, by correspondence, take charge of affairs there by sending missionaries of his own institute to New Orleans, by naming their superior his Grand Vicar. Mornay acted quite independently of Saint-Vallier, informing the latter of his decisions after they had been executed. Thus, for example, in 1722 he had the Carmelite missionaries removed from Louisiana, with the support of the Company of the Indies, because they had gone there under the aegis of the Propaganda in Rome and their superior had obtained a brief of vicar apostolic from Rome "which we do not recognize in France".[22] The proposal for the creation of a separate diocese of Louisiana was again discussed, and it was definitely decided against erecting a second bishopric. Increasing the colonial sees was seen as merely increasing problems for church–state relations.

Mornay was not entirely without interest in New France. He entertained good relations with the representative of the Quebec cathedral chapter in Paris, Canon Hazeur de l'Orme, and he obtained from the King an increase to 5,000 livres in the annual subsidy according to the chapter after 1724. In March, 1728, he decided to resign as coadjutor, but Saint-Vallier having died in December 1727 at Quebec, Mornay learned shortly afterwards that his resignation was invalid and that he had automatically succeeded to the episcopal see of Quebec. He had the Archdeacon Lotbinière formally take charge of the diocese, having decided not to come to Canada himself, but the cathedral chapter raised countless obstacles and even attempted to enlist the support of the Sovereign Council to block the customary legal formalities. The Jesuits wrote to the Court to expose these local oppositions, stressing the detrimental effects of such wranglings on the prestige and influence of the national church.[23] Their comments were much influenced by the unedifying spectacle of Bishop Saint-Vallier's funeral which did little to strengthen the uncomprehending public's respect for the ecclesiastical estate.

Intendant Dupuy, who had been named executor by Saint-Vallier, proclaimed the beginning of the *régale* (which had been the source of bitter disputes between Louis XIV and the Holy See) according to which the revenues of the see devolved to the Crown until a successor were installed. (Louis XIV had by decree in 1673 extended his right to nominate to certain convents — *the régale spirituelle*, and his right to receive the revenues of all vacant sees, including the hitherto exempt provinces — the *régale temporelle*.) The cathedral chapter met immediately and elected Etienne Boullard capitular vicar. A dispute erupted between the newly elected capitular vicar and Archdeacon Lotbinière, who claimed that the honour of presiding at the Bishop's funeral belonged to him. Lotbinière appealed to the Intendant Dupuy, who advanced the date of the funeral, and the Archdeacon proceeded with the internment of the Bishop in the presence of the astonished nuns and paupers of the General Hospital where the ailing prelate had died. A long legal battle ensued between the chapter and the Sovereign Council, led by Intendant Dupuy, who indicated that the chapter's election was invalid because a coadjutor had automatically taken office on Saint-Vallier's death. Dupuy reiterated the Gallican position espoused by the royal intendants in an ordinance which restricted the ecclesiastical power to purely spiritual matters, leaving all temporal concerns to the civil power, and arguing that the competence of secular judges extended to all matters according to the long-accepted phrase of St. Optat that "the church is in the state, not the state is in the church".[24] Governor Beauharnois intervened and the King recalled the Intendant, the whole incident being judged to have accomplished little in securing the people's devotion to either secular or ecclesiastical institutions.

Bishop Mornay now decided to remain as titular of Quebec "receiving all the revenues of the bishopric" (the regalian rights not being applicable as Dupuy had first supposed) and administering the diocese from France to the continued detriment of the colonists. In 1729 he was given Pierre-Herman Dosquet, a former Sulpician who had spent two years at Montreal, as coadjutor. Dosquet had been named Bishop of Samos and had been destined for the Oriental mission field, but he indicated that he was willing to return to Canada to carry out the episcopal functions which Mornay refused to perform there. On August 4, 1733, the Minister of Marine insisted that Mornay proceed immediately to Quebec to take charge of his diocese; the Bishop responded on September 12 by submitting his resignation. During his incumbency he had issued no pastoral letters, no *mandements*, no circulars, and no ordinances for the guidance or government of the church of New France, and his feet had never touched the shores of the New World. It would appear that his real administrative talents, which were considerable, were employed instead in administering the see of Cambrai, which remained vacant for a number of years following the death of the illustrious Fénelon.

Dosquet now found himself in full charge of the diocese. He returned to Canada with a retinue of domestic servants and established himself on his seigneury near Trois-Rivières, where he had built a church and residence which gave rise to the village of Villa de Samos. This example from a bishop led a number of the Canadian clergy to acquire seigneuries and sawmills in the hope of supplementing their meagre incomes. Bishop Dosquet inaugurated an important liaison service for the colonial church. He named a permanent vicar-general, stationed in Paris, to represent the interests of the diocese at the Courts of Versailles and Rome. The most outstanding of these ecclesiastical diplomats was the *Abbé* de l'Isle-Dieu.

Dosquet's years in Canada were unhappy and marked with controversy. The Superior Council pressed home the fact that he was a foreigner — a "Belgian" born in the principality of Liège — and therefore he was required to become naturalized before he could take his seat on the Superior Council. He quarrelled with the nuns of the General Hospital, who according to the terms of Saint-Vallier's will were obliged to keep the episcopal palace in good repair, and finally obtained the necessary financial assistance from the Court when the Hospital Nuns refused to pay. Then, in an attempt to assert the dignity of his episcopal office, he tried to keep the general public off his terrace which for some years had been used as a public park. He had a high wall and gate built, but the populace tore these down and forced him to accept the continued invasion of his privacy. As for ecclesiastical discipline he found it sadly wanting — "the canons acknowledge neither rules nor statutes nor superiors: they treat the dean as their inferior and the Bishop as their equal" — and a bad example for a hierarchical society.

Dosquet made every attempt to reassert the political rights and privileges of his church. He began by attempting to set order in the parishes. A *mandement* dated December 12, 1730, was read from all the pulpits admonishing churchwardens and directors of fraternities to have their prospective account books and regulations ready for the Bishop's inspection on the occasion of his pastoral visit.[25] The following year, he protested vigorously against the naming of a civil judge to investigate circumstances in which certain prisoners were able to break out of jail reportedly because they had been furnished with files by the Brothers Hospitallers. Dosquet maintained that according to French procedures the inquiry must be conducted jointly by a civil judge and the Official of the church court. Then, there was a quarrel with the Seminary of Quebec when he suggested that in order to relieve its debt burden it be amalgamated with the Sulpician seminary at Montreal. This controversy took on overtones of colonials versus metropolitan French, as the Seminary clergy were Canadians whereas the Sulpicians, Jesuits and bishops were French. The Canadians presented the case as one in which Canadians did not wish to see their training school closed or absorbed by what was regarded as a French institution. At this point, Dosquet pleaded ill health and returned to France.

For the next four years the colony was without a resident bishop. Dosquet travelled between Paris, Liège and Rome and spent much of his time trying to augment the meagre revenues of the abbeys which were destined to the support of the Canadian diocese. Maurepas, the Minister of Marine scolded him:

> You cannot be ignorant of the fact that your diocese is not in the position of being able to get along without a bishop. . . . It is finally time that we know what to expect. If you wish to stipulate conditions for your resignation, say so. I expect a prompt and positive answer.[26]

The bluntness of this communication elicited no reply, so Maurepas took up the issue three months later saying that the government intended to appoint a successor who would sail to Quebec the following spring. Dosquet shuffled his feet and proposed a rather complicated arrangement whereby he would be engaged as a sort of secret diplomat for the Crown. The Minister of Marine offered him an abbey with 5,000 livres annual revenues in return for his resignation. Dosquet resigned on February 6, 1739 and the Court proceeded with plans to assure to the colony the leadership it required.

In New France there were no longer any confirmations or pastoral visitations, many parishes were without priests, twenty or more seminarians were awaiting ordination and three of these — at their own expense — crossed the Atlantic to be ordained by the Bishop of Vannes. Governor Beauharnois and Intendant Hocquart kept insisting on the political expediency of having an Ordinary resident at Quebec as quickly as possible. Louis XV named

François-Louis de Laubervière as Dosquet's successor and at the young age of twenty-eight, he was consecrated fifth Bishop of Quebec. Here was a young, healthy, zealous prelate of good family and sound theological training who would give the colony the kind of leadership it had so long required and had so long not received.

He sailed from La Rochelle in June 1740 but when the transport reached the Grand Banks a violent epidemic erupted. Laubervière did not spare himself in tending to the crowded, wretched passengers and crew struck down by the infection. When he landed at Quebec the entire town rejoiced for they saw in him another Bishop Laval who would give the colony the steady and long-term guidance and direction it lacked for many decades. Twelve days later he was dead from the plague; he was buried the same day, without ceremony, because of the nature of his disease. So were dashed the hopes of the Court, the church and the colony.

The Canadian church, as one author expressed it, was again a widow, although two former bishops — Mornay and Dosquet — were still alive. Many of the Seminary clergy, ignoring the French church's practice of naming Frenchmen to colonial episcopal vacancies, hoped that their agent in Paris, a Canadian, would be appointed bishop. Meanwhile, the nationalist feeling in the colony was permitted to express itself in terms of office-holding. The Grand Vicars at Quebec and Montreal, who in the absence of a bishop administered the diocese, were Frenchmen who resigned and left for France in 1740, leaving the way open for the canons to elect Canadians to replace them. Louis XV nominated the *Abbé* de Pontbriand in December 1740, on the advice of the Sulpicians and Cardinal Fleury, to the see of Quebec. Pontbriand sailed on the first available ship to Canada in the company of four fellow Breton priests. Upon his arrival in the colony, he made it clear that he intended to raise the spiritual tone of the colony and to refrain from political intrigue.

Pontbriand chose not to attend most of the sessions of the Superior Council, but when he did accord the Council the honour of his presence, the occasion was felt to be a particularly important one in which the church would express its support of measures undertaken for the general welfare. Thus, in 1743 Pontbriand attended the Council session which condemned "the odious cupidity of some of the inhabitants of the *côtes*" who profited from the scarcity which had plagued the colony, by charging exorbitant prices. He proposed that a reserve supply of wheat be stored in the King's warehouses for such times of emergency. The following year he cooperated with the secular authorities in screening the immigrants who had been sent to the colony — of these he was instrumental in having sent back to France a renegade priest from the Order of Charity and a notorious adulterer. In 1746 he joined with the Governor and Intendant in proposing an increase in the import duties on wines and spirits in order to procure for the colony an additional revenue of thirty to forty thousand livres required for the fortifications.[27] The Council of State acquiesced and an increase was granted for an initial three-year period, but the Bishop was unable to obtain the prohibition of the brandy traffic which he had hoped might be decreed for the chief towns and seigneuries, if not for the entire expanse of the colony. Regarding the internal government of the church, he retained some of the convictions of his countrymen: he remarked to Maurepas that in nominating an archdeacon it might be wise to return to the rule "that he not be a native of this country".[28] Governor La Jonquière took advantage of this situation by suggesting to the court one of his nephews, the *Abbé* du Cabanac-Taffanel, who returned to France soon after the death of his uncle. The Governor's death marked a triumph for the church because La Jonquière had made a good confession of his avarice to the Bishop and asked the latter to publicly indicate from the cathedral pulpit that he asked pardon for all the mistakes made during his administration.

The Bishop was more exercised by the threat to his church from an external enemy. In 1745 he ordered public prayers for the success of Louis XV's armies and the defeat of the Anglo-American force threatening the French possessions in North America. In a *mandement* to be read from all pulpits, he sketched for the faithful the probable consequences of an enemy victory — "our children raised in the midst of heresy, our churches overturned, our sacred vessels profaned, the Lord's ministers proscribed, and ourselves deprived of the sacraments".[29] It was an effective approach for rallying support and animating flagging patriotism. It also left the inhabitants with a reinforced prejudgment of British and Protestant intentions and helped create the psychological context which prevailed at the time of the actual Conquest in the next decade. Again in 1755, prayers were ordered throughout the diocese of Quebec — this time for the dispersed Acadians and against the "detestable errors of Luther, Calvin and Wiclef". From 1757 onwards, special prayers were recited at all masses for the success of Louis XV's armies in the Seven Years' War.

As the invaders closed in on Quebec and Montreal, the Bishop granted his clergy a wide range of discretionary powers to enable them to deal with an emergency situation. These powers included receiving abjurations of heresy, and the power to dispense from irregularity any priest accused of the homicide of an enemy. The clergy were permitted to say mass anywhere, to go about their spiritual duties in disguise, to swear temporary allegiance to the conqueror, and to permit Protestant services in their churches. On the other hand, they were to do nothing to assist the enemy in achieving his military objectives, they were to refrain from bearing arms, and they were to have no part in marriage ceremonies between Catholics and Protestants.[30] The Bishop, sensing his approaching death, also gave his Grand Vicar specific instructions for the administration of the diocese.

Bishop Pontbriand died on June 8, and on July 2 the canons of Quebec met at the Ursuline monastery to name regional administrators for the vacant see: Briand for the regions under British rule, Perreault for Trois-Rivières and parts of Quebec still under French rule, Montgolfier for Montreal and the upper country, Maillard for Acadia, Beaudoin for Louisiana, and Forget for the Illinois country. Following the signing in 1763 of the peace treaty which ceded New France to the British Crown, the chapter met to nominate Montgolfier as successor to the vacant see. He proceeded to England to seek support, but when Governor James Murray objected to his candidacy, Montgolfier withdrew in favour of *Abbé* Briand. Briand was quietly consecrated in France and did not arrive back at Quebec until June 28, 1766, by which time the 181 priests at the time of the fall of Quebec had been reduced to a mere 138. It would not be until 1793 that the British government would permit a few priests from France to come to serve in the unchurched regions of the colony.

The arrival of another bishop was widely acclaimed and marked an important concession derived from the royal prerogative of George III, not from Parliament, on behalf of his "new subjects". The official report said:

> It was really affecting to see them congratulate each other wherever they met . . . and to see them afterwards run in crowds to the Parish Church to see this bishop, whom they look upon as the Support of their Religion, and as a Pledge of the King's Paternal goodness to them. In fact, at the same time that they publicly bless the Lord for having given them a Bishop, they loudly proclaim their Gratitude to His Majesty

for having attended to their Requests: It is likely that this Favour confer'd on the Canadians by the King, will effectually attach them to the British Government.[31]

Governor Murray, in recognizing the disabilities of 85,000 Catholics under British laws and the prohibition of a Catholic hierarchy in the British Empire, had wisely proposed, as a compromise intended to satisfy all parties, the consecration of a bishop in France who would be the "superintendent of the Catholic church in Quebec".

The Conquest raised another question of a political order. The Canadians had feared the worst treatment imaginable at the hands of heretical English, and their last Bishop, Pontbriand, had sought to prepare them for any eventuality. To their surprise and relief, they found that the British standing orders to their troops enjoined not only a strict discipline but also required the utmost public respect and courtesy regarding religious matters. The British stressed strict discipline and exemplary behaviour to "win over" the "new subjects", to ensure a moral conquest and psychological victory. The Canadians were regarded as British subjects by choice, since they had refused the option to return to France or a French possession. The standing orders of November 1759, for example, that when Catholic processions passed in the streets, "it is ordered that the Officers pay them the compliment of the hat, because it is a civility due to the people who have chosen to live under the protection of our laws", stood in sharp contrast to the French laws which had forced Huguenots to kneel in the streets as the sacrament passed.[32]

Yet another problem had been raised by the Conquest. After the fall of Quebec in 1759, the British had gathered for a service of thanksgiving in the Ursuline chapel, ironically only ten feet from Montcalm's grave, conducted by the chaplain Rev. Eli Dawson who used Psalm xviii:49 as his text: "Therefore will I give thanks to Thee, O Lord, among the heathen and sing praises unto Thy name". An ensign in the Black Watch regiment recorded in his diary that "several French merchants, said to be of the Reformed Religion, and commonly called Huguenots, attended, though unacquainted with our language".[33] The Protestants had been among the first to show an interest in the Americans but they had long been driven underground as a dangerous political party and a divisive element in the realm detracting from the uniformity and orthodoxy which the monarchs wished to conserve.

The first French colonization schemes had been launched under the supervision of Roberval in 1541, Villegaignon in 1555, Ribault in 1562 and Laudonnière in 1564 — all were largely Huguenot enterprises, and all were marked with failure. Many of the early unrecorded fishing expeditions, which also initiated the fur trade of New France, were undoubtedly manned by Protestants. The early monopoly holders such as Chauvin, De Monts, La Pierre and Lomeron were all members of the "alleged Reformed religion". In 1621 the Recollet missionaries and Champlain petitioned Louis XIII to exclude Huguenots from the colony, and in 1627 the charter of the Company of New France included a clause drafted by Cardinal Richelieu which permitted only "natural-born French Catholics" to settle in the colony.[34] Protestant merchants and fishermen continued to visit the colony although it was clear that they might not settle there and that the Edict of Nantes did not provide for their toleration in New France. Protestant worship was specifically prohibited in Acadia in 1659.[35] The presence of a Bishop and of an Intendant brought great pressure on those Protestants who were living quietly in the colony without open exercise of their religion. As more Protestants arrived with the troops, contingents of settlers and even the "brides" recruited in the *hospices* of France, efforts to secure abjurations redoubled with secular and ecclesiastical persons competing for conversions.

In 1670 Bishop Laval pressed the home government to prevent French merchants dealing with Canada, (many of whom were obviously Huguenots), from sending Protestant agents and crews to the colony because the men held "seducing discourses", lent devotional books, impressed the Amerindians and colonists favourably, and even held religious assemblies among themselves. His main thrust, however, was political:

> Upon examining the matter from the viewpoint of the State, it appears to be no less consequential. Everyone knows that the Protestants in general are not as attached to His Majesty as are the Catholics. Quebec is not very far from Boston and other English cities; to multiply the number of Protestants in Canada would be to give occasion to foment revolutions. Those who are there have hardly appeared to take a prominent part in the success of His Majesty's arms; we saw them noise about with a certain haste all the setbacks that occurred. A prohibition to French merchants to send out Protestant agents would suffice to remedy this abuse.[36]

Laval had expressed widely accepted views of the "alleged Reformed religion" in France. The King congratulated him for working to build a strong loyal colony and declared that the implementation of his suggestions would correct "the vices and imperfections which could prejudice to some extent" the royal authority.

Following the revocation of the Edict of Nantes in 1685, Louis XIV ordered Governor Denonville to have all the Huguenots in the colony abjure their heresy. The following year Bishop Laval met with Seignelay to plan the uprooting of persisting Huguenotism in the Acadian fishery. Nevertheless, the colony was never without some Protestant leaven, although it never had an open Protestant worship or continuous Protestant community. The attempts to impose religious uniformity had no sooner uncovered an individual or wiped out a pocket of Protestantism than a few more individuals slipped into the colony from some unsuspected source. In 1699 a group of Huguenots who had taken refuge in the Carolinas asked Louis XIV for permission to return to French territory in the lower Mississippi region, but they were denied their request. After the death of Louis XIV, the regent Philip of Orleans showed himself more lenient in his treatment of the Protestants, and a trickle of Huguenot immigrants to the colonies resumed. By 1741 the number of Protestants in New France had again increased, especially since Huguenot commercial firms in La Rochelle, Montauban and Rouen had started trading with Quebec, and the Council of Marine instructed the Governor and Intendant to conduct a secret survey of the numbers and circumstances of the Protestants in Canada.[37]

In the years which followed, more Protestants arrived among the troops, the captives, the suppliers, the deserters, the artisans, and the women sent as "King's daughters". Bishop Pontbriand raised all the former arguments of Bishop Laval for excluding them, but Intendant Bigot sent an unequivocal defence of the Protestants to the Minister of Marine. Bigot said they were a mere handful in number, that they were loyal, had never distributed "bad books" nor interfered with Catholic practices, and that to prosecute them would be equivalent "to diminishing the commerce and abundance in the colony".[38] He also wished to protect the Jews who had been banished from the French colonies in 1683, although this was a dead letter in New France since there were no Jews there. Bigot had a sister married to a Jew, and in 1748 he had formed a joint stock company with Abraham Gradis of Bordeaux for the Canadian trade. Bigot had probably reduced the numbers in his report because in 1753 the home government decided to recall "numerous" Huguenots. Nothing seems to have happened and four years later the Bishop again complained of the great number of Protestants in New France. It was now widely accepted that the Protestants presented no grave threat to the unity of the realm or the authority of His Most Christian Majesty.

Looking back over the political involvement of the church in New France, it would appear that the greatest problems did not grow out of friction and misunderstanding between ecclesiastical and secular authorities, or even out of imagined threats emanating from dissident communities such as the Huguenots or libertines. The absenteeism of the bishops prevented the church from asserting a dominant role in political affairs, even if other factors had been favourable to such a development. Presumably, an activist bishop could give the clergy leadership, and through his control of the institutions of learning, welfare, and education, as well as his participation in the Sovereign Council and his consultations with the Governor and Intendant, he could wield influence. Only Bishops Laval, Saint-Vallier and Pontbriand spent a significant period in New France. Bishop Mornay never came at all during a six-year episcopate, and Dosquet came for only one year of another six-year episcopate. Lauberivière came but died twelve days after his arrival at Quebec. Moreover, although Laval had a long episcopate and lived many years in retirement in the colony, it should not be forgotten that he was absent in France for no less than twelve years. Saint-Vallier was absent seventeen years from his diocese. These were significant lapses in episcopal control and direction which may have been more significant for the spiritual health of the colony than was the much more publicized six-year lapse which followed the death of Pontbriand in 1760. The absence of a bishop from 1760 to 1766 came at a politically critical moment, it is true, but the more than forty years of absences prior to the British Conquest coincided with religiously and socially critical periods.

Chapter IV

The Church and Economic Life

New France had its beginnings in the fishery and the fur trade — in the commercial exploitation of depletable natural resources, the pursuit of which did not require extensive settlement or elaborate institutional frameworks. Because the foundations of Canada were commercial rather than agricultural, the missionary church had to concern itself with economic matters, to an extent it might not otherwise have done. An often-sketched picture of the colony is that of a relatively primitive frontier subsistence community in which the church owned large tracts of the most arable and productive land. Even the visual impression is of the massive stone monasteries and tall-spired churches dominating the landscape.

These external impressions do not give a completely accurate view of the church as it was in the seventeenth or eighteenth century. Some of the religious communities, notably the Jesuits and the secular priests of St. Sulpice and of the Foreign Missions, acquired important properties when they initiated their activities in the colony. This they did to become self-supporting as rapidly as possible, an important consideration given that the fires of the religious revivalism which had fed the Canadian missions were already burning low by the time a royal administration was created at Quebec and troops and settlers were being sent out at royal expense. None of the lands of the St. Lawrence valley were particularly fertile compared to French agricultural returns or to later North American agricultural development. If the lands owned by the clergy were among the first cleared and put into cultivation, it was in good measure because, out of their own financial resources, they invested capital to build up their farms and mills to provision the settlers whom they were able to attract to the New World, and to meet the deficits of the early years until the seigneuries became economically viable. In becoming a seigneur through its institutes and communities of seculars, the church aided in the transfer to New France of the traditional French seigneurial system, which rapidly became modified in its new environment. It provided a continuation for the historic association between property, social class and honours. The system required the transfer of the accepted hierarchical class system and entailed a juridical body of legislation and procedure which, although diffuse at first, soon saw the emergence of select sections of the Custom of Paris as "Canadian law". Furthermore, the church by virtue of its early application, relatively substantial investments and sustained interest, provided the colony with models of seigneurial success.

How wealthy was the church? How much arable land and other property was in the hands of ecclesiastical seigneurs? At the time of the institution of royal government in 1663, the several religious communities held about a million and a half square arpents of land among them. These lands had been acquired as outright gifts, as charitable donations, as dowries for young women entering convents, and through purchase. The Company of New France conceded a score of seigneuries to the church, the largest concessions being those of Batiscan and Cap de la Madeleine. Although the church held about 11 per cent of the conceded lands of Canada in 1663, that proportion did not represent fairly the value, the development, or the productive capacity of the church-held property. For example, the religious seigneurs held about one-third of the conceded river frontage along the St. Lawrence River. The Jesuits held the largest area of farm land, the Sulpicians were in possession of the important island of Montreal, and the Seminary of Quebec had been able to acquire some of the most fertile and productive lands. Few church lands were left undeveloped or held for speculative purposes.

Once the colony reverted to the Crown, very few land concessions were made to the religious institutes or communities. The cathedral chapter at Quebec was conceded half of the seigneury of Petite-Nation, along the Ottawa River, but this meant little in economic terms because the state forbade the agricultural settlement of this area which lay along the northern canoe route. Louis XIV, anxious to keep the church within its jurisdictional bounds, therefore resolved (and was reminded from time to time by his Gallican bureaucrats) not to extend unduly the holdings of the church. Ruette d'Auteuil advised in 1705 that the realm would be better served if vacant lands were granted to a lay seigneur or kept in the royal domain.[1] Royal policy in this context was further strengthened in 1743 by Louis XV's declaration forbidding new religious foundations and forbidding "a multiplication of acquisitions by the existing ones" because "these withdraw from commerce a considerable part of the wealth of our colonies and can only be regarded as contrary to the common good of society".[2] Despite the fact that even gifts and sales of land required express royal sanction after 1743, the church continued to acquire property.

Between 1663 and 1743 the King had granted only five new concessions to religious institutions, yet the amount of land they controlled had more than doubled in the same period. In 1680, Bishop Laval gave the seigneuries which he had recently acquired himself, Beaupré and Île Jésus, to the Seminary of Quebec. The Jesuits bought Belair in nine transactions spread over 35 years while the Ursulines at Trois-Rivières bought Rivière-du-Loup outright in 1727. The church also acquired *arrière fiefs* (concessions within a large seigneury which were held from the seigneur rather than from the king) and *rotures* (concessions which could not be subconceded) within lay seigneuries. By the end of the French régime, the church, through its various institutes and individuals, controlled slightly more than 25 per cent of all lands conceded in Canada, and about 34 per cent of the total population lived on these lands which were generally located within a fifteen-mile radius of Quebec or a ten-mile radius of Montreal.[3]

Apart from their more auspicious beginnings and greater initial capital investment, the church seigneuries had several advantages over lay seigneuries. Unlike lay seigneurs, the church seigneurs if they were institutes or seminaries, did not die, and thus the seigneury was not divided according to the inheritance provisions of the Custom of Paris. According to canon law these lands were inalienable, being held in mortmain. To continuity was added efficient control. Most of the institutes and seminaries, including women's communities, appointed a priest to manage each of their seigneuries. These directors were knowledgeable about the production, value and revenues of each *roture* within the seigneury and kept meticulous accounts of each *censitaire's* dues and payments. (A *censitaire* was a farmer who made a token cash payment, or *cens* for his concession of land.) This worked to the advantage of both *censitaire* and seigneur.

During the early "mystical period" of missionary work in the colony, the Ursulines, Hospital Nuns, Jesuits and Sulpicians established themselves by means of the support offered by their wealthy patrons in France who were directed in their charitable giving by missionary-minded confessors and coteries of *dévots*, such as the

Company of the Holy Sacrament. This metropolitan support diminished in the 1650s, in both money and evangelical labourers coming to the colony to pioneer in missionary work. Other sources of support became proportionately more important. In the 1660s Louis XIV proscribed the activities of the Company of the Holy Sacrament, and in the 1670s the *Jesuit Relations* ceased being published, thereby putting an end to one of the most influential appeals for support of the missions.

The religious institutes or orders, of course, enjoyed revenues from their mother houses in France. These came usually from the interest on reserve funds and bequests and from revenues from properties. The Seminary at Quebec, the diocese of Quebec, and the cathedral chapter were all granted property in France designed to furnish them with revenues for their subsistence in New France. Towards the close of the episcopate of Saint-Vallier, the Bishop enjoyed annual revenues of about 9800 livres, the cathedral chapter 5000 livres, the Seminary of Quebec 20,000 livres, the Jesuits about 25,000 livres, the Recollets about 3000 livres, the Sulpician Seminary a revenue of about 12,000 livres (not including tithes from various Montreal island parishes), the Hospital Nuns at Montreal 5000 livres, the Sisters of the Congregation 4000 livres, the Hospital Nuns at Quebec 6000 livres and the Ursulines about 5000 livres. In other words, the church, while not fabulously wealthy, did enjoy a measure of economic stability.

Another important factor in this stability was the contribution of the Crown. The King had always been generous to the religious institutions which carried his religion to the New World. The church, like the colonial administration, relied on royal subsidies to carry out its mandate effectively in a region where labour and transport were expensive, where imports were substantial, and where local investment possibilities were limited. The royal subsidies were part of the colonial budget, and after 1665 they were sent to the Intendant for distribution according to the King's directives. These subsidies were an effective instrument in keeping the religious institutes alert to royal policy because their share of the *gratification* was dependent upon their "usefulness to the King's service". Thus, during Talon's administration the Ursulines were considered much less "useful" to the state than were the Hospital Nuns. In 1705, for example, the Governor and Intendant made an urgent appeal to the Crown for the continuation of the annual subvention, indicating that if it were permitted to lapse completely the role of the church would be seriously undermined:

Sieurs Vaudreuil and Raudot represent to you that unless you make available funds next year and until such time as the affairs of the colony are in a better state to meet the necessary charges of this country, there will be a terrible disorganization. The curates not having received their supplements are abandoning their parishes. The Seminary which takes in children without charging them board, in order to bring relief to poor families, no longer receiving the King's gift will close its college and will receive no more children. The Hotel-Dieu and the hospitals being deprived of their ordinary subsidies will take in no more sick or paupers . . .[4]

Needless to say, Louis XIV resumed the annual donation. Under the Regency, and under Louis XV the policy was continued. In fact, Louis XV was most generous in his support of the Canadian church. Throughout the 1720s for example, the Crown granted a total of about 15,000 livres for the building of the cathedral at Quebec, 3000 livres annually for the parish churches and rectories, 1500 livres for the church in the lower town of Quebec, and about 15,000 livres for the construction of an episcopal palace. Royal subsidies continued throughout the French régime and presented the British conquerors in the 1760s with a dilemma — if they wished to have the church continue its spiritual, educational and charitable work under the Crown, it would be necessary to find means of providing additional revenues to replace the royal subsidy from France, which had been cut off.

The commercial origins of the Canadian colony imposed on the French church a measure of participation in the exploitation of New World resources which, at first glance, was incompatible with Tridentine principles. In order to overcome the reluctance of the commercially dominant Huguenot merchants to provide them with transport to their mission field, the first Jesuit missionaries to Acadia actually entered into a commercial contract with Biencourt and his associates. This manoeuvre enabled Jacques Michel, a Huguenot pilot, to accuse them, in 1629, of coming to the New World "to convert beavers rather than savages", an accusation often repeated in succeeding decades.[5] The reply to such accusations, which became the standard response to all similar charges, was that beaver pelts were an accepted medium of exchange in the colony, and that the Papacy itself had recognized the right of religious institutes to engage in some trade "in order to lessen the expenses of their establishments" in heathen lands. This did not prevent the rival Recollet order from challenging the Jesuit defence:

> This proposition is captious because it is certain that although the Jesuit Fathers are very wealthy and receive large gifts to give to the savages, they nevertheless never give them anything of their goods, not even the alms they have been given for distribution, unless they make them pay six times as much as the value of the merchandise which they distribute to them upon the return from their hunt. This is something the Recollet Fathers would not have done for they run not after furs nor after possessions.[6]

The Company of New France permitted the circulation of peltry as "the coin of the country", to employ Father Paul Le Jeune's expression, on condition that all the skins would eventually reach its warehouses and cross the ocean on its vessels. The Recollets employed it also, their accusations against the Jesuits notwithstanding (and meaningful only in the later context of efforts to resume their missionary activities in what had become an exclusively Jesuit field), and rationalized that "what is a scandal in one country is not so in another", also that "necessity knows no bounds".[7]

In its origins, the fur trade was probably non-economic, at least for the Amerindians who gave the first European visitors furs as gifts, accepting gratefully from the fishermen whatever they gave in exchange. Gift exchanges were viewed as symbolic and "diplomatic" by the natives, even after European materialistic concepts as shared by Huguenot and Catholic alike, and trader and missionary alike, had been adopted into native value systems. The introduction of missionary work among the Amerindians was viewed as a means of attaching the tribesmen more firmly to the French politico-military system and trade. Champlain and the Recollets saw no incompatibility between the French fur trade and the Catholic mission to the Hurons — indeed, one would strengthen the other. Champlain went so far as to threaten to cut off trade with the tribes unless they accepted the missionaries in their villages. The Jesuits succeeded the Recollets in this role, and wherever the missionary went in search of new tribes to evangelize the fur trade followed; conversely, when the *coureurs de bois* ventured among new tribes and regions in pursuit of beaver pelts, the missionary was soon asked to follow. The fur trade became so important to the colonial economy that the church found it difficult not to involve itself in some of its activities.

Canon law and the decrees of the general councils made it clear that members of the clergy should not have entangled themselves in commercial affairs; nevertheless, the temptations were too great for a number of individuals. Papal bulls in 1633, and again in 1669, in reaction to irregularities and commercial activities by Jesuit missionaries in Japan, forbade the clergy to engage in commerce. Both the clergy and nobility, as privileged classes, were regarded as being above the pursuit for commercial gain; to have broken the rules would have meant a derogation of one's social status. When the nobility was permitted to trade in the monopoly sphere of North America in 1669, and more generally in 1685 when the King sanctioned engagement in trade by *gentilshommes* in Canada, the clergy retained its original status. The Intendant Talon reported that the Jesuits traded actively in the Ottawa region and at Cap de la Madeleine but, he added, he was unable to give definitive proof of such activities. The clergy of the Foreign Missions in Paris speculated that the papal prohibition of 1669 would probably have little effect in New France because the seculars of the Seminary at Quebec would continue to dissimulate their commercial activities.[8]

A closer examination of these activities reveals the truth of Father Le Jeune's justification to his superiors concerning alleged violations of "the rule of the seventh general Congregation of our [i.e. Jesuit] Society, which absolutely forbids all kinds of commerce and business, under any pretext whatever", that his colleagues used furs as currency but did not invest in the trade in order to make huge profits. He protested the accusations brought by "unnamed persons in France" that Jesuits' "hands are not clean from this traffic" and the unrealistic assumption of superiors in the order itself that "we must not even look at from the corner of our eyes, or touch with the tips of our fingers the skin of any of these animals, which are of great value here."[9] In 1645, the Jesuits were reassured by the Community of Habitants that they would not be disadvantaged by the transfer of the fur trade monopoly from the Company of New France, but they were advised to "go about it quietly", a counsel that was to be transmitted to the superior at Trois-Rivières where large numbers of Montagnais, Algonkins and even Iroquois came to trade. The registers of the mission at Tadoussac indicate quite clearly the nature and extent of the Jesuit involvement with fur trading. As early as 1646 beaver pelts were presented as offerings, as reparations for sins confessed, and as contributions toward building and furnishing the church. Every year thereafter, similar gifts of beaver pelts were made, which the missionaries would dispose of through normal fur trading channels.[10]

The question of clerical involvement in the fur trade was an aspect of Jean Peronne Dumesnil's investigation in 1660, which tended to point to the existence of a friendly relationship between Bishop Laval and Father Ragueneau and the chief traders of the colony, whom Bishop Laval had also succeeded in having named to the first Sovereign Council at Quebec. Dumesnil's office was looted, the evidence he had accumulated was destroyed and he managed to return to France with little more than his life. Louis-Gaudais Dupont was appointed royal investigator but his unconvincing report (no longer extant), was challenged by the Marine bureaucrats who tended to believe the unsubstantiated charges made by Dumesnil. Governor Mézy's papers, which were intended for the information of Lieutenant-General de Tracy, were also seized, torn and burned. Thus, evidence of unknown value was effectively destroyed.

Radisson gave some indication that the Jesuits were interested in the Hudson Bay trade, and Dutch and English sources confirmed a Jesuit involvement in trade with the colonies to the south of the St. Lawrence valley. Ruette d'Auteuil accused the Jesuits of active trading along the Ottawa in 1704, and in the following year, he followed these charges with accusations of important commercial ventures among the Illinois, and at Michilimackinac. The illicit trade which flourished between the English colonies and New France, notably between Albany and Montreal, employed the domiciled reservation Amerindian converts as intermediaries, especially during the first half of the eighteenth century. Governor Beauharnois and Intendant Dupuy even enlisted the aid of the chieftains to curb this illegal trade with the English colonies. In 1727 a large illicit shipment of furs was seized in France itself. Baron Lahontan was convinced that the Jesuits in the Illinois country engaged in active trading "for increasing the revenues of their houses by the prodigious number of canoes of beaver which they send to Quebec under the name of Tiber and Gautier".[11]

More than the Jesuits were involved. Although the domestic servants and *donnés* (voluntary lay helpers) at the missions always had the right to trade, their activities were often difficult to distinguish from transactions carried on for their masters and employers. In 1677, for example, the Sulpicians were warned to have their domestics cease all trading, and not long afterward, the Superior in Paris advised the Montreal community to abstain from the very appearance of trafficking in furs. The chaplain of the Ursulines was required to surrender 260 pounds of pelts in his possession in 1647, while the spiritual advisor to the Hospital Nuns at Quebec in 1658 was revealed to have entered into commercial transactions for the nuns. There were apparently opportunities for the clergy to make money in the colony. The *Abbé* Louis de Norey Dumesnil, a professed Recollet at Quebec for ten years who in 1741 had, with papal permission, entered the Regular Canons of Saint-Augustine, died at Quebec in a private residence in August, 1743, leaving assets of several thousand livres. How a former Franciscan vowed to poverty could have accumulated such wealth is unknown, but it was evidently possible.

The church became involved early in its New World activities in a dispute with the fur traders over the use of alcoholic beverages in trading with the Amerindians. The disputes were not always moralistic versus materialistic in nature because the missionaries came to realize the competitive role of this traffic, and the traders were much aware of the violence and crime which grew out of the trade. The ecclesiastics were as much imbued as the laymen with the French concept of the civilized man being able to handle liquor. The only possible compromise solution to the confrontation was to gradually accustom the natives to French habits, and to restrict the brandy traffic so as to ensure successful competition with the Dutch and English without simultaneously undermining the work of the missionaries and creating too great social disorganization among the Amerindian communities. In fact, this solution was never realized.

Initially the church blamed the Huguenots, and then the Dutch and English, for introducing the "nefarious traffic" to the Amerindians. This was propaganda, of course, as was the charge concerning the first introduction of firearms. The Micmacs had been introduced to alcohol, which was quite unknown in precontact days to all the tribes of the area that became New France, before the first Jesuit missionaries arrived. The fishermen had discovered the material gains to be reaped through bartering wines and brandies for pelts and furs. By the time missions were established at Tadoussac, Quebec and in Huronia, the brandy traffic was already a serious obstacle to evangelization. In 1644, Governor Montmagny grasped the threat posed by unrestricted trafficking in intoxicants, and won the admiration of the clergy by prohibiting the sale to the Amerindians, whether or not converted, of intoxicants and of firearms.[12] This ordinance was followed by a series of ordinances designed to implement the policy and enforce compliance. The pattern had been set for the entire French régime. The clergy would continue to complain of irregularities, violence and non-enforcement, while the civil officers would alternately relax regulations and then re-impose prohibition. Attempts to regulate the traffic would continue to the Conquest and always the problem remained unsolved.

The Recollets and Jesuits spoke out against the trade in intoxicants, and also against the excessive drinking of French seamen, traders and settlers. They urged state regulation of imports and controls on the sale of intoxicants to the native peoples, but they stopped short of demanding absolute prohibition because their cultural background presumed a reasonable use and enjoyment of wines and liquors. The problem of drunkenness became very acute in the French settlements in the late 1640s. Notorious troublemakers were pilloried, and it became known that the drowning of sailors who threw themselves into the sea, the suffocation of imprisoned soldiers and the burning down of a warehouse in Quebec were all related to misuse of alcohol. On one Christmas eve, the men who were to sing at midnight mass caused a shameful commotion and were too drunk to perform. Some native chiefs came to the missionaries with the complaint that Frenchmen were not required to undergo the same severe penance for drunkenness and disorder as were Amerindian converts. The Jesuit missionary at Tadoussac was demanding three beaver pelts by way of reparations for drunkenness, but no similar penance was imposed on French inhabitants nor would such a penalty have been accepted by them.

The reports from ecclesiastical, official and private sources on the attraction which brandy had for the natives and the disastrous effects it produced among them are unanimous in their conclusions. Pierre Boucher was among the first to write that the Amerindians drank "only to become drunk", an observation that was constantly repeated thereafter by both missionaries and laymen. Du Creux summarized some of the Jesuit reports on the matter in these words:

> . . . in addition to the drunkenness which it causes there come many grave and dangerous diseases, for their vitals are scorched by the brandy and injured by the quantities of wine and unfamiliar dainties with which they gorge themselves for several days at a time each year, on the arrival of the ships from France.[13]

The military officer Lahontan observed that the brandy sold to the

Amerindians was "murdering stuff" because it was greatly adulterated, yet was so powerful as to "extinguish their natural heat", to reduce them to a state of "consumption" and in some cases bring rapid death. Much of the "brandy" sold to the natives was brewed from wheat in the colony itself, mixed with cheaper brandies and such foreign substances as urine. Belmont, the missionary to the Algonkins and Iroquois at Oka who wrote a treatise on the subject, referred to cirrhosis of the liver when he warned the domiciled converts that the evil liquors the traders offered them would turn their livers and intestines black.[14]

Neither the Amerindians nor the French were able to understand fully the nature of alcohol addiction and the consequent social disorganization among the tribes which had contact with the French colony. The missionaries theorized about native physical intolerance to alcohol, dietary patterns, cultural drinking and eating customs, and some even considered responsible the Amerindians' "brutish nature" and presumed "diabolical possession". Although the missionaries who came from France usually held that trading intoxicants to the natives was permissible, they rapidly came to the conclusion, after living and working a few years in the colony, that such traffic constituted a mortal sin. Like the French laymen, however, they emphasized the Amerindian deficiencies rather than the materialism of the Europeans, as the touchstone of the problem.

In 1660 Bishop Laval issued a *mandement* threatening those who persisted in disregarding Governor Avaugour's prohibitions with excommunication, and reserving to himself the power to grant absolution in such cases. The civil power soon had some disagreements with the Vicar Apostolic over the enforcement of the ban, and Laval took the matter directly to the French Court. The Sorbonne had been asked to pronounce itself on the validity of such an episcopal ban, and the decision rendered by the theologians on February 1, 1662 was that the civil officers had been unable to maintain peace and order in the colony, that the Amerindians were under tutelage, and that the church had to bolster state legislation. Therefore, in their opinion, selling intoxicants in an infant church of newly converted tribal peoples was a mortal sin and the Vicar Apostolic was justified in making a reserved case of brandy trafficking.[15]

On September 15, 1663, the newly-created Sovereign Council issued its first ordinance of prohibition providing for a 300-livre fine, flogging and banishment in the case of relapse. There were arrests and fines, well below the amount prescribed in the ordinance, but the practice continued unabated. New ordinances with increased penalties were issued each year from 1665 to 1668, all to no avail. Bishop Laval again made a reserved case of supplying intoxicants to the Amerindians and encouraged his clergy to attack the abuses in their Sunday homilies. The state attempted control through a policy of restricted leaves or *congés* for trading in the upper country and through the prohibition from taking intoxicants into the woods for the native trade. Meanwhile, in 1675 the University of Toulouse had given a theological opinion of the brandy traffic. This judgment stressed that although the sale of intoxicants was legitimate, abuse thereof was not. A distinction was made between those Amerindians who were subjects of the French King, and to whom the sale of intoxicants could legitimately be forbidden, and those Amerindians who were in the English sphere of influence and to whom it was necessary to sell brandy in order to obtain their trade.[16]

In 1678 the King and his Council ordered the Governor and Intendant in Canada to call a consultative assembly of the twenty leading inhabitants of the colony to discuss the brandy question, to submit a full report with recommendations to the Crown, appending thereto a list of all the crimes committed in the colony during the last six years. Fifteen of the twenty consulted *habitants* believed the trade should not be restricted, and five favoured some measure of prohibition, although all agreed on the disastrous moral consequences of trading brandy to the Amerindians, and all agreed that the Bishop's interventions had been futile. Laval, meanwhile, consulted his clergy before going to France to lay his case before the King. He argued that the Amerindians presented an exceptional problem of intolerance to alcohol, that he was within his episcopal rights to have made a reserved case of brandy trafficking, and that the eighty ecclesiastics consulted in the colony were overwhelmingly agreed that the trade should be outlawed and absolute prohibition should be enforced. The result of these consultations and representations was the proclamation of a royal edict in 1679 — in the drafting of which the Archbishop of Paris and the King's Jesuit confessor (Father LaChaise) each had a hand — forbidding Frenchmen to carry intoxicants to the dwellings of the Amerindians.[17] The royal compromise avoided both absolute prohibition and unrestricted trade; it did nothing to provide more effective control over the *coureurs de bois* and the soldiers who sold liquor to the natives.

Forbidding the brandy trade in the woods but permitting it in the towns soon proved to be no solution at all to the problems raised in the colony. The brandy traffic went on unabated at the military forts, clerical censures and state regulations notwithstanding. Even the French settlements were gravely affected by the remunerative traffic. In 1685, Trois-Rivières was a village of some twenty-five houses of which at least eighteen were cabarets. The Iroquois raid on Lachine in 1689 gave them an inordinate quantity of brandy, and the following year, the missionaries at Michilimackinac complained of the disastrous effects at that far distant outpost of the arrival of a shipment of 100 barrels of brandy. There was no means of combatting this commerce, however prejudicial to the physical and spiritual welfare of the native peoples, so long as it was viewed as an essential concommittant of the fur trade and military alliances. The King explained his position again in 1689 following appeals from Bishop Saint-Vallier for prohibition enforcement:

> With regards to the disorders caused by the use of brandy . . . His Majesty is pleased to inform them that he does not find it appropriate to change anything . . . nor to deprive his subjects in France and in Canada of the advantage which they obtain from this commerce which would not fail to fall into English hands the moment the French relinquished it.[18]

In 1696 the Sorbonne was once again asked to deliberate the pros and cons of the question. The previous decisions of the university had been based on the premise that the tribesmen drank only to become drunk and once inebriated, that frightful consequences ensued. The case, as presented in 1696, turned on the question of responsibility of the wholesalers who imported large quantities of intoxicants for sale to the Amerindians, but who salved their own consciences by leaving the actual retailing of the brandy to the consumers to lesser merchants and colonists. The importers pretended that all the liquor imported was for the consumption of the French and that if some traders did sell it to the natives in the upper country, the wholesalers could not be held responsible for such infringements of the law. They did not explain, at least to the satisfaction of the clergy, why such large quantities were imported, why stocks were held until the annual fur brigades came down, and why there was so much evidence that much of the brandy eventually went to the Amerindians, not to Frenchmen or Canadians. The only recommendation the learned doctors of the university made was that the wholesalers import smaller quantities of intoxicants and that they refuse to sell brandy to lesser merchants and colonists when the fur brigades came down to Montreal.[19]

Throughout the eighteenth century the problem remained a serious one, no new solutions were proposed, and the previous prohibitions were retained with the same ineffectiveness. The Intendants Bégon, in 1721, and Dupuy, in 1726, employed the same legislative tactics as their predecessors in office with no more successful results.[20] On November 26, 1730, Bishop Dosquet attempted once more to resolve the question for all time. He forbade all confessors to absolve any persons who directly or indirectly contributed to the drunkenness of the natives, reserving to himself the granting of absolution in such cases.[21] His efforts met with no more positive reformation than had the efforts of Laval and Saint-Vallier before him. And Pontbriand who succeeded him also adopted the same policy in the closing decade of the French period with no better results. The church had been as ineffective in dealing with this matter as had been the state officials who wished to curb excess and disorders, because it was not only a social or religious matter, but also, in the eyes of many, it was a crucial economic matter. The importation of wines and spirits was a significant portion of metropolitan trade with the colony, and there was no disposition to curtail it however strong the protests of the ecclesiastics or the complaints of the missionaries might be. Duties on wines from the Bordeaux region, Languedoc and the Canary Islands, on brandies from La Rochelle and Cognac, and on other spirits from the West Indies, for example, accounted for 49.2 per cent of the revenues of the Domaine d'Occident in 1735, an amount which surpassed its revenues from the fur trade. In 1738, Quebec imported about three thousand barrels of wine, and in 1753–54 Louisbourg alone received 7,288 barrels of Bordeaux wines.[22] The economic magnitude of this trade explains the inability to enforce any effective curbs or restrictions.

Thought had been given as early as 1646 to the creation of parishes which would be financially supported, on the metropolitan model, through tithing. The Company of the Holy Sacrament, in recommending the creation of a seminary for the colony, had also obtained permission to collect the *denier de Dieu* for the church of New France in all the markets, fairs and houses of exchange where trading contracts were negotiated. In 1647, it was planned that, instead of tithes, one-sixth of all lands conceded in the colony should be reserved for the clergy with special attention being paid to advantageous locations for the erection of parish churches. The few domiciled converted natives were to be taught to follow the example of the most pious inhabitants and give the first fruits of their harvests to the missionaries.[23] These arrangements did not provide much stability for the development of a parochial system with resident curates and solvent *fabriques* capable of supporting their pastors and teachers, maintaining a church, rectory and school. Indeed, the experiences of the first secular priest, the *Abbé* Jean Le Sueur, indicate the primitive situation which prevailed in 1651:

> There is here a priest who says mass for us each day. He has no revenues or regular honoraria. Nevertheless, he receives his visitors magnificently. He earns his living by weaving nets, which are used greatly in fishing; and this industry brings him more than would any of the chief curial benefices of France.[24]

His case illustrated the need for ecclesiastical organization.

When Laval arrived in 1659 as Vicar Apostolic of the vast territory of New France, he found no parish organization, nor a single church edifice on the south bank of the St. Lawrence or on the island of Orleans, only small wooden edifices for religious services at Montreal and Trois-Rivières, and he learned that most missionaries were saying mass in settlers' cabins. The whole region was served by 25 priests of whom 16 were Jesuits and nine were seculars. Into this vast and sparsely populated region Laval attempted to bring some organization and progress. He decided to provide for parochial charges while avoiding the creation of benefices and circumventing the suggestion that wealthy patrons be found in France. Patronage, if widely promoted, would result in a recurrence of the proprietary church system of early mediaeval Europe which Laval abhorred; he dreamed of implementing a utopian plan worthy of the religious reformation of his time.

On March 26, 1663, Bishop Laval issued letters-patent for the erection and establishment of a seminary at Quebec which would train a colonial clergy and would act as the ministering body of the colonial church. His plan called for superiors chosen by and directly answerable to himself, the eventual creation of a cathedral chapter with the King's approval, the supplying of priests for all the parishes of the colony from this institution, the collection by the seminary of all the tithes of the colony in return for the support and care of the parish curates and the "evangelical workers, as well in health as in sickness, be it in their appointments or in religious communities".[25] He wanted the seminary to be "a continual school of virtue", a reserve of well-trained and diciplined priests worthy of the standards set by the Council of Trent, which would supply the spiritual needs of the colony in both parishes and missions. He proposed with the directors of this institution to retain control over the appointment, tenure and disposition of the parochial clergy who would remain "removable, revocable and subject to dismissal at the will of the bishops and of the seminary". Each parish and mission would still have its *fabrique* (or church council) responsible for providing and maintaining a suitable place of worship, but the seminary would distribute the tithes equitably throughout the colony so as to assure each parish of regular financial support whatever its local revenues might be. The seminary as a community of diocesan clergy would also administer any surplus revenues for the construction of parish churches and rectories and would administer diocesan charities. Laval saw in such a system not only the centralization of control necessary in an unorganized territory but also a return to an apostolic primitiveness in which the clergy "had all things common".

During the primitive period, all the holdings of the church were indivisible, administered by the clergy under the direct and personal authority of the bishop, all disbursements to the several parishes were made by the same administration under the bishop's authority, and all personal and individual enjoyment of ecclesiastical property was forbidden. This was the model that Laval had in mind in endowing the colony with a seminary capable of revitalizing the old faith in a New World.

Since Laval wished to avoid the introduction of benefices, which he regarded as a mediaeval violation of the primitive spirit of apostolic poverty, both he and the secular clergy grouped around him voluntarily renounced their personal possessions to the benefit of the whole diocesan community. In return, the seminary assumed full responsibility for their temporal needs not only when in active service but also in illness and in retirement. When the Sulpician secular clergy instituted a similar organization on the island of Montreal, the Vicar Apostolic had reason to hope that this primitive model would become the permanent form of ecclesiastical organization for New France. The royal letters-patent confirming his establishment "so that the bishops who succeed us may not judge that the bishop alone has bound them to it", provided for a tithe at the rate of 1/13 of the fruits of human labour and production from the soil to be collected and distributed as Laval had planned.

There was a marked difference between the amount officially levied, in conformity with the royal edict, and the amount the habitants would pay. Many colonists complained about the lack or the inadequacy of spiritual services; therefor Laval made some concessions on a local and special basis which were very soon appropriated by all the colonists collectively. The inhabitants of Petit Cap, for example, were permitted to pay at the reduced rate of 1/20 for six years, and the receiver of tithes there was permitted to employ the tithe directly for the upkeep of the local church. This alteration in both the rate and the application of the tithe was also granted to Quebec parish, and this practice was widely interpreted as applying to the entire Vicariate. When Laval contested this interpretation, a rumour began to circulate that he planned to extend the tithe to such items as eggs, cabbages, planks, cordwood and all kinds of manufactures. When an Intendant, Jean Talon, was sent to the colony in 1665, he was instructed to enforce the tithe at the newly accepted rate of 1/20 and to assess whether this was still too onerous a levy for the colony.[26]

Laval hoped to enlist the support of the Intendant in establishing his original plan for the colonial parishes, and he urged the Holy See to elevate the Vicariate to a bishopric because with the influx of immigrants and troops there was being formed "a society of merchants" who allegedly wished to usurp the rights of the church by "pretending to erect parishes and appoint priests in them" on the grounds that New France did not have an Ordinary or resident titular bishop. There was a great popular outcry against the suggestion that the tithe be collected at the rate of 1/13; the Sovereign Council ordered widespread consultation of the colonists while the Lieutenant-General, Governor and Intendant drew up a plan, which Laval approved. It was generally agreed in principle that the rate should be 1/13 (the rate exacted in the Viscounty of Paris), but that for an initial 20-year period it should be levied at 1/26, subject to the King's approval and with "the common consent of the peoples of the aforesaid country". To this greatly reduced rate was added a clarification that it should not extend to manufactured goods or to the fishery. The civil officials also regulated the mode of collection: two elected assessors in each parish computed the tithe; the tithe was paid in threshed grain, and it was to be delivered by the habitant either to the rectory or to the mill.[27]

The problem was that the habitants did not pay their tithes as stipulated. The clergy appealed to the Intendant Duchesneau who issued ordinances in 1675 and in 1677 enjoining the habitants to pay their dues. In the latter ordinance he included a proviso that "the Bishop be obliged to appoint resident curates in each quarter". This reopened the question of resident tenured curates, and the provision of regular services, as a condition for the payment of tithes. Laval argued that without an annual stipend of 600 livres no parish priest could be expected to survive, and none of the parishes to date had collected sufficient tithes to meet such a minimum requirement. In October 1678, the Intendant convoked a special assembly to which the Bishop was invited to consider a plan for erecting twenty-five parishes and to consult some of the leading inhabitants. In the end, only nine parishes were delimited by the Bishop, Governor and Intendant, but Laval was forced into conceding that the resident curates might receive the tithes and offerings instead of the Seminary of Quebec. The arrangements agreed upon at this Quebec conference were given royal sanction by an edict of May 1679, registered by the Sovereign Council at Quebec on October 23, which superseded the letters-patent of April 1663, decreeing that the tithes should be paid to the *fabrique*, that tenured curates be named to the parishes, and that the rights to patronage of churches be observed as in France.[28] However, the secular priests appointed to parish charges agreed to render a full account of the finances of their benefices to the Seminary, which in turn guaranteed them an adequate income. In this manner, Laval's original plan was not totally abandoned.

Although the Sovereign Councillors registered the edict, they discussed at length the fourth clause, which made it their responsibility to provide minimum stipends to resident tenured curates. They communicated all the relevant documents to each *fabrique* and invited comments during the spring of 1680, a measure of popular consultation and discussion of metropolitan policy which the Ministry of Marine might take unkindly. The following year, consultation confirmed the clergy's claim that a minimum stipend of 800 Canadian livres would be required to assure a modest standard of living to parish priests and the regular provision of religious services to the colonists. Intendant Duchesneau communicated the consensus that if the King would accord a subsidy of 4,000 livres, the pressure would be relieved in the poor parishes, and in places where resident pastors could not be appointed, missionary service would be continued. The clergy also complained bitterly about the manner in which tithes were levied and paid. In many cases, the procedures laid out in the edicts and ordinances notwithstanding, the *habitant* harvested his crops, declared the gross product, computed his tithe and took the harvested and cleaned grain to the receiver of tithes for the parish. According to reports received from several parish priests, the colonists were not always honest in declaring their crops, they paid off their debts before computing their tithes, some moved away without paying their dues, and some paid only on a portion of the fields they cultivated. The method of collecting the tithe invited fraud and deceit, could bring financial disaster to a parish, and led in some cases to interminable legal proceedings.

By 1681, of twenty-five priests in regular parish assignments only nine held letters of provision from the Bishop of Quebec. Moreover, Laval had stipulated that patron founders of parishes would have to build stone edifices and supply an endowment. Colonists in many parishes and missions still refused to supply the tithe as required, and there were persistent rumours that a return to the original rate of 1/13 would be instituted in 1683, especially after it became known that the Bishop had asked the Ministry of Marine for a thorough survey of the financial conditions of each parish in the spring of that year. Intendant de Meulles discovered that only ten parishes had been canonically erected, that there were only eight stone churches and seven *presbytères* in Canada, that seventeen seculars from the Seminary at Quebec (among them seven Canadians), three Sulpician seculars and one Recollet served as parish priests, and also that twelve of the priests lodged with their parishioners. Only six parishes collected 500 livres or more in tithes; eleven collected 300 livres or less — overall, for twenty-three areas outside the town of Quebec, the average tithe was about 340 livres per parish.[29] The response in France was the usual injunction to create more parishes, but this was accompanied by the more practical announcement that the royal subvention was being increased to 6,000 livres to supplement the revenue deficiencies in many parishes to assure the clergy a minimum stipend.

In 1685, the Bishop-elect Saint-Vallier toured the colony and reported on the state of the church. He noted that there were "about thirty resident priests in the colony" and that, since the 1685 tithes amounted to 6,196 livres, computing at the very low rate of 400 livres minimum stipend, the provisioning of fifty parish priests (as requested by Louis XIV) would mean a deficit of 13,804 livres. He did not believe that adequate services and decent living standards for the clergy could be assured for less than 20,000 livres annual subsidization by the Crown.

In 1686 Bishop Saint-Vallier obtained from the King an increase to 8,000 livres of the subsidy allocated for minimum stipends for parish priests. The principal problem requiring his immediate attention was the extension of the parochial system so that colonists would hear mass more frequently than "one Sunday in a month or in six weeks" as Intendant Duchesneau had reported. Parish priests were designated to parishes in three different manners. In both Quebec and Montreal, the nominations of parish priests belonged to the respective seminaries in those towns. Also, since 1679 the common French patronage system had been introduced, and Bishop Laval had provided that any person, especially a seigneur, who paid the construction costs of a stone church would enjoy the right of nomination to the cure whenever vacant. As it turned out, neither seigneurs nor *censitaires* rushed to undertake such an expense in return for the few privileges and honours it bestowed. The Seminary of Quebec, as seigneur at Saint-Joachim and Ile Jésus, took up the patronage rights. At Terrebonne the *curé* and seigneur Lepage fulfilled the requirements to obtain the patronage rights. In other words, lay patrons were not forthcoming and the system attracted only ecclesiastical patrons. Bishop Saint-Vallier, therefore, decided unilaterally to drop the system in 1699. Finally, the most direct system was for the bishop to nominate the parish priests. The secular power insisted that the Ordinary should make appointments "irrevocable and immovable", that is, they should be life-time appointments with security of tenure.

In 1690 the Intendant Jean Bochart de Champigny, reported that Saint-Vallier had done nothing to expand the parochial system, therefore he suggested withdrawing the annual subsidy unless twelve new parishes were erected. Saint-Vallier responded by canonically erecting three more parishes. Then a dispute erupted over who should distribute the royal *gratification* to the parishes to supplement their revenues from tithing: the Bishop felt it was his responsibility to do so, the Seminary claimed it held the legal right, and the Intendant believed his charge over colonial finances entitled him to oversee the distribution. A compromise solution saw the churchmen carry out the actual distribution with Champigny scrutinizing the entire proceedings.

The bitterest quarrels were not between secular and ecclesiastical officials but among the clergy themselves and between the clergy and the colonists. In 1691 Saint-Vallier publicly denounced all parishioners who refused to pay their tithes and threatened to personally investigate such cases. However, at the synod of 1698 it was decided to leave such investigations in the hands of the parish priests. The Sovereign Council had to intervene in 1705 to appease aroused parishioners at Beauport and Ange Gardien who threatened revolt unless their pastors, Boullard and du Fournel, retracted their assertions that the tithe should be computed at the original rate of 1/13 and should include cattle, sheep, hay, fruit, flax, hemp and other agricultural products. The popular outcry was that the rate of tithing had been fixed and could not be altered, that it could not be extended to articles hitherto not taxable, that Boullard had added a seventh and unauthorized commandment of the church requiring the payment of tithes, and that if the colonial income from tithing was insufficient to meet over-all needs, the exemptions granted the religious institutes and seminaries on their productive lands should be repealed. The attorney-general reported that the claim of the clergy to the right to augment and extend the tithe was founded on a regulation of August 23, 1667, which had never received approval but had been superceded by another settlement reached on September 4 of the same year. By an ordinance promulgated on February 1, 1706, the Sovereign Council forbade any alterations in the tithe, a position which was upheld by the Council of State in France the following year.[30]

Saint-Vallier continued to fight to have the colonists pay their tithes and to have the Seminary clergy agree to permanent parish charges. In 1713 the Intendant, Bégon, had to take affairs into secular hands by ordering the colonists to deliver their tithes as required by the royal edict to the *presbytères*. In 1717 Saint-Vallier ordered the clergy to refuse to give absolution to those who came to perform their Easter duties but who were guilty of what he now called "the inveterate and virtually irremediable abuse" of refusing to pay the prescribed tithes in the appointed manner.[31] Saint-Vallier indicated that many defrauded the church, that they reported only a portion of their harvests, and paid "often with the worst quality of their grains and paying only when and how they are ready to comply". His *Rituel* had taught the faithful to pay the entire amount assessed with the best quality of grains at Eastertide, but large numbers seemed to ignore these teachings completely.

Neither in the matter of tithes nor in the establishment of parishes were the difficulties ever resolved. In 1727, recourse was had again to the Intendant for an ordinance requiring the colonists to pay and deliver the full tithe as prescribed. In 1730 another civil order was sought to require the colonists to tithe on all cereals, not just on wheat as, some contended, had been the original understanding. In 1742 Bishop Pontbriand found it necessary to establish once again that several religious houses and seminaries had been exempted from paying tithes in their holdings.[32] As for delimiting parish boundaries, an effort in 1721 to define 82 parishes drew protests from the seminaries at Quebec and Montreal and from the poorer parishes. By 1730 there were still no more than 20 tenured curates and the remainder of the parishes were being served by missionaries. The bishops never gave up their right to remove at will the priests (curés) they appointed to parish charges; therefore, apart from Notre-Dame parish in Quebec, in a canonical sense there were no irrevocable cures in the colony before 1763.

The burden of the tithe in France fell unevenly on the population as it was levied on cereals generally, but in some districts it was levied also on cattle, sheep and vineyards. In Brittany it was extended to the fishery in the sense that dues were claimed by the clergy on the harvest of the sea, and this practice was extended to Placentia and Louisbourg in the 18th century. An unofficial tithe of "one quintal of cod per chaloupe" was exacted in 1731 at the request of the Recollet missionaries and St. Ovide, who observed that "there is perhaps only Isle Royale in the world which does not pay the tithe to its priests", since it possessed neither grainfields nor vineyards. The Ministry of Marine regarded this tithe as a voluntary almsgiving or *donation*, which had become the customary contribution at Placentia for the provision of religious services at that output. The Ministry was willing to force captains to pay it and it upheld those ecclesiastics who withheld services and withdrew privileges from those who neglected to provide this kind of financial support. This tithe was paid in flour or biscuits, sometimes in wines or salted meats, at the discretion of the captain. The problem was to convince the inhabitants of Louisbourg proper that they ought to pay a similar tithe for the support of their clergy. One of the reasons for preferring Recollets from Brittany to secular priests for Isle Royale was that seculars would have required more substantial financial support from the *fabrique* than did the members of a religious institute.[33] There does not appear to have been any move to apply the tithe to the fur trade in New France although such an imposition could have been defended logically and rationally, particularly in the period prior to the development of agriculture in the colony.

As already indicated, every parish and mission had its board of trustees called the *fabrique*. The churchwardens who composed this local council were elected by parishioners, except at Quebec and Montreal where the outgoing council and former churchwardens formed the electorate. The office carried no stipend, could not be refused, and afforded but few honours in ceremonies and processions. The *fabrique* was responsible for the temporal affairs of the parish, such as the maintenance of the church building, the rectory, the school (if there was one), and the cemetery. The parish income consisted of the weekly collections, the annual collections at the time of the priest's parochial visitation, pew rentals, offerings, burial fees, one-third of the fees for the singing of high mass, and the profits from cultivated lands if the parish owned any. If major repairs or new construction were necessary, the normal income of the parish could not suffice. In such cases, a meeting of the parishioners was called to agree democratically upon the contribution of each. The upkeep of the parochial schools and the salaries of their teachers were met by the same self-taxing system. There was strong opposition to any externally imposed taxation — indeed, the colony had no direct taxes or levies, and rumour of imposing the *taille* (a form of direct royal taxation levied on non-privileged subjects) had at one time evoked revolutionary talk.

Local control was not necessarily beneficial to the development of the institutional church. In 1720, for example, the bishop had to remind the inhabitants of Detroit that their church was in a lamentable state, and that the cemetery was in a deplorable condition because they had not so much as enclosed it. The general state of affairs in the closing decades of the French period is a good indicator of the problems which existed. During his visitations, Bishop Pontbriand emphasized the need for suitable places for divine worship and the decent upkeep of all church-owned properties. Wherever he went he gave specific directions for their maintenance: sometimes it was the church that required repairs, or the cemetery that stood in need of weeding and fencing; in other places, it was a confessional to be built, pews to be repaired, a belfry to be erected, or a fence to be mended. The advice was direct and practical, and it indicated a certain degree of negligence on the part of the populace regarding church affairs. During years of poor crops and war conditions, both of which were numerous in the eighteenth century, it could also be that the burdens on the poorer people were sufficiently heavy to arouse feeling against any additional contribution of either money or labour for the church.

The *fabrique*, while providing a democratic form of trusteeship, also made it difficult to enforce collection of dues from one's neighbours and relatives.

There were other economic problems too. Building materials for new churches or for repairs were never easy to obtain from the parishioners, who did not appear to have flocked willingly and in large numbers to provide the labour required. When it came to *presbytères*, the habitants were loath to contribute in any way. The Bishop had to decree minimum dimensions for rectories, had to threaten to remove curates unless a residence were built and then had to forbid Sunday labour or the use of old materials. At Baie-St. Antoine the building material was collected but left to rot on the spot as none would volunteer labour. At Sorel, which was threatened by Pontbriand with the removal of a resident priest, the parishioners took four years to put a roof on the rectory. The church frequently resorted to the secular arm for support; from 1709 when an ordinance was issued by Raudot until 1751 when one was issued by Bigot, there were no less than 31 orders to recalcitrant and stubborn parishioners to build and repair *presbytères* in over twenty different parishes. The effectiveness of this state intervention was evidently less than desirable because several orders had to be repeated.[34]

In addition to considerations of time and cost, the *habitants* may have objected to voluntary labour and special levies because construction could be a seemingly never-ending process. By 1750, parishes like Ste. Famille, Cap Santé, Pointe Claire and Lotbinière were building their second, or even third in the case of Sorel, church chargeable to the *fabrique*.[35] Perhaps if better materials had been furnished in the first instance, and more care had gone into construction, there would have been less need to rebuild at such short intervals.

Finally, there is the question of the church's teaching in the sphere of economic justice, especially with respect to usury and just price. The various religious orders, including the Ursulines and Hospital Nuns, employed letters of exchange and rescripts in their financial dealings. These did not fall under the condemnation of usury because French merchants distinguished between interest and *change* — the latter being charges levied for exchanging currencies or bills of exchange and therefore not in the same category as outright interest on borrowed money which was still defined as usury by the royal declaration of December 1665.[36] As far as laymen were concerned, the church forbade the taking of inordinate and excessive interest, as opposed to a legitimate return on an investment, loan or service rendered. The church seigneurs in New France lent money to their *censitaires* at a 5 per cent interest rate. Sometimes a *censitaire* in need of money sold his land to his seigneur, but remained on his *roture* as long as he paid the 5 per cent annual interest on the sale price. It is estimated that the religious orders may have averaged 50 to 100 livres from these interest charges for each one hundred *rotures*.[37] Usury was condemned but its meaning was not extended to the point of undermining completely the profit motive and the economic foundations of the political order.

The church had always been concerned by shortages, high prices, and economic hardship when these touched the common people. In maintaining a teaching of social and economic justice, the churchmen sometimes risked offending the secular officials who failed to distinguish between private gain and the perquisites of civil office. Many quarrels with Governors and Intendants could have been avoided had the clergy closed its eyes to the exploitation concommitant with the fur trade. Towards the end of the French régime, war, famine, epidemics and corruption in high office weighed heavily on the common people. During the famine which struck Quebec in 1742 the ecclesiastical authority came to the support of the secular arm by means of a *mandement* attacking the exorbitant prices charged by rural inhabitants for the foodstuffs which the town dwellers sorely required. The *mandement* indicated some rural-urban tension:

> The towns are, Our dearly beloved Children, like the heart of this colony; would you become unrighteous members who would refuse to a strained heart the blood which it requires? It is in the towns that you will find what is lacking in your countryside, it is in the towns where many of your children receive a Christian education; would you be so ungrateful as to violate the laws of perfect gratitude which heaven will reward a hundredfold? It is in the towns where the hospitals are open to receive you in your infirmities; offer to these houses, which will forever be august monuments of the piety of your forefathers, the help they impatiently await; it is in the towns that justice settles your differences and renders to each what belongs to him; it is there that resides in a special manner the Royal authority and where His Majesty supports a large number of troops for the defence of this colony, in order to

maintain peace and public tranquillity; finally, it is in the towns that the poor of the countryside take refuge at the public charge.[38]

Although no effective means of enforcing the Christian ideals of brotherly love and communal sharing were prescribed, the appeal did hold before the populace a standard which contrasted markedly with the egoism, avarice and hedonistic considerations then rampant.

Bishop Pontbriand gave his official blessing, the following year, to state measures to alleviate the bread shortage and to provide the colonists with seed grain, and took the occasion to remind his clergy that it was their obligation "to have the people understand that if the harvest is not abundant, it often is a punishment of God"; nevertheless, they could appease Divine retribution by sincere penance, redoubled prayers and acts of charity to those less fortunate than themselves. In 1758, the Bishop was dismayed that Marine officers required the inhabitants to swear solemnly to supply the armies. The scarcity of food in the colony was a major problem as the war dragged on. Pontbriand issued a circular encouraging his clergy to sacrifice their tithes to the King's service, so that victory might be obtained for the French arms; nevertheless he remained convinced that few habitants would pay their tithes in kind because they required what they had for their own seed and food and the church could not fault them for such behaviour.

Thus, in every aspect of economic life and activity, the church in New France found itself involved and its message relevant.

Chapter V

The Church and Public Welfare

The primary responsibility of the church was to minister to the spiritual needs of the colony. In recognition of this duty of the church, the state cooperated by assuring that sufficient personnel — missionaries, secular priests, chaplains, nursing sisters, teachers and lay helpers — were permitted to emigrate to New France. It was the state which gave permission for new religious foundations, opened new mission fields, and regulated religious professions. Besides affording the religious protection, the civil power gave assistance in the way of open passages, freight allowances, exemptions, special concessions and subsidies. Contemplative orders, however, came to be regarded by mercantilist administrators like Colbert as parasitical and unprofitable. All the religious communities, male and female, came to expect that a utilitarian standard would be applied by the government bureaucracy in evaluating their normal requests for the various types of authorizations they required.

Colbert expressed himself unequivocally on this matter:

> If Your Majesty can manage to reduce all his subjects to these four sorts of occupations (agriculture, trade, war, seafaring), one can say that [he] can be master of the world, while striving at the same time to diminish quietly and imperceptively the religious of both sexes who produce only useless people in this world, and very often devils in the next world. . . .[1]

The objective of every community was to establish that it was "useful to His Majesty's service." One could be useful in achieving stated royal objectives over a wide range of activities — chaplaincy duty, discovery of new lands, nursing the sick, educating the youth, assimilating the native peoples, serving as translators or ambassadors, advising the state officials on local conditions, etc. But apart from utility to the Crown there was little hope of prolonged activity in the colony.

Growing out of this situation was the fact that an enduring tradition of religious involvement in the domain of public welfare developed early in the colonial period. The reforms begun in the seventeenth-century French church increased the duties and responsibilities of the parish priests as well. They were expected to preach, to instruct the young, to stimulate religious practices, to exercise control over public morality and matrimonial discipline, to engender respect for the confessional, to set a personal example of piety and temperance, as well as to keep accurate parish registers indicating the vital statistics of their charges. In other words, they had an important social role to fill and they were reminded frequently of their special ecclesiastical dignity. It was natural that they should sometimes consider themselves apart from and superior to the laity. This probably had direct consequences for their conduct which was, in the colonial context, remarkably exemplary on the whole, and very rarely reprehensible. There were a few parish priests about whose conduct the parishioners complained, fewer religious who were sent back to the metropolis or who left their orders, and still fewer recalcitrants who caused any public mischief.

The parish clergy, moreover, do not appear to have been great charismatic leaders wielding unusual influence for moral reform or fervent religiosity among their parishioners. In general, they could barely overcome the indifference of the *habitants*, and testimonials to external social conformism in religion are legion. Some priests were unhappy when assigned to parish charges. The *Abbé* François Seguenot, for example, complained when posted to Pointe-aux-Trembles, which he felt isolated him from the fellowship and intellectual stimulation of the seminary.[2] Seguenot's concern was that as an educated individual, a leader in the parish, a guide in many everyday affairs, a counsellor, and a man with whom the colonists would exchange ideas and even argue, he might have much to give but could expect little in return. The function of the church, at this level, was to indoctrinate the young and initiate them into the life of the church, developing their reason and stirring an appreciation of the beautiful in nature, in the liturgy, and also in thought. If the church could succeed through the catechetical method in imparting some facility with abstract ideas and self-expression, then the *curés* would not find their parishioners such dull people from the intellectual standpoint. Seguenot's experience seems to indicate that parish life could be a deadening and unbearable charge compounded by the economic hardships imposed by a high cost of living and very inadequate revenues.

Three colonial bishops — Laval, Saint-Vallier and Pontbriand — were particularly interested in the close supervision and strict regulation of the religious institutes, secular communities and seminaries. Laval and Saint-Vallier, in particular, instructed their clergy to indoctrinate their parishioners in the basic principles of the faith and the fundamental doctrines relating to penance, the eucharist, and the mass. None of the bishops equalled Saint-Vallier in his devotion to the achievement of this objective. His clergy gave special Lenten sermons and instructional sermons on high festivals and during retreats. Special catechism classes held in each parish for at least three weeks preceding confirmations started in the episcopate of Dosquet, if not earlier. But not all parents sent their children, and Pontbriand had to upbraid the inhabitants of St. Thomas in 1741 for their negligence in this respect.[3]

The women's communities came under particularly close scrutiny. Indeed, both Ursulines and Sisters of the Congregation resented what they considered "unwarranted interference" in their rules and customs by Laval, but the greatest outbursts of resentment and defiance were reserved for Saint-Vallier. Pontbriand often visited their monasteries, examined minutely their accounts and regulations, as counselled by the Council of Trent and the ordinances of the Assembly of the French Clergy, and inquired into their disciplinary methods and conformity. He was particularly strict in his supervision of the Sisters of the Congregation and of the Sisters of Charity (founded by Mme. d'Youville) because they were both communities of recent and Canadian origin.

This attention, however, was not a form of discrimination. Pontbriand dealt just as meticulously with his clergy. He was so interested in the moral and theological training of the clergy that he personally gave lectures in dogmatics and moral philosophy to the seminarians. In 1752 he inaugurated a plan for ecclesiastical conferences and retreats. His sermons during the 1757 retreat for the diocesan clergy, for example, dealt with such topics as the salvation of souls, paradise, the duties of confessors, penance as a virtue, the glory of God, and the small number of the saved.[4] These were the ideals and standards set before a clergy which was expected to give leadership in the parishes of the colony.

Education was of paramount importance in the colony, and thus, nearly all the religious institutes, including the orders of Hospital

Nuns, undertook some educational tasks. In 1626 the Marquis de Gumaches and his wife provided the Jesuits in Canada with an annual income of 3,000 livres and promised to give them a capital fund of 48,000 livres when their son took his final vows in the Society. The Jesuit missionaries in the colony, however, were not legally constituted as a novitiate, or as a college or as a professed house, therefore they were technically unable to administer such a capital fund. For this reason, their Provincial in Paris decided to found "a college within the residence of Canada" in order to capitalize on the generous bequest. Thus it was that in 1635, prior to the founding of Harvard, the small town of Quebec, which could not have boasted more than ten or so boys of school age, was blessed with a college. It would be both inexplicable and manifestly premature, apart from this institutional requirement, for the Jesuits to found a classical college in an embryonic colony.

The original plan was to have the college for French boys at Notre-Dame des Anges, the former Recollet residence near to Quebec, proximate to a "seminary" for Amerindian boys. Classes for the French boys opened in Quebec, not at Notre-Dame des Anges, in response to parental demands. The instruction seems to have been of a practical primary level suitable to an outpost where self-reliance, innovation and practicality were at a premium. The Jesuits found it necessary to become involved in this primary schooling in order to raise up a clientele for their more advanced type of instruction. Not until 1650 was the Jesuit residence and college in Quebec completed and ready to provide the youth of the colony with the disciplined scholastic curriculum of the *Ratio Studiorum*.

In 1651 Martin Boutet opened a boarding school for the parish of Quebec and the boys enrolled came to the Jesuits for most of their instruction. This school started with sixteen pupils. Two years later, the Superior described this instructional program in these words:

> Especially here at Quebec, because of the greater numbers of our colleagues, the college gives a consequential idea of one of the more important colleges in Europe, particularly in what concerns religious discipline. For what relates the teaching of *lettres* we have up to the present only two classes, one in grammar, the other in mathematics, although I could add a third where we taught the children to read and to form their letters. This responsibility is left entirely to two Fathers . . .[5]

Boutet would certainly have given the boys a grounding in French, arithmetic and music and it was probably this practical primary instruction that became the mathematical class described above, while the grammar class was most likely the more traditional Jesuit teaching of Latin and Greek as outlined in their syllabus of 1599. The so-called "mathematics" class was in reality to become a commercial and technical education serving the needs of the merchants and seafarers of the colony.

In the autumn of 1659, at the urgings of Bishop Laval, the Jesuits started classes in humanities and rhetoric, and in 1665 philosophy and theology were added to round out their program. Thereby was opened to young Canadians the full range of educational prerequisites for the priesthood. The fact that Amerindian children could not meet the cultural requirements of this educational program accounts for the complete absence of an Amerindian clergy in New France. In 1666 Louis Jolliet and Pierre de Repentigny were publicly examined in logic by the Lieutenant-General, the Intendant and the Bishop, an impressive panel of judges who handled Latin well. The following year the first class was publicly examined in the entire philosophy course. Three students were then ready to enter theology — Jolliet, Martin and Véron — but the results were not too encouraging for Jolliet decided to go into the fur trade and exploration, Véron disappeared from historical records, and Martin preferred the seculars to the Jesuits.

Then in 1667, Bishop Laval gathered together at the Seminary of Quebec three students in theology and two in philosophy to form the nucleus of his Major Seminary. This, in effect, undermined any Jesuit aspirations of controlling the formation of a Canadian clergy because henceforth nearly all of the boys desiring to enter the priesthood would go to the Seminary of secular priests at Quebec. It was not until 1713 that a student at the college entered the Jesuit order. On the other hand, among the missionaries who came from France there were a number who had not yet completed their studies and they did so at Quebec.

The Jesuit college at Quebec maintained its high reputation throughout the French régime. It was forced to close in 1759, although it did manage to maintain its associated elementary school until 1776. In 1685 the Minister of Marine asked the cartographer Franquelin to teach courses in navigation at the college. Franquelin was succeeded in 1696 by Louis Jolliet who was named professor of hydrography. The Ministry even sent cadets from France to train at Quebec in this period. In 1703 Jean Deshayes assumed the task of teaching navigation and pilotage to the colonial youth and held this position until his death. The four most renowned teachers in this area had all been laymen; thereafter, Jesuits themselves continued to offer courses in basic physics, chemistry, geometry, and navigation, and in 1732 had no less than thirty boarders as well as a large number of day-scholars including Marine cadets, officers and petty civil officials. The colonial surveyors and assessors took special classes at the college. Over several years, Attorney-general Verrier gave a course of lectures in law, designed to give rudimentary knowledge to the assessors of the Superior Council.

By 1750 both the college and the order itself were held in high esteem. Peter Kalm, the Finnish botanist whose accounts of travel in New France have provided much interesting material on contemporary social behaviour, left the following account of his visit and impressions:

> The building the Jesuits live in is magnificently built, and looks exceedingly fine, both without and within, which makes it similar to a fine palace. It consists of stone, is three stories [*sic*] high, exclusive of the garret, is covered with slate and built in a square form like the new palace at Stockholm, including a large court. Its size is such that three hundred families would find enough room in it, though at present there were not above twenty Jesuits in it. . . . There is a long corridor along all sides of the square, in every story [*sic*], on both sides of which are either cells, halls, or other apartments for the friars. There are also their library, apothecary shop, etc. Everything is very well regulated, and the Jesuits are well accommodated there. On the outside is their college which is on two sides surrounded with great orchards and kitchen gardens, in which they have fine walks. . . . The Jesuits dine together in a great hall. . . . They dine very well, and their dishes are as numerous as at the greatest feasts. In this spacious building you do not see a single woman. . . . The Jesuits are usually very learned, studious and civil and agreeable in company. In their whole deportment there is something pleasing. It is no wonder therefore that they captivate the minds of people. . . . Their conversation is very entertaining and learned, so that one cannot be tired of their company. Among all the Jesuits I conversed with in Canada, I have not

found one who was not possessed of these qualities in a very eminent degree. . . .[6]

The chief cause of disappointment in the colony was that the Jesuits at the college and residence at Quebec were all from metropolitan France, and that of the five or six Canadian-born members of the order none had ever been sent back to New France. When one of the secular priests left the Seminary community to join the Jesuits it was reported that "the other priests were very ill pleased with this, because it seemed as if he looked upon their condition as too lowly for himself."

The other religious communities were no less active in the field of education. It was the *Abbé* Gabriel Souart, for example, superior of the Sulpicians at Montreal and a physician by training, who opened the first boys' school on the island. From this beginning in education, the Gentlemen of Saint-Sulpice assumed teaching charges throughout the island and in the adjoining seigneuries where they were also parish priests. They also took a very special interest in the education of Amerindian children, notably at their missions to the Seneca, at their reservation at La Montagne (which was successively moved to Sault-au-Récollect and Lac des Deux Montagnes) and at the Algonkian mission at Ile aux Tourtes founded by the *Abbé* Michel Barthélemy. The latter had been in charge of the Sulpician primary schools on the island of Montreal. Between 1693 and 1699 it was the *Abbé* Léonard Chaigneau who administered the school system, wrote a long memorandum on the equipment of schools for the bishop's information, and fitted out a model school. Also, in 1686 the *Abbé* de La Faye had been instrumental in organizing a community of teaching brothers, similar to the community of Jean-Baptiste de La Salle in Paris, at the principal boys' school in Montreal. This experiment within the Sulpician community collapsed in 1693 because of insolvency.[7]

The Sulpicians also contributed to schooling in Acadia where the *Abbé* Louis Petit, from the Seminary of Quebec, had been sent as Laval's vicar-general in 1676 and where he had organized a school at Port Royal. A layman named Dubreuil was an outstanding teacher at this school. Then, in 1685 Bishop Saint-Vallier invited the Sisters of the Congregation to take charge of the girls' school at Port Royal and the *Abbé* Louis Geoffroy of the Montreal seminary to act as pedagogical advisor with the responsibility of organizing *petites écoles* throughout Acadia. Geoffroy pursued this assignment zealously until the British intervention prevented further development of the French schools.

The Recollets had schools in Montreal, Trois-Rivières and Isle Royale, in addition to sponsoring and teaching in parochial schools when named to parish charges by the bishops. When they assumed the chaplaincy duties at Fort Frontenac and Detroit, they opened some of the first schools for French and Amerindian children at posts in the upper country. These early schools required that they set aside the traditional pattern of segregated schools for boys and girls and the newly acquired bias for segregated schools for Europeans and natives. All the children at these posts were educated in common schools.

There was a plan to establish an arts and trades school at St. Joachim, near Cap Tourmente, for boys desiring an education which stressed the manual arts and fine arts, and also a fine arts school for girls in the Upper Town of Quebec. Some arts were taught at Quebec by the Jesuits, Ursulines and the Seminary clergy. In 1685, Bishop Saint-Vallier and Governor Denonville opened a minor seminary at Cap Tourmente. Within a few years its students of philosophy and rhetoric were transferred to the Seminary in Quebec, while a few students at Quebec, unsuited to classical studies, were either apprenticed out or sent to the elementary school at St. Joachim where they also worked on the seminary farm. Bishop Laval gave some financial support to this project in 1693. It was probably this latter school — which trained colonial boys considered unsuited to the classical course — that Peter Kalm visited in 1749. He left an enlightening description of its objectives and limited success.

> In order to fit the children of this country for orders, there are schools at Quebec and St. Joachim where the youths are taught Latin and instructed in the knowledge of these things and sciences, which have a more immediate connection with the business they are intended for. However, they are not very particular in their choice, and people of a middling capacity are often received among them. They do not seem to have made great progress in Latin; for notwithstanding the service is read in that language, and they read their Latin breviary and other books, every day, yet most of them find it difficult to speak it. . . .[8]

He was not convinced that such mediocre schooling merited all the financial support forthcoming from royal subsidization or the income from lands conceded to the Seminary at Quebec by the Crown.

In 1694, the Brothers Hospitallers of the Cross, founded by François Charon, a Canadian, were given permission to open a school for orphans in conjunction with their hospice for men and boys at Montreal, "to teach crafts to the aforesaid children and give them the best possible education." The pursuit of these educational objectives in addition to their hospital work proved to be an unwise decision because it dispersed their funds and sapped their energies. Moreover, it brought the disfavour of the King, who forbade them to take religious vows and wear a distinctive habit, an opposition which undermined their morale. Specific permission was given in 1699, nevertheless, to teach crafts to orphans and foundlings, and consequently the Brothers attempted to operate a stocking factory, a brewery and a flour mill in conjunction with their apprenticeship program. These were all failures. In 1718, Louis XV approved a 3,000 livres subsidy for the maintenance of schoolmasters, provided they maintained *petites écoles* dispensing primary education in at least six rural parishes.[9] Charon went to France to recruit six schoolmasters in 1718, and the following year he succeeded in finding six more teachers for the primary schools. Unfortunately, most of these lay teachers taught only for a few months or a year, then found other employment, or engaged in commerce in the colony, making it necessary to continually recruit new schoolmasters. By 1721 Hospitallers' schools had been opened in Boucherville, Longueuil, Pointe-aux-Trembles, Batiscan and Trois-Rivières, in addition to the main school just outside Montreal. Claude de Ramezay, Governor of Montreal, on the other hand, reported that they did nothing for the cause of education in the colony, therefore the Council of Marine ordered certificates to be obtained from the priest of each parish where schools were operating in order to qualify the Brothers Hospitallers for the subsidy of 375 livres per schoolmaster which had been assured them.[10] Bishop Dosquet had also forbidden the Brothers to accept any new members into their community.

Eight more teachers came from France the following year, and the King, in stipulating that education was to be free for the habitants' sons, permitted the Brothers to accept gifts and donations in return for services rendered, although fixed fees were prohibited. In 1724 another six teachers came to the colony although the new superior, Brother Chrestien, had failed to negotiate successfully a proposed union with the Brothers of the Christian Schools.

On his return to the colony, the superior found his community to be indebted about 25,000 livres and, in panic, he fled to the West Indies. In 1730 the King cut off the annual subsidy on the grounds that the education provided was of inferior quality.[11] The remaining teachers and brothers struggled to keep the schools open until more optimism was generated in 1736 with the agreement to incorporate the community with that of the Brothers of Christian Schools in France. Their work continued to diminish as no new recruits were sent from France. By 1745, when the community dissolved, no fewer than twenty-four teachers had been sent from France and there were still ten parish schools operating in New France which traced their origins to the Brothers Hospitallers.

Religious women were active in teaching and hospital work in Canada twenty years prior to the arrival of the first bishop. The Ursulines were destined in 1639 to provide both a popular primary education and operate a finishing school for the daughters of the colonial elite, just as in France they operated schools for girls of the upper classes side by side with schools for the daughters of the poor.[12] Their *petites écoles* grew out of the prescription of the Council of Trent that "in every church in the city in the country" there be established a primary school where trained teachers "will freely teach poor children reading, writing grammar and calculation". Du Creux's comment on the special task of the Ursulines in the colony is relevant:

> The special task of the Ursulines is the training of young girls and to their schools of religion, which are a kind of public school, little girls are sent from all the communities of the country. The Ursulines also receive some pupils as boarders, who occupy a separate part of the convent, to be trained in religion and good manners.[13]

This concept of the "collective education of little girls" was innovative, but Du Creux's description of their school organization failed to indicate the initial or primitive pattern in the colony whereby the French girls were to be given an élitist education in the *pensionnat* and the Amerindian girls were to be given a basic and practical training, destined to prepare them for marriage to Frenchmen or entry into the relogous life, in what was called the "seminary".

Boarders paid about 120 livres board and tuition per annum, this being paid more often in kind than in cash. Marie de l'Incarnation (whose example of piety and devotion did much to retain official support for the order when it was assailed by both ecclesiastical and civil officials for being "less useful to His Majesty's service" than the other communities of religious women in the colony), concluded that were it not for the Ursulines, the young women of the colony in the first thirty years of colonization would have lost their faith and their children would have slipped into the permissive ways of the New World. The Amerindian work was soon abandoned as a separate project because the girls who were brought to them ran off; the French work was also slow and often discouraging because most of the girls remained only a year or two at the convent.

In 1697 the Ursulines extended their élitist type of education for girls to Trois-Rivières, but in order to obtain royal approbation, also agreed to open a hospital there at the instigation of Governor Frontenac and Bishop Saint-Vallier.[14] Conversely, when the Hospital Nuns of Dieppe arrived at Quebec in 1639, they were requested to provide a school for Amerindian and French children at the reservation of Sillery in addition to their hospital work. They found the costs of operating both a school and a hospital outside the town of Quebec extremely high; therefore, in 1646 they ignored the wishes of the Jesuit missionaries and assumed what they conceived to be their proper role in the colony — to establish and maintain a hospital at Quebec which would serve as a military and naval hospital.[15] When New Orleans was founded, the Ursulines were given charge of the education of girls and young women in Louisiana, a responsibility in which they were upheld by bishops Mornay and Dosquet.

In 1653 a secular association of devout women, commonly known as the Sisters of the Congregation, undertook a ministry of teaching in the Montreal area under the guidance of Marguerite Bourgeoys. They organized themselves along the pattern of the Sisters of Charity in France which had brought together women of high birth, considerable wealth and much leisure time to initiate a work of primary education of the poor in the rural parishes. Under the guidance of Vincent de Paul, they encouraged simple, frugal, "tough country girls" to dedicate themselves to the service of the unfortunate and to go from village to village teaching the poorest children the little they themselves knew. Marguerite Bourgeoys had joined such a "congregation" at Troyes and through it learned of Maisonneuve's work at Montreal. She sailed for Canada in 1653 and, according to her own account, was soon duplicating the

French experience with popular education:

> ... four years after my arrival Monsieur de Maisonneuve
> wanted to give me a stone stable to make a house to lodge
> those who would teach school. I had a chimney built and what
> was necessary in order to lodge the children there.[16]

The courses of study were not very advanced as Marguerite
Bourgeoys herself had had little formal education, but they did
provide for a kindergarten and nursery school, and a study circle
for adolescent brides.

She returned to France to recruit three young women of
middle-class background who would take care of most of the teaching assignments and one "strong girl" of humble origins destined
for the more menial but necessary work in the embryonic community. In 1666 a second school was opened at Trois-Rivières, and the
following year the inhabitants of Montreal successfully petitioned
the bishop to give the women a *mandat* authenticating their association for service throughout the colony, so pleased were they with
the schools. They obtained letters-patent in 1670, but Bishop Laval
steadfastly refused to support their request to become a religious
institute taking solemn vows and wearing a distinctive habit. In
1676, the Sisters opened a boarding school in Montreal, and
shortly thereafter, a school for domestic sciences called "La Providence" at Pointe St. Charles. Within a few years they were operating schools at Lachine, Batiscan, Champlain and Pointe-aux-
Trembles, also a school for Algonkian girls at Sault-au-Récollet.

When Saint-Vallier succeeded Laval as Bishop of Quebec the
Sisters of the Congregation were able to extend their school system
to Ile d'Orléans, the south-shore seigneuries and into Acadia and
Isle Royale. With his blessing they also opened a school for domestic sciences at Quebec. Their schools at Louisbourg, Saint Famille
and Château Richer drew most favourable commendations from
the colonists and the Intendants in the eighteenth century. The
Sisters of the Congregation also resisted successfully both Bishop
Saint-Vallier's efforts to make of them a cloistered institute, and
the general pattern of segregation of the sexes in schools. These
Sisters went in twos to the rural areas to teach boys and girls. By the
end of the French régime, they had a score of schools in the
Montreal area, four near Quebec, one at Trois-Rivières and one at
Louisbourg. They were not subject to the royal restrictions on re-
cruitment applicable to cloistered communities so their growth was

not held in check for political reasons. In any case, they were a popular community whose services to the common people were highly appreciated, who seemed to be more attuned to the colonial life-style than were the cloistered religious, and who attracted more novices because their dowries were modest and their rules were relatively liberal.

In addition to the *petites écoles* already mentioned, there were itinerant schoolmasters, and parochial or *fabrique* schools taught by the parish priests, or hired lay teachers, to provide a basic elementary education in the rural areas. Peter Kalm reported that every parish had its school, but he had visited only a small number of the seventy parishes in the colony and had presumed that all were as well developed and endowed as the few he had seen. Quebec at the time had at least six schools, Trois-Rivières had three, and Montreal had at least three primary schools. New France probably compared favourably in educational establishments with rural France and this would account for the laudatory comments of visitors such as Lahontan, Charlevoix and Bougainville. The Intendant Jacques Raudot informed the Minister of Marine in 1705 that the Seminary at Quebec took in the brightest of the poor children from the rural parishes and gave them a free education. The Sisters of the Congregation also itinerated during the summer months bringing instruction to seigneuries and parishes where no permanent schools were yet established. Raudot wrote pessimistically in 1707 that Canadian society was divided into "oppressors", made up of merchants, administrators, seigneurs and clergy, who cared little for the general welfare of the colony, and "the oppressed" who were without discipline due to a lack of proper upbringing and adequate schooling. To remedy this exaggerated imbalance he suggested that the state place schoolmasters in each seigneury who would be trained at public expense by the Brothers Hospitallers.[17]

While it was true that inequality of opportunity existed, there are indications that church and state cared about educational provision and about educational standards. When an itinerant schoolmaster named Le Chevalier, reportedly of dubious conduct, offered his services in the parishes, the Intendant Deputy thought it essential to restrain him. He forbade any schoolmaster to teach without a licence from the Intendant. By an ordinance of 1727 he requested that all itinerant schoolmasters submit to an examination administered by the ecclesiastical member on the Superior Council, and specified that unmarried schoolmasters were permitted to teach boys only. People who were exiled to Canada sometimes took up teaching temporarily in the 1730s and 1740s. One young man, aged only sixteen or seventeen, was exiled to Canada in 1736 for salt smuggling and he took up the profession of itinerant teacher along the Beaupré coast, until stopped by the provost court of Quebec two years later.

Bishop Dosquet took a particular interest in education during his brief sojourn in the colony. He was anxious that educational opportunities should be extended to more seigneuries and to a wider segment of the youth, therefore issued a *mandement* in 1735 urging the creation of *fabrique* (presbyterial) schools.[18] There were already twenty-four such schools in the colony but this number was quite inadequate, forcing parish priests to give instruction themselves in music, catechism and the liturgy. Although Dosquet was pleased with the opening of a new college in Quebec and the establishment of "Latin schools" in Montreal (i.e. primary schools taught by the Sisters of the Congregation and the Brothers Hospitallers which were oriented towards admission to the Jesuit college), he urged the parish priests to teach more Latin to more boys, and to prepare for admission to the seminaries all promising students who demonstrated any great intellectual ability and possible religious vocation.[19]

Bishop Pontbriand was very disturbed by what he called an increasing illiteracy in the colony, a decline in intellectual life and educational standards. It would seem that the relatively high standard of literacy which prevailed in the mid-seventeenth century, at the time of recent and selective immigration when perhaps 40 per cent of the inhabitants could read and write with facility, had slipped badly with the cessation of the trickle of well-educated immigrants and with the process of "Canadianization", a phenomenon which Frenchmen viewed as progressive barbarization. Pontbriand insisted on the catechetical method of instruction, which Saint-Vallier had done so much to promote in New France. It not only provided the colonials, he believed, with a set of reasoned beliefs and standards, but also equipped them with a system of reasoning which they could turn to good advantage in the secular aspects of life. Pontbriand did not find the spiritual health of his diocese very promising and he castigated the cloistered orders for not observing their regulations more closely, for engaging in jurisdictional strife, for making unfavourable comparisons between French and Canadians or between members of their own institutes and other orders, and for perpetuating long-standing feuds. In the schools he insisted on the segregation of the pupils and the teachers by sex and went so far as to threaten with censure and reservation of the sacraments any who ignored his regulations on the matter.[20] The rule was more difficult to apply to itinerant schoolmasters or to the Sisters of the Congregation, hence some of his reservations regarding this type of schooling.

What about the standards of education? Hocquart had commented in the 1740s that the children of *gentilshommes* could scarcely read and write and that they were ignorant of the basic elements of history and geography. Charlevoix, who taught at the Jesuit college at Quebec from 1705 to 1709, gave a more considered judgement, although he too was critical. He wrote:

> Many are of the opinion that they (Canadians) are unfit for the sciences, which requires any great depth of application, and a continued study. I am not able to say whether this prejudice is well-founded, for as yet we have seen no Canadian who has endeavoured to remove it, which is perhaps owing to the dissipation in which they are brought up. But nobody can deny them an excellent genius for mechanics; they have hardly any occasion for the assistance of a master in order to excel in this science; and some are every day to be met with who have succeeded in all trades, without ever having served an apprenticeship.[21]

Education for the Canadians was appreciated insofar as it was practically-oriented to their everyday needs and occupations, and only a small minority valued the more intellectual training dispensed in the major educational institutions. Iberville, whose handwriting was atrocious and whose spelling was based on his own phonetic rendition of words, knew more about North American geography and natural science than any professor at the Jesuit college. The explorer Nicholas Perrot boasted that he had learned more living among the Amerindians and running the woods than on the hard benches at school. Even Jean Nicolet, who possessed a large library at Quebec, said he was happy only in the woods. Here were early manifestations of Canadian anti-intellectualism.

One should remember that the educational and charitable institutions of New France had their origins in the revivalistic fires of the French Counter-Reformation and the *dévot* movement of the early seventeenth century. The zealous reformers, who thought in terms of a rechristianization of French society and of conversion of heathens and heretics, promoted pious practices, sponsored projects for charitable assistance, and spearheaded moves to repress vice, impiety and all manner of disorders generally attributed by the spiritual elite to the lower classes of French society. The unfortunates, unemployed, and alienated were often viewed as the source of all manner of evil, sedition and revolt against established authority:

> . . . a *canaille* composed ordinarily of people who do not know God, who are without religion and without instruction, who live in license and the unruliness of all kinds of vices, even in a shameful and horrible mixture, one with the other, without distinction as to sex, kinship or marriage, like beasts, who bred and raised in vice spend their lives therein and are readily given to all sorts of crimes.[22]

It was to cure these social ills that the colony's religious began and supported public welfare programs and sought the approval and supervision of civil authorities.

In 1639 the first three Hospital Nuns of Dieppe arrived in New France to establish a hospital and hospice. Although at first directed towards the Amerindian mission at Sillery, they soon returned to the chief town of the colony to set up their institution as a military and naval hospital in which the pay of the officers and soldiers treated by the religious would help defray expenses. Jeanne Mance, a lay worker who had connections with the Company of the Holy Sacrament, opened a small clinic near the fort at Montreal in 1642. In 1658 she went to France to recruit hospital workers, and during her absence two Hospital Nuns from Quebec kept her small Montreal hospital in operation. The Hospital Nuns of St. Joseph, from La Flèche, soon had Jeanne Mance's small hospital established on a firmer basis.[23] Bishop Laval tried unsuccessfully to unite the two congregations and the two hospitals under one administration. The state officials were generally pleased with the services offered by the Hospital Nuns for they cared not only for the sick and wounded, but also for orphans, foundlings, the infirm and mentally retarded. One of their reinforced cells was even used as a woman's prison. They were obviously "useful to the King's service" in the words of Intendant Talon. Some of the colonists complained that they unduly influenced young girls to enter their order contrary to parental wishes but neither the Vicar Apostolic nor the Intendant made any move to investigate these charges.

The Hospital Nuns did not favour extending their nursing services to encompass the correctional aspects of hospices in France. Some of them had chaperoned the "King's daughters" sent to the colony as brides for the soldier-settlers and they did not always have a kindly view of the inmates of such charitable houses as those from which these young women had come. One of the great campaigns of the *dévots* was the building of General Hospitals to combine charity with police action. The objective of the General Hospital was the incarceration of all lower-class indigents in quasi-penal institutions of correction and treatment. The civil officers were anxious to have such an institution in the colony because they had no correctional institution to deal with the lazy, the beggars, and the troublesome, as well as the sick and infirm, whose numbers, according to civil reports, increased each year. In 1676 an ordinance was promulgated against the beggars, and in 1683 the Sovereign Council issued another edict because "the same beggars who left Quebec have returned" and prohibited them from loitering in the city.[24] Driven out of the city, they resorted to building shanties outside the walls which were commonly referred to as "places of scandal and disorder". It was not until April, 1688, under the leadership of Bishop Saint-Vallier, that a Bureau of the Poor was organized on the Paris model, administered by the parish priests and some leading *habitants*, to deal with the problem of poverty and to find employment for the "sturdy beggars".

The church traditionally took care of the paupers, and state subsidization in New France was dependent upon the church fulfilling its role as the dispenser of public welfare and education. But by 1688 the problem of poverty was too great for the Hospital Nuns to handle unaided; therefore, the Sovereign Council took steps to establish a relief program parallel to, and supplementing the institutions conducted by the religious.[25] The Bureau of the Poor acted as relief centre and employment agency in each of the principal towns of Quebec, Montreal and Trois-Rivières. In Quebec, a House of Providence was also opened to shelter the poverty-stricken unemployed who had sought refuge in the town. In 1693 this institution made way to the General Hospital, but five years later the Bureau was re-established, and it continued to function throughout the remainder of the French régime as an additional welfare service to the hospitals and monasteries.

When the Bureaux of the Poor were abolished in Montreal and Trois-Rivières, the problem of illegitimate births was one of special concern. In each parish, the church was expected to look after its poor and needy, and this presumably included foundlings and bastards. Unwed mothers often abandoned their children to the Amerindians or even killed them. In 1717, Jean Françqis de Lino was so disturbed when a woman tried to reclaim an illegitimate child she had left at the Lorette reservation that he appealed directly to the Council of Marine to extend to Canada the edict of 1706 permitting royal officers to care for foundlings and later apprentice or indenture them to honest settlers. The suggestion was well received, and by the 1730s illegitimate children were being placed in foster homes under direct state supervision. It was still the local clergy, of course, who decided which homes were worthy of receiving such children and who made certain that such children were properly provided for and educated.

Saint-Vallier bought the original Recollet monastery outside Quebec for the General Hospital, and in 1693 five nuns from Hôtel-Dieu went to the new hospice to assume its management. The Sisters of the Congregation who had a House of Providence in the upper town of Quebec since 1687 were now able to turn over their inmates to the General Hospital and to close down their old establishment. The General Hospital was administered by a board of directors formed according to conventional French practice for the administration of similar institutions: the board consisted of the Bishop, the Governor, the Intendant, the parish priest at Quebec and three lay administrators. In this way the laity maintained some direct control over an institution run by religious under royal jurisdiction. Not until 1701 did the Hospital Nuns at the General Hospital organize a community distinct from that of their Sisters who continued to operate the original Hôtel-Dieu hospital. Peter Kalm, the Finnish botanist, visited this institution in the mid-eighteenth century and left this description of its appearance and activity:

> A hospital for poor old people, cripples, etc. makes up part of the cloister and is divided up into two halls, one for men, the other for women. The nuns attend both sexes, with this difference however, that they only prepare the meal for the men and bring it to them, give them medicine, clear the table when they have eaten, leaving the rest for male servants. But in the hall where the women are, they do all the work that is to be done. . . . Most of the nuns here are of noble families and one was the daughter of a governor. She had a grand air. Many of them are old, but there are likewise some very young ones among them, who looked very well. They all seemed to be

more polite than those in the other nunnery. Their rooms are the same as in the last place except for some additional furniture in their cells. The beds are hung with blue curtains; there are a couple of small bureaux, a table between them, and some pictures on the walls. There are however no stoves in any cell. But those halls and rooms in which they are assembled together, and in which the sick ones lie, are supplied with an iron stove. . . .[26]

Kalm also commented that the Hospital Nuns accepted a number of small girls who were sent to them for instruction in "the principles of Christian religon and in all sorts of ladies' work". He found that "the convent at a distance looks like a palace".

It is interesting that although the Ursulines were the elite order by tradition, the girls from the better families in the colony gravitated to the Hospitallers, and the most popular institution for religious vocations from this class by the end of the French period was the General Hospital of Quebec.

The Hôtel-Dieu at Quebec never lost its reputation, however, of being the foremost hospital in the colony. The Hospital Nuns had their convent joined to the Hospital proper, which by 1750 was a large stone building three storeys high, consisting of the nuns' cells — small, unpainted, unheated, hung with paper pictures of the saints and Jesus, scantily furnished, and strung out along a long centre hallway — on the top floor; a middle storey with a large well-decorated and comfortable work-room for needlework, embroidery, gilding, flower-making, a large instruction hall, a refectory, and a chapel, the whole being surrounded by an outside balcony running around almost the entire building where the cloistered nuns could get some fresh air; and a lower storey where were located the more functional rooms such as the kitchen, bake-house, butteries, and storerooms. The hospital, which formed a part of this impressive convent, elicited from the European traveller a laudatory description:

> It consists of two large halls, and some rooms near the apothecary's shop. In the halls are two rows of beds on each side. The beds next to the walls are furnished with curtains, the outward ones are without them. In each bed are fine bed clothes with clean double sheets. As soon as a sick person has left his bed, it is made again to keep the hospital in cleanliness and order. The beds are two or three yards distant, and near

each is a small table. There are good iron stoves, and fine windows in this hall. The nuns attend the sick people, and bring them food and other necessaries. Besides them there are some men who attend, and a surgeon. The royal physician is likewise obliged to come hither once or twice every day, look after everything and give prescriptions. They commonly receive sick soldiers into this hospital, who are very numerous in July and August, when the king's ships arrive, and in time of war. But at other times, when no great number of soldiers are sick, other poor people can take their places, as far as the number of empty beds will reach. The king provides everything here that is requisite for the sick persons, viz. provisions, medicines, fuel, etc. Those who are very ill are put into separate rooms, in order that the noise in the great hall may not be troublesome to them.[27]

The fact that the Intendant often inspected the hospital to ascertain its right to the royal subsidies and payments no doubt aided in the maintenance of such comparatively high standards. The so-called "welfare state" is not a creation of the twentieth-century — church-operated institutions provided vital services under state supervision and with public funds for the general welfare in the seventeenth and eighteenth centuries in Canada.

In Montreal in 1692, François Charon had gathered around him Pierre Le Ber, Jean Le Ber and Jean Fredin with the intention of founding an almshouse for indigent elderly men and had obtained the authorization of the Sovereign Council to build a hospice. In 1694 a large three-storey building containing 24 rooms in addition to offices, was opened at Pointe-à-Callières, just beyond the town walls of Montreal. In 1700 Charon and his associates were permitted by Bishop Saint-Vallier to form a religious community according to canonical rules but some of the brothers refused to take vows and wear a uniform habit. Moreover, Louis XIV objected to the creation of a new religious community, and therefore new recruits were difficult to find. Financial mismanagement brought about insolvency until, in 1747, the General Hospital was turned over to Mme. d'Youville and her sisterhood for management.[28] The Brothers Hospitallers had also expanded their hospital work to Louisbourg and approved of establishing a hospital at Detroit until the French government rejected the plan. Another community of Hospitallers, the Brothers of Saint-Jean-de-Dieu, came from France to administer the hospital at Louisbourg and they remained in charge until the British conquest of the fortress in 1758.

When the Brothers Hospitallers were forced to disband in 1747, another community of female seculars was founded by Mme. d'Youville, wealthy widow of a well-known trader and brandy trafficker. Because of their grey habit, or because they were ridiculed as the "tipsy sisters" (*soeurs grises*), their name remained Grey Nuns. The Sulpicians invited them to assume the direction of the General Hospital of Montreal and soon the sisters had old folks, orphans and "women of Jericho" at the Pointe-à-Callières institution with which they associated supporting farms at Chambly and at Pointe-St. Charles. The Intendant Bigot decided in 1748 to close down this General Hospital and obtained the consent of Bishop Pontbriand to transfer all the assets to the General Hospital at Quebec. The Sulpicians in Paris, however, were able to make known the wishes of the inhabitants of Montreal and of the Grey Nuns, as well as their own desire to see such an institution maintained on the island of Montreal. Louis XV's advisors reversed the colonial decision and on January 3, 1753 a new religious institute, a truly Canadian order, was granted royal letters-patent. Not only had Montreal retained a valuable institution: but an order destined to play an important role in Canadian nursing had been granted a new lease on life.

The role of the hospitals and hospices cannot be over-emphasized in a consideration of the public welfare services of the colony. The hospitals were particularly busy during epidemic years which were frequent in the seventeenth and eighteenth centuries. Typhus struck in 1685, 1743-46, 1750, 1756-7 and 1759; smallpox or "purple fever" struck in 1688, 1702, 1734 and 1755; influenza swept the colony in 1700 and certain undetermined fevers ravaged the St. Lawrence valley in 1710 and in again 1718. In each case the hospitals were over-crowded, the nuns overworked and the grave-diggers over-taxed. Foreign prisoners of war and Protestant captives, and French who had secretly held to their Huguenot beliefs, were pressed to abjure. The lists of such conversions attest to the religious zeal, if not nursing skills, of the Hospitallers.

People went to the hospital as a last resort because it was associated more with death than healing. There were few doctors — indeed only four graduates of French faculties of medicine practiced in New France between 1608 and 1760 — who served the officials, the troops and any others who had recourse to the hospitals. Under the care of the Hospital Nuns, Grey Nuns or Ursulines, patients suffered usually as much from the purges, bleedings and enemas as from the original malady or wound. There were quite a number of barber-surgeons who dispensed such routine medical treatments as bleedings, lancings, poultices, and amputations, and prepared broths, herbal teas and ointments. Sometimes there were special services associated with the hospitals. The Hôtel-Dieu in Montreal, for example, engaged a Jean Martinet as surgeon in 1681; he had opened a school for surgery in 1674 and he now transferred it to the hospital where he trained apprentices until 1699, at which time surgery was elevated from a manual trade to one of liberal arts. The occupation of midwife, although not associated with the hospitals or the para-medical guild of barber-surgeons, was controlled to the extent that, in order to practice and to be entitled to their stipend from the colonial budget administered by the Intendant, the midwives had to have the attestation of an ecclesiastic. In the towns where there was a hospital, the chaplain usually issued these certificates.

Utility to the Crown and the colonials was a measuring rod that kept religious workers aware of their social responsibilities and the need for what is now called good "public relations". The small colony of a little over three thousand inhabitants had 41 religious women, of whom 33 were stationed at Quebec, at the time of the first census in 1663. Two years later several councillors of state advised Colbert in France that the number of religious in the realm should be reduced, and a subsequent edict (issued in December 1666) restricted the foundation of convents and regulated religious professions. Great, therefore, was the consternation of the Ursulines in 1668 when it was learned that a rumour circulated in Paris that they were "useless in this country" — for such an opinion could cost them their royal subsidies, freight allowances, patronage and eventually letters-patent. Marie de l'Incarnation defended her order in a letter to her son sharing with him her anxieties:

> Those are the fruits of our labour, of which I wanted to give you some details, to answer to the rumours which you say are spread about that the Ursulines are useless in this country and that the Relations do not speak of them as accomplishing anything. Our Reverend Fathers and Monseigneur our Prelate are delighted with the education we give the young. They allow our girls to take communion as early as eight years of age, finding them as well instructed as they could be. . . .[29]

In remarking on the incompleteness of the accounts given in the

Jesuit Relations and the favouritism shown by the publisher in Paris for the Hospitallers she added the argument that "a hospital which is open shows to everyone the good done there" whereas educational achievements were more difficult to evaluate.

Official views towards numerous religious professions never changed. In 1754 a Sieur Boucault ressurrected the argument that the royal *arrêt* of 1670 favouring early marriages had been instituted, with provisions for fines for obstinate bachelorhood, in order to overcome the excessive number of religious vocations.[30] Since the foundation of the colony, the King had always supervised regulations regarding vows, dowries, length of novitiates, and the location of convents. As a matter of fact there were, in 1760, about 70 Sisters of the Congregation, 56 Ursulines, 74 Hospital Nuns and 15 Grey Nuns in New France living in seven convents (five of which were cloistered) and all of these religious were Canadian-born. Bishop Pontbriand was more concerned about adequacy of personnel to meet the challenges of the day than about any overpopulation of religious.

In France the church was in complete control of the delimitation of parishes, but in New France the secular authority took an active part in the creation of parishes insofar as the defining of their boundaries was concerned. The parish was, naturally, the ecclesiastical unit of local administration, and curiously it tended to become the local civil and military unit, displacing the seigneury. This development would aid the church, during the ensuing British period, to assert a leadership role in the ethno-cultural society *vis-à-vis* socio-political affairs. The militia, for example, was organized on a parochial, and not seigneurial, basis, so, in the eyes of the general public, the captain of the militia, by the eighteenth century represented at the local level the double authority of Governor and Intendant. He held a commission from the governor of the colony and he reported in civil matters to the sub-delegate or the Intendant. His announcements were made from the church steps and militia service was organized according to parochial units. The parish priests had at first been required to publish from their pulpits all state decrees, but in 1717 the captain of the militia was assigned this duty. Because the militia captain was a civil and military leader in the parish, just as the curate was its religious leader, he was accorded a place of honour in the parish church, his pew being next to the seigneur's.

Clearly, the parish was intended to be a social unit with the centrally located church, ideally frequented by all the people of the district, serving as the meeting place for the dissemination of information and for socializing. There were many complaints that the churches were too distant to hear mass weekly or to keep abreast of news and gossip. In 1721 an inquiry was conducted in each parish and new boundaries were assigned so that a church was located in the centre of an area of between 200 and 500 souls.[31] The inhabitants of each parish had been given an opportunity to voice their opinions and grievances, but still there remained unchurched areas. In a few cases the boundaries of seigneuries and parishes coincided; in populous areas like the island of Montreal, the Ile d'Orléans and the Beaupré coast there were a number of parishes; and in a number of rural areas several seigneuries with small populations were grouped into one parish. In fact, these parishes were not units which greatly facilitated social control.

On the contrary, some of the parishes proved to be quite unruly and independent. Château-Richer and Pointe-aux-Trembles seem to have been areas where Protestants managed to "live quietly as Catholics" without being too disturbed in their private devotions. In 1706, the parish priest at Château-Richer asked the Intendant to issue an ordinance requiring his parishioners to show proper respect in church, and requiring them to denounce all those who sold intoxicants unlawfully and especially on Sundays. The parish of Saint-Thomas was, towards the end of French régime, one of the most difficult to control. Although regular catechism classes were scheduled, the parents did not send their children to them. When the parish priest denounced those who failed to perform their Easter duties, he was faced with a virtual revolt. Then, the parishioners refused to pay their tithes. Finally, the bishop intervened but it is not known with what success. The parish was evidently not a model unit of social control.

Economic and political necessity could drive the church to take extraordinary measures. The last years of the French régime were years of crisis. Bishop Pontbriand saw the misfortunes beginning with the fire that destroyed the Hôtel-Dieu at Quebec in June 1755. The hospital had scarcely been rebuilt when a smallpox epidemic struck with disastrous consequences, taxing the hospital facilities to the limit. To the misery of the colonists was added a famine so severe that by May, 1757, the daily bread ration was down to four ounces per person. Conscious of being on the brink of a great disaster, Bishop Pontbriand administered confirmation to approximately 1,200 persons in the cathedral on September 4, 1757, including a number of young children and even infants in arms.

The British bombardment of Quebec in 1759 was disastrous for the church. When it was over, the cathedral was a heap of smoking ruins, only the kitchen of the Seminary was intact, the church in the lower town gutted and the churches of the Recollets, Jesuits and of the Seminary required extensive repairs. The episcopal palace was gutted, and all the convents and monasteries were heavily damaged. Even more distressing with respect to immediate needs were the facts that four of the Seminary's farms and three of its mills had been burned by the invaders, that all the lands of the Hospital Nuns had been ravaged and the crops destroyed, and that the whole Beaupré coast and the Ile d'Orléans had been laid waste. Moreover, the nineteen parishes on the south bank below Quebec had suffered a similar destruction of crops, seizure of livestock, and burning and pillaging of farmsteads. The church found itself least capable of alleviating the suffering and want of the people when these were of unparalleled enormity in the history of the colony. Bishop Pontbriand fled in late 1759 to the comparative safety of Montreal, where he died a saddened and exhausted man on June 8, 1760. He is reputed to have said on his death-bed, "You will tell the poor that I leave them nothing in death because I myself die more poverty-stricken than they!"[32] In its hour of greatest trial, the Canadian church was left without a chief shepherd, and bereft of the resources to assume its assigned public welfare role.

Chapter VI

Colonial Manners and Morals

The church was expected to furnish not only spiritual comfort and guidance to the colonists but also to provide an ethical and moral code of behaviour, a sound grounding in the principles of the historic national religion, and to imbue the faithful with a proper respect for all "the powers ordained of God". Its first responsibility was, obviously, to set an example and standard itself, for it was the instrument of human salvation. The bishops, religious and the seculars could be expected to represent orthodox belief, exemplary practice and an approximation of the ideals of post-Tridentine Catholicism. Laval set a high standard of personal piety and of conscientious administration for his successors which Saint-Vallier and Pontbriand honoured, but which the other bishops by their absenteeism tended to devalue. Saint-Vallier, in particular, lived like an austere devout ascetic, and at his death left only a bed, table, cloak, bureau and a few chairs and a library of 300 volumes, having spent his considerable personal fortune on his colonial diocese, the Seminary of Quebec, and various charitable institutions. The bishops and canons of Quebec were not like so many of their contemporaries in France who ran off to comedies with ladies "the moment they get out from sermon" and who mixed the vanity of the world with the external piety which their calling imposed upon them.

It was not uncommon in France in the years following the spiritual revivalism of the early seventeenth century to hear of the gross ignorance of the rural clergy and their parishioners, to perceive the lack of spirituality or religious understanding of the courtiers, and to hear of the drunkenness, concubinage and general debauchery of some of the ecclesiastics. New France had come under the strong currents of Catholic revivalism from the time of its origins with the result that its clergy was singularly well behaved and disciplined, dedicated and devout. Generally, the priests set a good moral and spiritual example for their parishioners and gave their flocks few occasions for complaint. The Jesuits and Recollets defrocked only one or two of their company, and of the priests and nuns who would not remain in the colony only a few also left their institute. A few priests appeared in the colony under suspicious circumstances and these were soon expatriated. In 1647 a Benedictine monk who had "converted at La Rochelle", falsely represented himself in England, and then appeared in New France where he "pretended to wish to become a heretic again," departed hastily — leaving some unpaid debts — when confronted with his incorrigibility. In 1718, Saint-Vallier was disturbed to learn that another defrocked Benedictine was being harboured in the rural parishes near Quebec, and he issued a warning to the parish clergy to bar him from the sacraments and from hearing mass.[1] When the inhabitants of Beaupré complained in 1654 about their curate, Vaillant, Governor Argenson set up a commission of inquiry which found the complaints justified. Consequently, the governor reprimanded the priest and fined him the court costs. The Jesuits, who were the chief missionaries in the colony and the zealous guardians of its morals, carried out their own investigation, although Vaillant had been sent to the *Officialité* for trial. He returned to France on the first vessel.[2] There was also the renegade Recollet priest who accompanied the British invasion fleet in 1759 about whom Pontbriand warned his flock.

During his brief stay in New France, Bishop Dosquet believed that there was a certain laxity in ecclesiastical discipline. In order to remedy "abuses", he issued a *mandement* to his clergy drawing attention to such practices as parish priests being served by women domestics in their rectories, as priests wearing wigs, and permitting schoolmasters to teach female students. The grand vicars were charged with giving special dispensations to priests who felt it necessary to wear hairpieces and with licensing all schoolmasters who wished to teach boys.[3] Pontbriand came back to the charge in 1752, condemning the clergy who ignored the church ordinances respecting the age of women servants employed at the rectory. He deplored cases where women domestics even slept in the same room as the parish priest. There were numerous disorders against which he took action: for example, in 1742 he disciplined the parish priest of St. Anne de la Pérade for his drunkenness. The superiors of religious orders issued detailed instructions for the proper behaviour and deportment of the clergy and seminarians. Tronson told the Sulpicians to show more respect and orderliness by walking two by two and not in hurried groups when going to mass, to avoid wearing wooden shoes or white stockings at divine service, to wear clean vestments and cuffs when hearing mass, and especially to avoid the immodest posture in church of which the inhabitants of Montreal accused them. They were even instructed to carry a handkerchief at the belt and not to blow their noses through their fingers, especially while at the altar and when handling the Host. Also to be avoided was the carrying of brandy on their persons and during processions and visitations. He added:

> And if the procession is somewhat long and you require some refreshment you may have a few servants carry some bread and wine as this would not set a bad example to the laity as does the carrying of brandy for several reasons.[4]

The following year Tronson admonished his secular community at Montreal, telling them not to spend too much time with women in the confessional "speaking to them in too tender a manner, engaging them at hours when they ought to have been at home." Such practices were scarcely edifying. One of the rules strictly enforced in France was that the clergy were forbidden to bear arms; Governor Lauzon encouraged the Jesuits of Quebec to fortify their residence and arm themselves with stones and other missiles. There is no record of the clergy's active participation in warfare or skirmishing in the colony.

On the other hand, the excessive zeal of the clergy had to be curbed occasionally. When the *Abbé* Fénelon undertook to enlighten the parishioners of Montreal on the matter of Frontenac's unwarranted commercial activities, abuse of his gubernatorial office and high-handed intervention in judicial affairs, in his Easter sermon in 1674, he brought down the full wrath of the Governor and a reprimand from the Ministry of Marine. When the *Abbé* Jacques Hingan, a youthful French priest at Grondines, was so incensed by the unseemly behaviour of a couple of his parishioners in 1757 that he denounced them publicly from the pulpit, he found himself being sued and only the bishop's intervention to have the case transferred to the church tribunal enabled him to escape with paternal admonition.

It is difficult to imagine today the relaxed and uninhibited atmosphere that prevailed during mass, and especially during the sermons, in New France. The churches were places of public meeting for a highly gregarious, somewhat undisciplined population which loved all the pomp, ceremony, display and ritual of the Roman liturgy, but which generally took little account of what might be described as solemnity. The secular priests were given a guideline of conduct in 1679 which sought to instruct their congregations in modesty and reverence in church and which included warnings against crossing legs, making movements intended to attract attention to themselves, staring at people, untidy dress and noisiness during the divine office.[5] One secular priest noted that at least one-quarter of the parishioners at St. Michel left during mass to go out to compare and discuss their fine horses, that at least as many who remained inside during the sermons shuffled their feet and coughed noisily out of annoyance with the preaching, and that very few paid their tithes and heeded the warnings against fancy balls and rowdy wedding parties.[6]

In 1706, the *Abbé* Gauthier complained that his parishioners at Beaupré showed little respect in church: two of them had come to church drunk and had disrupted mass; many left during the sermon to smoke and gossip noisily at the entrance of the church; a few even talked loudly and quarrelled during the saying of mass.[7] Raudot issued an ordinance ordering them to be respectful in church, but the effects of this reprimand and warning can only be guessed from ensuing legislation. Four years later the Intendant found it necessary to issue a general ordinance applicable to the entire colony, and providing for prosecution by the Sovereign Council in case of non-compliance:

> To correct all these disorders, we order that our previous ordinances be executed and herewith prohibit all persons, of whatever rank or station they be, to talk in church or to show a lack of respect due in such a holy place; to smoke at the doors or near them; to leave the church when the priests are giving their sermons, except in cases of great urgency, under pain of a fine of ten livres levied against the offenders, payable by the fathers in the case of minors, and of imprisonment in the event of relapse. We order the priests of the parishes in question to publish the present ordinance, to renew it each Christmas and Easter, and to inform us forthwith of contraventions. We order the captains of militia to see to its execution.[8]

Saint-Vallier had in 1691 counselled preachers to restrict their sermons to one-half hour because the habitants had their horses waiting outside. Again in 1732, the Archdeacon Chartier de Lotbinière felt compelled to issue a circular prohibiting parishioners from leaving the churches during the sermons and from wearing heavy oversized capes and hoods which they pulled over their heads during mass. He noted that it was the young people, more often than the older people, who insisted on wearing these unconventional clothes to church.[9] It must be remembered that Canadian churches were barely heated and that the cold winters did require both men and women to dress warmly, and even the priests wore mittens in mid-winter to say mass. However, there was no excuse for the men to race their horses around the church during the singing of high mass, and when an ordinance forbidding such an "amusement" was issued, the recalcitrant *habitants* challenged the facts by suggesting they had done so only during the saying of a low mass, thereby requiring a more explicit piece of legislation.

There were those who felt that the church sought to impose a puritanical morality on the colonists which differed from the accepted religious standards of the mother country. An anonymous Sulpician said that the colonists "in truth lead a more regulated life ordinarily in that country than they do in France." Colbert warned the Intendant Bouteroue in his instructions about the legalistic conformity and dead-centre orthodoxy which the clerical leaders sought to impose in New France:

> With regard to the spiritual estate, the information from that country has it that the bishop of Petraea and the Jesuits establish their authority too powerfully by means of the fear of excommunication, and by the excessive severity of life which they wish to impose there.[10]

It has since been suggested that this arose out of Jansenist influences which traversed the Atlantic.

Rigourism, not Jansenism, was the motivating force behind the religiosity which the church sought to implant in New France. It grew out of the 1645 Assembly of the French Clergy condemning the laxity in the Gallican church, and the decision of the 1665 Assembly to publish and distribute to the clergy St. Charles Borromée's instructions to confessors. The Jansenists, of course, drank from and were nourished by the same wellspring of revivalism. In 1676 Pope Innocent XI, an austere man, condemned sixty-five propositions which favoured laxity in moral theology. Then, in 1687 the Jesuits chose as their General a zealous Spanish champion of the moral system of probabilism who embarked on a long campaign to root out what he interpreted to be laxity in the

Society's life and teaching. At this juncture, Saint-Vallier became Bishop at Quebec and he brought his rigouristic views to a colony where moral standards and religious practices were probably at a low ebb. This was the context of the numerous *mandements* and ordinances of a puritanical and legalistic flavour which gave the colonial church the inappropriate reputation, in later years, of having been deeply influenced by errors of Bishop Cornelius Jansen. In the mid-eighteenth century, the waves of intellectual skepticism and deism which swept over France did not make an appreciable contact with New France. War and relative isolation from the metropolis, both physically and intellectually, explain the colony's venerable fidelity to a fervent Catholicism, and to high ideals and narrow orthodoxy among the clergy and religious leaders.

The Jesuits and Bishop Laval have been represented as the sworn enemies of Jansenism although there is evidence that the differences between Jesuits and Jansenists were more political and partisan than doctrinal. Moreover, Laval, while espousing many of the practical devotional attitudes of the Jansenists, had managed to avoid signing any of the formularies condemning Jansenist doctrines. Saint-Vallier has more often been represented as tending to Jansenism and five specific charges of doing so were made against him during his lifetime. His *Rituel de Québec*, published in 1703, was based on Rituels published in Alès (1667) and in Rheims (1677), the former having been suspected by Pope Clement IX of tending to heresy. When the Jesuit Superior at Quebec accused Saint-Vallier of Jansism in his *Rituel*, the prelate referred it to the Sorbonne where he obtained a judgment upholding its orthodoxy. The church's attorney in Paris, Dudouyt, accused Saint-Vallier of being too attached to Bishop Le Camus of Grenoble, a known Jansenist. Father Chauchetière added that Saint-Vallier wanted confessors to refuse communion without any reason, apart from the fact that "communions are too frequent in Canada." Saint-Vallier had long crusaded for better confessions and preparation for receiving communion, but Chauchetière hinted that the Bishop had been influenced by Jansenist teachings on communion. In 1700, another Jesuit accused Saint-Vallier of having created problems for the order in New France following the example of the French bishops "especially the Jansenist bishops". Then in 1715 the Minister Pontchartain told the French clergy that Saint-Vallier had not immediately issued a mandement publishing the papal bull condemning Father Quesnel's *Réflexions morales*, which was censured only fourteen years after its first publication. As a matter of fact, Saint-Vallier issued a *mandement* in 1714 promulgating the papal constitution *Unigenitus* which condemned a number of Jansenist teachings.[11] Two years after Saint-Vallier's death, Bishop Dosquet had all the clergy of Quebec sign the formulary condemning Jansenism. By way of explanation he said:

> ... by the grace of God the diocese ... [having been] to the present time shielded from the errors of our time ... our Lord Bishops, our predecessors, had not believed it necessary to require the signing of the formulary nor to take other precautions against the heresy of Jansenius. ...[12]

There were other ecclesiastics accused of Jansenism who either cleared their names or hurriedly left the colony. The *Abbé* de Merlac, for example, who came to New France in 1693 and soon became a canon at Quebec and confessor to the women's communities, found himself being called "a bad priest" by the Hospital Nuns. The canon Glandelet was also suspected of Jansenism because of the austerity of his life and his bitter opposition to the Jesuits, but he also condemned Jansenist traits in Merlac. Mother Juchereau de Saint-Ignace suspected the priest Thibault of Jansenism. Dom Georges François Poulet, a Benedictine who found his way to the colony in mysterious circumstances, refused the Bishop's orders to sign the formulary renouncing Jansenism and found himself expelled in 1719. The missionary Dominique Varlet from the Seminary of Foreign Missions in Paris served as Saint-Vallier's vicar-general in Louisiana and returned to France in 1718 to be consecrated Bishop of Babylon. Because he then confirmed some known Jansenists in Holland he was suspended from office in 1719; he replied to this censure by consecrating a Jansenist bishop in Utrecht. However, during his years in the colony he had demonstrated no sign of Jansenism and left no following there. These cases, while all indicating connections with the feared heresy of Ypres, tend to prove by their very nature the orthodoxy that prevailed in New France.[13] There was very little opportunity for Jansenism to take root in Canadian soil, and very little chance for it to profoundly influence the colonial clergy. In fact, probabilism was taught at the Jesuit college of Quebec as early as 1699 and seems to have been influential in the major seminaries.

There were colonials, on the other hand, who firmly believed that the clergy wielded undue power, that they exercised unnecessary supervision and censorship and that a general atmosphere approaching a theocracy prevailed. The soldier Lahontan wrote from Montreal in 1685 in that vein:

> ... here we cannot enjoy ourselves, either at play, or in visiting the Ladies, but 'tis presently carried to the Curate's ears, who takes publick notice of it in the Pulpit. His zeal goes so far, as even to name persons; and since he refuses the Sacrament of the Holy Supper to Ladies of Quality, upon the most slender pretences, you may easily guess at the other steps of his Indiscretion.[14]

Even the Ursulines were inclined to believe that Bishop Laval was being too conservative when he discouraged congregational singing and instrumental music at mass and when he forbade the nuns to sing parts and harmonize.

Although the church did not forbid the faithful to dance, the clergy did not encourage it and regarded it more as an occasion to sin than an expression of joy or a form of harmless recreation. As early as 1645, at the wedding of a soldier from Montpellier, five soldiers had danced a kind of ballet. Two years later, there is record of another so-called ballet at the warehouse at Quebec, but the Jesuits who reported the event were careful to add that none of the priests or nuns saw fit to attend this function.[15] The first ball in the colony took place on February 4, 1667, when Louis-Théandre Chartier de Lotbinière decided to celebrate his installation as provost judge of Quebec. The Jesuits were very annoyed by his decision and the Superior indicated in their *Journal* that they hoped it would not result in "consequences".[16] Saint-Vallier advised Governor Denonville and his wife in 1686 that "although balls and dances are harmless by nature", they were not profitable to conscientious Catholics because of "the corruption that almost always steals into consciences as a result of this amusement." He continued:

> This being so, it is of great importance for the glory of God and the salvation of souls that the Governor and his wife, on whose conduct most people will pattern their own, not only firmly refuse to enter houses where people have assembled for balls and dances, but also shut out from their own home this kind of entertainment. ... Nevertheless, since their daughter needs recreation because of her age and vivacity, she may be allowed a few decent and moderate dances, but only with persons of her own sex, and always in the presence of her mother as a safeguard against indecent words and

songs; but never with men and boys because, to speak plainly, this mixing of the sexes is the cause of the disorders which flow from balls and dances. . . .[17]

One aspect of dancing came under severe clerical censure throughout the French period. Masquerades were denounced as immoral for they resembled too much the licentious amusements of Marly and Versailles. Lahontan complained:

> They excommunicate all the Masks, and wherever they spy 'em they run after 'em to uncover their Faces, and abuse 'em in a reproachful manner: In fine, they have a more watchful eye over the conduct of the Girls and married Women, than their Fathers and Husbands have. They cry out against those that do not receive the Sacrament once a month; and at Easter they oblige all sorts of persons to give in Bills to their Confessors.[18]

His complaint was the common reaction of the garrison officer and soldier. At military posts like Detroit the *libertinage* was just as great as, if not worse than, at Quebec or Montreal. In distant Acadia, the bishops deplored unrestricted dancing and "nocturnal festivities." At Quebec, of course, the aping of French court life was impossible to uproot.

Dancing became so popular among the governing class at Quebec that some confessors exacted promises from their penitents never to attend such festivities again before granting them absolution in an effort to prevent the practice of dancing from spreading to all classes of the population.[19] A nun at Quebec in 1753 voiced the following opinion to a correspondent in France:

> We are witnesses here of much misery and I regard Canada as the echo of France in the matter of vices, self-interest, bad faith and disoluteness, luxury, high living, all the pomp of the devil being displayed. . . .[20]

Bishop Pontbriand in proclaiming the jubilee of 1751 opined that "religion is becoming extinguished" in New France.

> I do not fear to say it and many among you deplore it as we do, that never has the colony merited less the grace of heaven: crimes are multiplied and appear vividly, virtue is despised and its maxims are a source of shame, religion is becoming extinguished; what frightful assertions are made

with authority, sustained by continuous example, to attack the most solid fundamental! Was there ever in this diocese a greater dissipation in morals, thefts of all kinds, assassinations, duels, perpetual murmurings against authority; one sees on every hand only matters capable of irritating the Almighty.[21]

Saint-Vallier would have disputed some of these claims, however, asserting that the closing decades of the seventeenth century was the ebb-tide of dissolution and immorality in the colony. Pontbriand could only employ prayer and persuasion in most cases. He realized the limitations of both ecclesiastical and secular authority to change a whole society. He often repeated in his circulars and public pronouncements the phrase, "God alone can bring the remedy".

The luxurious dress and vanity of women in church was a subject of Bishop Laval's *mandement* of February 26, 1682.[22] He attacked such deportment as contrary to their baptismal vows to renounce Satan and all his works, as tending to many sins of the flesh, and as condemned in Holy Writ as a sign of slavery to the devil. Women were widely regarded as likely subjects for satanic subversion. Laval was particularly scandalized by the nudity of arms, shoulders and bosoms, and the wearing of transparent clothing, especially at the communion rail. Curled hair decked with many bows and ribbons he found more appropriate for the ball or theatre, neither of which he could heartily recommend.

Saint-Vallier echoed these sentiments in the advice he gave Governor and the Marquise de Denonville. He asked the governor and his wife to set an example of piety for the colonists by "expressing in both word and deed the indignation they feel for such an abuse" and privately reprimanding those who appeared in ostentatious dress. He elaborated on ostentatious dress because much of the dress of that age could pass for being excessively elaborate:

> Ostentation in dress appears first of all in the rich and gaudy fabrics which exceed the means and condition of the women who wear them. Also it appears in the excessive clothes they put on, in the extraordinary way in which they dress their hair, which they fill with bodkins and leave uncovered showing those immodest curls which the Epistles of St. Peter and St. Paul so expressly forbid, as do all the doctors of the Church, and which God has often severely punished, as may be seen by the example of the unhappy Pretextate. According to St. Jerome, who knew her, her hand was withered and five

months later she died suddenly and was dashed into Hell, as an angel of God had warned her, because on the orders of her husband she had curled the hair and dressed in worldly fashion her niece.[23]

Saint-Vallier took up Laval's earlier denunciation of "indecent and immodest dress" in church and particularly in receiving communion. He remarked that "this profligacy begins at an early age when little girls, even those of humble birth, are dressed and adorned like dolls," that girls continued these habits into married life, and that only "lewdness and a great number of sins" were perpetuated in the colony by such behaviour. The visionaries who in laying the foundations of Catholicism in New France dreamed of the Third Age of the Holy Ghost, the millenial age approaching the Parousia, and a return to the pristine purity of the Apostolic Age would have been sadly disillusioned by the turn of events. Some of the bitterness expressed in the idealistic pronouncements of the first two bishops is also indicative of the eschatological views of the founders.

What Saint-Vallier said to the Governor and châtelaine of Château St. Louis he proclaimed to all:

> But what has caused us above all a great sadness is the excess of luxury in dress and the vanity manifest throughout the country, among the young girls and women of the world, with greater license and scandal than ever before; not satisfied with wearing clothing of which the cost and splendour are far beyond the wearer's means and standing, they affect also immodest head-dress, appearing outside and inside and often even in church bareheaded, or head covered only with a transparent headdress with a collection of ribbons, laces, curls, and other vanities, the which is completely unbecoming a Christian person; and what is still more to be deplored and pierces our soul with grief is that they do not hesitate to make themselves the instruments of the devil, and co-operate in the loss of souls redeemed by the blood of Jesus Christ, by laying bare their necks and shoulders and scandalizing thereby and causing the loss of an infinite number of persons who unfortunately find in these scandalous objects the cause of their sins and eternal damnation.[24]

At his last synod, Saint-Vallier remarked on the "little exactitude" with which the colonists had observed his admonitions, and his

Grand Vicar added that he did not believe "our advice and remonstrances had any effect at all." Dire warnings had never been accompanied by repressive measures, and therefore there had been little evident reform in colonial manners and behaviour.

Smoking, though very common among the *habitants*, was not regarded with much respect by the clergy, and perhaps by some of the leading inhabitants, because it was engaged in somewhat furtively at first.[25] In the mother country the Company of the Holy Sacrament led a campaign against tobacco because of "the great disorders which it occasions." It was also seen as a concession to Amerindian ways and was associated in some quarters with a barbarization of Europeans. Du Creux repeated the informed opinion of his day:

> This tobacco has a wonderful effect in drying up the brain, as European explorers were the first to learn; today both Europeans and Canadians use it to produce intoxication. The Indians will not go anywhere without the longish pipe through which they inhale the smoke, generally to inebriation, for the smoke affects the brain and finally produces an intoxication like wine. . . .[26]

Use of tobacco and brandy in excess were regarded as dangerous both physically and morally. By the mid-eighteenth century, boys of ten or twelve years of age smoked openly and both men and women used snuff.

The church also sought to control the theatre, especially the popular drama and comedy with its ribaldry and violence both on stage and in the audience. The religious revival in the early seventeenth century did not attack the upper-class, classical and established theatre, however. Dramatic performances had been the subject of legislation in France in 1559, 1609 and 1641 which regulated the conduct of actors and forbade indecent language and behaviour. Corneille and Racine were not only staged in the colony by the religious teachers, but they were part of the literary curriculum. The theatre was employed as an instrument of religion, short Latin plays being performed for the colonists and the Amerindians. On New Year's Eve, 1647, for example, the Jesuits had their pupils stage a play and they were able to comment that "all went off well and there was nothing that might not edify."[27]

In France, the Company of the Holy Sacrament advised its members not to attend comedies or other spectacles, but Molière was the only playwright specifically censured for ridiculing asceticism and religious zealotry. The *dévots* were particularly aroused by his *Tartuffe*, lampooning religious zealots, and "each agreed to speak about it to such of his friends as had any credit at Court" with the result that they succeeded in having the play banned for three years in 1664, for another two years in 1667, but when finally staged in 1669 it was a prodigious success. In New France in 1694, Governor Frontenac created a storm by arranging to have an unsavoury officer of his household staff named Mareuil play the leading role in this controversial comedy as part of the winter festivities preceding the Lenten fasts. During his second administration as governor he had encouraged the Carnival week roistering to prolong itself throughout the winter months in a round of balls, parties, masquerades and amateur theatricals. It was therefore quite predictable that the bishop would intervene and seek to have the production of *Tartuffe* stopped.[28] It was unusual, however, that Saint-Vallier should have offered Frontenac more than a thousand livres (100 pistoles) to have the play stopped, and that Frontenac should have accepted the payment and then started proceedings in the Sovereign Council for an investigation of the theatre in the colony in order to determine if the plays which had previously been enacted had been wicked or vicious. Mareuil was arrested on charges of impiety and blasphemy but he escaped from prison, broke into the Seminary grounds to do mischief, smashed some windows at the episcopal palace and performed some impious acts on the bishop's doorstep. The whole case was appealed to Versailles where the bishop's right to denounce the theatre and the profession of actor was upheld, but where no assistance from the secular arm in enforcing the moral code was offered. There was some expression of fear that over-zealousness would result in a type of Inquisition being introduced into the colony, a move which would be repugnant to the Gallican principles. Saint-Vallier's admonition to Dennoville a decade earlier about not permitting his daughter to take a role in a play especially when "boys and girls recite together" seemed rather tame compared to the invective he employed against Mareuil and those ladies of the administrative circle in Quebec who used the stage to defy the bishop. It is only against the backdrop of the events of 1694 that Saint-Vallier's condemnation of the theatre as "absolutely evil and criminal", and the warning that "one cannot attend without sinning" make sense.[29]

Lahontan expanded the charge that the clergy prohibited "the reading of Romances and Plays" and that they burned all books which were not devotional in character. There was censorship in the colony as there was in France; also books were rare, there being few libraries. The better stocked ones, such as the Sulpician Seminary library, were not encouraged to lend books — even to members of their own communities. There was royal censorship, regulated by the Code Michaud of 1629, and church censorship exercised by the bishops, the Sorbonne, and the various religious orders. The *Index* of prohibited books issued in Rome was regularly communicated to nuncios and bishops, but in the realm of France these prohibitions were of non-effect unless also specifically confirmed and registered by royal authority. The first recorded case of censorship being exercised in New France occurred in 1626 when a copy of the anti-Jesuit pamphelt known as the *Anti-Coton*, attributed to a Huguenot pastor and accusing the Society of Jesus of regicide, was found circulating furtively from house to house in Quebec and was burned on the public square by the executioner.

Lahontan was of the opinion that ecclesiastical censorship was annoyingly effective. He complained:

> When I think of this Tyranny, I cannot but be enrag'd at the impertinent Zeal of the Curate of this City. This inhumane Fellow came one day to my Lodging, and finding the Romance of the Adventures of Petronius upon my table, he fell upon it with an unimaginable fury, and tore out almost all of the leaves, This book I valued more than my life, because 'twas not castrated: and indeed I was so provok'd when I saw it all in wrack, that if my Landlord had not held me, I had gone immediately to that turbulent Pastor's House, and would have pluck'd out the Hairs of his Beard with as little mercy as he did the Leaves of my book. These Animals cannot content themselves with the study of Men's Actions, but they must likewise dive into their Thoughts. . . .[30]

His attitude and reactions would indicate that the puritanical clergy felt it necessary to wage war against pornography and eroticism, against indecent songs and lampoons. Needless to say, Lahontan had to find a publisher outside France for his own works.

The publication of the Jesuit *Relations* was halted in 1672 on orders from the General in Rome, and although several suggestions were made by the religious institutes working in the colony for the setting up of a printing press, no measures were ever taken to realize this objective. Peter Kalm commented on the lack of newspapers and of a printing press in Canada during his visit in 1749:

> There is no printing press in Canada, nor has there formerly been any; but all books are brought from France and all the orders made in the country are written, which extends even to the paper currency. They pretend that the press is not yet introduced here because it might be the means of propagating libels against the government and religion. But the true reason seems to lie in the poverty of the country, as no printer could make a sufficient number of books for his subsistence; and another reason may be that France now has the profit arising from the exportation of books hither.[31]

This deficiency cannot be blamed on royal censorship alone because the religious orders and the universities were also anxious to control publication, especially in mission fields and in "exotic tongues".

The problems of enforcing a rigouristic moral code in relation to such matters as immodest dress, worldly amusements, smoking and proscribed literature, according to Saint-Vallier, gravitated about the question of weak confessors who in the face of continued disorders and vice failed to be sufficiently severe. In 1719 he cautioned that it was only after a confessor had refused to grant absolution and that no amendment had ensued in behaviour and attitude of the penitent that the other censures of the church, such as reservation of the sacrament, refusal to admit to communion, and excommunication, should be resorted to. Nevertheless, he held to the position that absolution should be withheld from all those who stubbornly persisted in behaviour "tending to sin, public scandal and habitual disobedience." The situation did not improve with the passage of time, nor was it any more commendable in distant Illinois country, Louisiana, Acadia or Isle Royale. In 1742, Bishop Pontbriand sent a circular letter to his clergy in Acadia (much of which was under British rule), urging them to stamp out the prevalent frequenting of cabarets, where quarrels and fights were common, evening parties attended by both men and women, and dances in which the sexes mixed. He expressed concern about the predilection to work on Sundays and feast days, and lashed out against the popular customs of "sprinkling" newborn infants at home, of avoiding performing Easter duties when in litigation with one's neighbours, and of having younger children share their parents' bed.[32] All these practices were in defiance of frequent sermons dealing with such matters.

How did the colonists conform to the sacramental system as conceived in their day? The prevalent teaching of the church by the seventeenth century was that infants should be baptized within three or four days of birth; however, practice lagged far behind precept — as witnessed by the frequent reminders to present children for baptism, and by the warnings against parents or relatives merely "sprinkling" the infants at home without presenting them to the priest at church for the full rite of baptism and the recording of the act in the register which was kept for the purpose at the command of the King and the royal administration. In 1664 Laval issued a *mandement* ordering the early baptism of children and he asked all the parish clergy to make known through the weekly announcements in church the obligation of parents to christen their children and to avoid sprinkling them (*ondoiement*) themselves — unless in danger of death.[33] In 1684, for example, a Jean Dumets and his wife of the parish of Côte de Lauzon, were reprimanded by the bishop himself for having ignored three admonitions to have their month-old child christened in accordance with the order of 1664 and a subsequent ordinance of February 5, 1677.[34] Laval went so far as to threaten them with interdiction if they did not comply within a week. The registers indicate that a number of children were baptized months after birth, and that some received the sacrament only before marriage. In the latter case, it is possible that the colonists in question were Protestants who had managed to hide their true religious convictions until the civil laws required them to present themselves at church to contract a valid marriage.

First communion and confirmation seem to have taken place usually around the age of puberty, and thereafter the person was required to take communion at least at Eastertide each year. The *dévots*, whose influence in laying the foundations of the institutional church in New France are well known, recommended frequent communion and the adoration of the Real Presence in the sacrament. Some of the purists, notably the Jansenists, placed more emphasis on the unworthiness of the communicant, the need for mortification and prayerful preparation, and the danger of "profanation of the sacrament if taken without adequate preparation and spiritual understanding." The colonists did not take communion very frequently, on the whole, and it is possible that in the minds of some priests there was an association between this avoidance of communion and the doctrines of the Jansenists, Quietists and mystics. The eighteenth-century clergy were aware, even if the majority of the colonials were not, that the doctrines of the mystics and spiritual purists — Quietists in France, and Quakers in England and her colonies — removed the necessity for an intermediary priesthood and the sacraments.

It was precisely on the point of proper preparation for receiving the sacrament that the Jesuits launched their attack on Bishop Saint-Vallier. They charged that his *Rituel*, based in good measure on one edited in Alès (a region of southern France which had both Albigensian and Protestant traditions in addition to a Jansenist penchant) was too severe in the matter. Therefore, it discouraged rather than encouraged frequent communion. All were agreed, on the other hand, that the faithful should fast before receiving communion, that the men should present themselves unarmed and the women should come modestly dressed at the rail with their long skirts (whose hems they buttoned up to their waists when going out) down over their ankles. Throughout the eighteenth century, the colonists should have been thoroughly instructed concerning the sacraments because both the *Rituel du diocèse de Québec* (1703) and the *Catéchisme du diocèse de Québec* (1702) — compiled and published by Saint-Vallier and used throughout the colony — gave ample and explicit treatment to the subject. In spite of this, abuses were constantly being cited. Dosquet noted that some parishioners feigned conscientious motives to refrain from taking communion and that most of the colonists failed to recognize the importance of confession and penance. The *habitants* never took communion frequently in great numbers because in 1756 Pontbriand had requested that at least once a month some member of the household should take communion.

Marriage, although restricted by numerous conditions, was highly recommended for those who did not choose to enter holy orders. The state officials, imbued with ideas of the mercantilist populationists, favoured early marriages and large families as a means of populating the colony, increasing its economic production and its military strength. Louis XIV reprimanded Governor Vaudreuil and Intendant Raudot in 1711 for the large number of unmarried young people in the colony. The church favoured the fines imposed on bachelorhood and the family allowances provided from the royal coffers for very large families. Although the colony had a high birth rate consequent on a high fertility rate, it should not be forgotten that it also had a high infant mortality rate, and that men married, on the average, at age 26 and women at age

22, not at 20 and 16 respectively as the edicts of Louis XIV recommended. Very few families ever qualified for the family allowances which applied to families with ten children living and not in holy orders, and to families with twelve or more children living and not in holy orders.

Although the decrees of the Council of Trent were never promulgated in France, the canons laid down governing marriage were adopted by the Gallican clergy and were given royal sanction by edicts of 1579 and 1580. Louis XIV, by ordinances of 1639 and 1667, confirmed the basic requirements insisted upon by the church: reciprocal consent of the contracting parties; consent of the parents or guardians; public celebration of marriage with witnesses and the benediction of the priest at the exchange of the marriage vows; and proper registration of marriages. The church, for its part, insisted on parental approval, on the observance of the canons respecting consanguinity and affinity, on the publication of banns over three successive Sundays prior to the nuptial mass, and on having the bride and groom interrogated and instructed in their duties and responsibilities by the parish priest beforehand. The Seminary of Quebec gave its priests a list of points to discuss with young men planning to be married. This advice to prospective bridegrooms included the admonition to set aside all desires of fortune, ambition and sensuality; to choose a partner whose piety, gentleness, modesty, cleanliness, frugality, and obedience to her parents were well known; not to court several girls at once and not to make rash promises; to obtain the consent of both sets of parents and, in case of opposition, to avoid threats and schemes; never to remain alone with the intended spouse "for only those who wish to do evil seek out darkness"; to pray frequently for guidance; and to beware lest human affections should replace the first love due to God.[35]

The instructions which both partners were given by their priests concerning marriage were even more explicit. They were reminded, first of all, that marriage did not permit sexual irregularities. Sexual intercourse could be enjoyed for two reasons: for the procreation of children; for the avoidance of committing a greater sin when desire for intercourse was great. Onanism was condemned and the "ordinary position" in intercourse was recommended so as to avoid the spilling of any of the seminal fluid. Intercourse was forbidden in daytime and in public view, during the woman's menstrual flow, soon after childbirth, and during the major fasts and days of abstinence. The prospective bride was instructed to offer her husband access, not to avoid pregnancies, to practice abstinence according to the church calendar, and to show a submissive spirit taking her problems and complaints to her confessor.[36]

Some couples circumvented the course of events laid out by the church by resorting to marriage *à la gaumine*. Since canon law required the exchange of vows in the presence of witnesses and the blessing of the priest, couples would go to church with their witnesses and when the priest turned to give his blessing to the congregation they would rise together, and audibly exchange their marriage vows. This met the canonical requirements and it remained for them to consummate their nuptials. The clergy found this to be not only an avoidance of religious obligations but also an affront to the sacrament, therefore they sought to eradicate the custom. In 1717 Saint-Vallier issued a mandement prohibiting marriage *à la gaumine*, in response to the Officialité's actions and the complaints of the missionary and parochial clergy:

> Having regard to the request of our promotor, and other remonstrances which were made to us, we declare excommunicated, by an excommunication consequent upon the act itself, and of which we reserve to ourselves alone the power of absolution, all those who henceforth shall dare contract such detestable marriages ... (we condemn) numerous young people, who despising civil and ecclesiastical laws, and contrary to the respect due to the church and their parents, have found at the instigation of the devil a detestable manner to contract marriages, which they call *à la gaumine*.[37]

Although the official prohibition made it more difficult for couples to enter into such alliances, and have them recognized subsequently as valid marriages, it did not eradicate the practice. The church court took action against offenders on at least three occasions, namely in 1724, in 1727 and in 1754. The state supported the church in the attempts to impose religious uniformity because it wished the edicts governing marriage to be observed, also the proper registration of marriages to be enforced.

Church and state cooperated closely in this area on a number of occasions. In 1672, the Grand Vicar at Quebec granted a dispensation to allow a couple to marry in spite of a fourth degree of consanguinity. He also rehabilitated a marriage which had been annulled, but neglected to consult the Sovereign Council. Governor Frontenac insisted upon the state's right to make a ruling first in these cases before the church took action. The Intendant always upheld the right of officers to give their permission before a soldier might marry. The state was vigilant in seeing that the publication of banns was adhered to, and when the clergy granted dispensations from banns, they consulted not only the bishop but also the Sovereign Council. Other dispensations were also referred to the Council: for example, when it was objected that an intended bridegroom suffered from epileptic fits, which did not constitute a canonical impediment to marriage, the Sovereign Council ruled that the person might marry but if the groom continued to suffer from seizures both he and his bride would be required to return to France.

Lahontan believed that one of the reasons for unhappy marriages in the colony was the lack of any opportunity for social intercourse between young people. He wrote:

> After a man has made four visits to a young Woman, he is oblig'd to unfold his mind to her Father and Mother; he must then either talk of Marriage, or break off all Correspondence; or if he does not, both he and she lie under Scandal. In this country a Man can't visit another Man's Wife without being censur'd, as if her Husband was a Cuckold.[38]

He added that eligible young ladies sometimes had insufficient dowries but they accused their suitors of scandalous conduct so that the clergy intervened and forced the soldiers to "swallow the bitter Pill and take the very same Girls in Marriage." Bishop Saint-Vallier, on the contrary, said that the garrison soldiers often courted young girls in order to obtain sexual favours and that these girls often consented because they hoped by so doing to be assured of marrying their suitors. Their parents then consented to their marriages in order to preserve their honour. The bishop ordered that all such cases should be reserved to his decision and that parish priests were not to perform marriages in these circumstances.[39] The clergy was also aware of the intolerable refusal, sometimes for periods of eight to ten years, of officers to permit their soldiers to marry. Saint-Vallier issued orders permitting soldiers to be married without their officers' permission or that of the Governor, so long as they met all the canonical requirements, in order to avoid what he believed to be an abnormal restriction and an invitation to licentiousness.

Wedding festivities tended to be noisy and sometimes rowdy. An established custom brought from the mother country required the priest to go to the newlyweds' home to bless their nuptial bed. The higher clergy found some of the social customs indelicate, although the parish priests of Canadian origin probably shared the earthy humour of their parishioners. Saint-Vallier's *Rituel* permitted the blessing of the nuptial bed, but while the entire marriage ceremony stressed the procreation of children as a chief function of the married state, it was also stipulated that the officiating priest should never wait until nightfall to give his blessing.

Another popular custom which the clergy found distasteful was the *charivari*, or noisome demonstration by the parishioners in cases of unseemly early remarriages or of a great disparity of ages between the spouses. Intendant Duchesneau issued an ordinance prohibiting the practice, probably on the insistence of the clergy, but his action drew a reprimand from Colbert:

> To go into details, the ordinance which you gave against charivaris cannot be upheld. If this event took place between domestic servants of Frontenac and garrison troops it is up to him to give such an order and not you; if it is by inhabitants of the town of Quebec it is up to the ordinary judges and the Sovereign Council; thus, no matter how it happens you ought not to have issued this ordinance.[40]

Bishop Laval was so disturbed by a week-long charivari in 1683, on the occasion of the remarriage of a widow only three weeks' after the death of her first husband, that he fired off a *mandement* threatening the populace of Quebec with excommunication for their part in "impious actions which constitute a complete derision of the mysteries and truths of our Christian religion and the most wholesome ceremonies of the Church."[41] During the tumultuous demonstrations the pranksters usually pontificated on appropriate texts relative to marriage, produced an actor to represent the spirit of the recently departed first spouse, asked for masses for the repose of the first spouse's soul, and so forth. But there was little amendment in popular behaviour for in the 1750s Bishop Pontbriand was still combatting the same practices.

Penance was a sacrament which engendered much dispute because one of the principal censures employed by the church was the refusal of absolution and the reservation thereof to the bishop, or his grand vicar. Confession to the parish priest was obligatory at least once a year at Eastertide. If confession were made to a priest other than the parish priest, a *billet de confession* was required in order to be admitted to communion. Those who engaged in illicit brandy trafficking with the Amerindians, for example, sought out confessors who were ignorant of their infractions of civil and ecclesiastical regulations or who were reputed to be lax in imposing penance and granting absolution. A Lachine trader named Rolland became involved in a lengthy suit involving his parish priest, the Bishop and the Sovereign Council for the alleged misuse of such a certificate of confession. It was the period when the Intendant and Governor were supporting the Recollets in their various altercations with Bishop Laval, who had done everything possible to block their return to the colony in 1670. The Recollets charged that when the townspeople of Quebec came to their monastery at Notre-Dame-des-Anges — for they were forbidden by the Bishop to hear confessions at their hospice in the upper town — to confess themselves, there were always gossips on hand to report the names to the secular priests of the Seminary and the Jesuits who made difficulties for the penitents by throwing some doubt on the validity of their confessions. Those who admitted having confessed to Recollets were "objects of scandal" and were informed that their absolutions were probably invalid. This was the "troubling of consciences" which so aroused Gallican bureaucrats in Versailles against what Frontenac represented as a Bishop's and Jesuits' clique.[42]

Frontenac accused the Jesuits and Laval of attempting to institute a form of Inquisition in New France, "a thousand times worse than that of Italy or Spain." Such language was calculated to arouse the sensibilities of Gallican officials who jealously guarded the national church and the state from Romanist intervention. The Governor charged that the curiosity of the priest in the confessional was limitless, that paid spies in every community reported to the Bishop, and that if such practices continued he was prepared to initiate proceedings against calumniators. Frontenac said that an enraged husband had threatened to kill his wife who had been wrongfully accused of unfaithfulness, and that he had questioned the informer. The informer admitted that it was a Jesuit who had urged her to make known the suspicions to the husband. Frontenac played up his own role of mediator, concluding his version of the affair with the claim that not only had the couple been reconciled, but also that the false witness had been forced to retract her accusations before a notary, and that the entire community had learned a good lesson.[43] The incident illustrates the feeling there was against clerical inquisition and use of the confessional to enforce social order. But even Frontenac had to admit that moral turpitude was widespread and that certain disorders followed naturally from a preponderance of males in the population and the long absences from home and family life occasioned by the fur trade and garrison duties. Frontenac himself had in 1672 written to Colbert that it was essential to send out more brides because the bachelors "are responsible for no end of licentiousness in the homes of their neighbours, and this particularly so in the remote settlements where the women are quite content to have several husbands, whereas many of the men have difficulty in finding wives."

However little attention some traders, soldiers and high-ranking administrators paid to the commandments of the church during their lifetime, they all tried to die in a state of grace. Mézy, the first governor under the royal administration instituted in 1663, quarrelled bitterly with Laval but he died reconciled to the Bishop and at peace with the church. There was a deep concern with salvation and obtaining eternal rest in Paradise even if there was a strong-willed independence manifested *vis-à-vis* religious restrictions on one's everyday behaviour. In New France the corpse was exposed in the coffin, not on a bed as in France, during a wake which retained some survival of pagan observances. It was then transported to the parish church for the solemn, lugubrious requiem mass. Burial was usually in the parish cemetry, although a few priests and seigneurs were buried under the church until there was a public outcry against the pestilential odours which were commonly believed to convey infections and cause epidemics. A few persons of note asked to be buried in the paupers' section of the cemetery, as a sign of himility and self-abnegation; and one secular priest requested to be buried face downwards in token of perpetual penance.

Attendance at mass (sometimes employed as an indicator of religious practice) was required by state ordinances, and since the 1620 decision of the Parlement of Paris, the church courts were not competent to try laymen accused of violating laws requiring attendance at divine service on Sundays and feast days. Religous behaviour ought to be a matter of routine activity rather than rational conduct. After all, a culture qualifies as rational all routine behaviour which conforms to a preconceived set of values and moralistic principles. Deviance and behavioural variation in colonial society caused great concern and led to persuasive measures and coercion to enforce what was conceived to be rational and

Christian conduct. In 1685 Intendant De Meulles alleged that the church, far from being over-staffed, lacked adequate personnel to provide the necessary services throughout the colony so that "three quarters of the people at least do not hear mass four times in a year." But where regular services were available there were those who did not attend.

No sooner had a Sovereign Council been established than cases of non-observance of the Sunday legislation were brought before it. An *habitant* found guilty at Montreal of hauling wheat for the militia on Sunday was fined 10 livres, and this infraction did not prevent him becoming a churchwarden a few months later. But, a Huguenot merchant convicted of having a vessel unloaded on a feast day, which was not a Protestant holy day, was fined 100 livres and incurred endless difficulties thereafter with the law. The Sovereign Council took action against its own baillifs and sergeants in 1672, warning them that all official business transactions concluded on Sundays and holy days were null and void, that the penalties for Sunday work applied to them, and that they were setting a bad example. The police regulations of Quebec, promulgated on May 11, 1676, repeated the injunction that all inhabitants were to attend mass regularly, that no business was to be contracted on Sundays and other feast days, and especially that cabarets were to be closed during the hours of divine service.[44]

In 1679 an ordinance made clear that the laws respecting manual labour on Sundays applied to servants and domestics, as someone had apparently contested the application of the regulations. That people complained of the enforcement of Sunday rest is evident from a letter of the Sulpician Superior to a parish priest on the island of Montreal in 1684 in which he reminded the curate that the people felt that mass was said too late in the day and that the sermons were too long, so that little was left of Sunday after they had fulfilled their obligations. Tronson suggested starting mass earlier and keeping sermons to about one-half hour because people judged the weight of their obligations by the time they got out of mass.[45] If some inhabitants worked at what they considered essential jobs on days of obligation, there were others who wasted their time drinking, card-playing and gambling in cabarets, some of which remained open — in spite of the regulations — during the hours of mass and vespers. Saint-Vallier deplored the excessive travelling, visiting and reunions of which the colonials were fond.

What did the common people believe? They had been catechized in the ten commandments, the seven sacraments of the church, and the creeds, and were acquainted with the liturgy and devotional practices of their religion. How much of this made a deep and effective impression upon the people, providing them with an everyday moral code, an ethical standard for public life, and a spiritual direction in their intellectual and religious life? Almost without exception, they were preoccupied with the idea of "working out their own salvation."[46] It would be a mistake to expect everyday conduct to conform exactly to the conditions the *habitants* believed to be essential for their salvation. They did not live up to their ideals, but this does not mean that they were not preoccupied with eternal destiny. Very few, after lives of transgressing the commandments of God and the church in the fur trade, the army, the social life of the towns, or the isolation of backwoods seigneuries, failed to seek reconciliation and the comfort of the last rites.

Were the *habitants* concerned about religious ideas or were they content with mere external conformity to inherited traditional observances, rites and forms which, they believed, would assure them the salvation they ultimately desired? During the closing decades of the French period, the church in France was shaken by deism, skepticism and indifference, yet so critical an appraiser as Pontbriand declared that there was no trace of error in his diocese. Those Canadians who communicated with France would surely have encountered some of the current religious thought of the metropolis. Just as astonishing is the fact that in the 1740s when communication with New England was frequent, there is no mention in New France of the Great Awakening. Perhaps to avoid all mention of Protestantism was a reflex action.

Wayside shrines dotted the countryside testifying the beliefs of those who erected them; few people ever passed them without at least some acknowledgment of their significance. Family prayers were recited morning and evening, and in the majority of homes grace was said before and after meals. The belief in the efficacy of relics, pilgrimages, novenas and the exposition of the Blessed Sacrament was firmly rooted in the popular mind. The shrine of Ste. Anne de Beaupré early became a centre of pilgrimage, and, by the end of the seventeenth century, there were scores of miracles attributed to her intervention. The relics of the Jesuit martyrs, though few in number, soon had miracles attributed to them — one nun claimed that a particularly stubborn Huguenot had become docile and converted readily after being given a broth in which a small fragment of Father Brébeuf's skull had been placed. Supernatural events were also connected with the tombs of Bishops Laval and Saint-Vallier. Reverence and awe were paid to Catherine Tekakwitha, Marie de l'Incarnation, Jeanne le Ber and Marguerite Bourgeoys — but a few of the outstanding women pioneers of the faith in New France. It was commonly believed that the blessed bread, which the parishioners presented in turn, and which engendered some competition among the women who prepared it, possessed special attributes. It could aid in "chasing demons" from the body of the possessed, in healing sickness, and giving strength. According to the *Rituel*, "the great Saints employed it successfully to these ends." To sell it at a higher price than ordinary bread was declared an act of simony. Stories of the Host stopping a fire at Quebec, or curbing a plague of caterpillars were fervently repeated. Although, to date, the church of New France has not produced a single Canadian canonized by Rome, Bishop Saint-Vallier was certain that Brother Didace's intercessions had obtained for him the cure he sought at Trois-Rivières.

It is always difficult to establish the extent to which a folk-belief may be a survival of the "old religion", that is, of pre-Christian paganism, or to determine whether it is a localized accretion with no particular religious connotation. Studies of European religious mentality and survival of magical pagan beliefs and practices would seem to indicate that the cultural baggage of colonists to the New World included a great variety of such beliefs and practices. The inhabitants of New France placed great stock in magical formulas, in healing waters, in natural phenomena as omens of Divine intervention, in the observation of taboos, and in the efficacy of witchcraft and sorcery. Such acceptance was not in any way separated from religious belief as evidenced by the fact that prayers and pilgrimages, along with religious processions and the public display of the Host in its sun-shaped ostensory, were employed to stop plagues of caterpillars and grasshoppers, to put out fires, to protect from violent storms and earthquakes. Although it might be noted that the earthquakes of 1663, remarkable for their severity, had no more long-range effect in bringing about a reformation in fur traders' and merchants' morals than did the fiery celestial apparitions which were widely reported at that time.

The Feast of St. John the Baptist was observed, as in France, with all the pagan observances recorded for the festivities of the night of June 23-24. Grasses long reputed to have magical qualities were tossed into the flames, the common people danced around the community bonfire, and the ashes were later carefully gathered, according to ancient Western European custom. In 1646, for example, the Jesuits accompanied the governor to the great bonfire at Quebec, which he lit, and they sang an appropriate hymn and prayer for the occasion before leaving the people to their celebrations. Each year thereafter, the clergy was present for the ceremonies, until, in 1650, the Jesuit Superior refused to attend — not wishing to light the fire himself — and set a precedent, although another member of the order attended in surplice and stole. Thereafter, the Jesuits made no mention of these festivities, and apparently they withdrew discreetly from participation in celebrations which took on more mundane characteristics.[47] This did not prevent the observances from developing into a sort of colonial national holiday.

A colony where popular religious belief sometimes bordered on the superstitious can be expected to have experienced serious outbreaks of witchcraft and to have engaged in the judicial pursuit and exorcism of sorcery. It is essential to recall that, during the Middle Ages, witchcraft was regarded as a superstition inspired by the devil. Pope Gregory VII, for example, condemned the popular belief that natural calamities were caused by diabolical intervention. The Council of Trèves (1310) decreed that the "sabbaths" did not exist but were mere hallucinations inspired by Satan; belief in their existence was therefore a sin. This attitude changed, notably among theologians and the educated elite, during the period between 1560 and 1620, when challenges from Protestantism and the old surviving pagan customs of the countryside coincided with witch-hunting. Suppression of witchcraft in France and the colonies fell entirely within the jurisdiction of the secular power from the 16th century forward, and from 1500 to 1670 not one year passed without some sorcerers being executed by orders of the Parlements. There were publicized cases of "possession" of nuns at Aix, Loudun and Chinon which greatly worried Mother Marie de l'Incarnation that the hysteria would spread to New France and to her convent inparticular.[48] By the seventeenth century, the Catholic revival brought the *dévots* to question these supposedly Satanic rites and powers, and there was a return among a religious elite to the mediaeval interpretation of witchcraft. Bishop Laval and most of his clergy in the colony tended to believe that mental disorders and the power of suggestion had much to do with popular belief in witchcraft. The essayist Montaigne had condemned superstitious practices, and had postulated mental derangement as the explanation for apparent devil possession. The Belgian doctor,

Jean Wier, had called into question the medical evidence given at witch trials and each passing decade saw a greater number of medical authorities share his skepticism. The Ordinance of 1682 put an end, for practical purposes, to witchcraft trials in France.

Marie de l'Incarnation, Jérôme Lalement and Paul Ragueneau all saw in the "possession" of a young girl who was probably subject to epilepsy, the "malignity of certain magicians and sorcerers come from France." The caterpillars which plagued Canada in 1646 were described in some texts as "nefarious spirits", the Amerindian religious leaders were regarded as "sorcerers" and some soldiers who were reputed to possess knowledge in bone-setting and healing were considered to be under diabolical influences. The inhabitants of Beauport and Bellechasse were reported to watch the goblins tripping away under the direction of Satan himself at sabbaths held on the island of Orleans.

At a time when witchcraft trials were shaking Connecticut and Massachussetts, authorities in New France showed a marked tendency to discredit popular belief in this form of supernatural activity, or to simply avoid prosecuting suspects. Bishop Laval and the Sulpician superior, Tronson, were influential in quieting alarms about diabolical possession and witchcraft. The clergy, as a whole, had a firmly rooted belief that the grace flowing from the sacraments could be employed against dangers of uncertain origin. Finally, there was a growing weight of informed opinion in France which discredited what sometimes passed for sorcery. The *Rituel* which Saint-Vallier gave the colony warned that charges of witchcraft were to be dealt with prudently; nevertheless, it did not deny its existence and provided that burial in consecrated ground be refused to sorcerers. The service of exorcism in the *Rituel* warned against "suspecting neighbours and other persons of having procured this evil", and cautioned the faithful "not to listen to vain promises made by certain people who hasten to assure them that they will discover the author of the spell."[49]

One of the popularly believed diabolical powers was that of *nouer l'aiguillette*, that is rendering a marriage barren and the couple impotent by a spell. In 1657 a rejected suitor and corporal of the garrison was said to have cast a spell on the marriage of Marie Pontonnier and the gunsmith Pierre Gadois. When no children were procreated, the troubled couple sought the advice of their parish priest, who — on the bishop's suggestion — had a new nuptial blessing given.[50] The results were still negative; therefore, the church annulled the marriage after three years of enquiry provided for in the sacred canons "for cause of and in consequence of perpetual impotence caused by witchcraft." René Besnard, the corporal in question, meanwhile, was charged in the seigneurial court of Montreal with the attempted seduction of three women, and it developed during his trial that he was believed to have been responsible for the aforementioned barren marriage. He escaped with a heavy fine and banishment from Montreal. If any needed further proof of the power of the spell he was supposed to have cast, it was provided by the fact that when Marie Pontonnier and Pierre Gadois each re-married, they both had very fruitful marriages blessed by numerous offspring.

A young girl named Barbe Halé was brought from Beauport to Quebec "infested with a wild demon since five or six months of age, but at divers times". Between 1661 and 1663, Bishop Laval had exorcised the devils several times, as had the Grand Vicar Lauzon-Charny, but with no evident improvement in her condition. Meanwhile, the miller of the seigneury of Beauport was arrested on charges of having cast a spell on her for refusing his amorous advances. She became so violent in her moments of "possession" that it was decided to keep her under surveillance at the Hôtel-Dieu in the company of a guard of Hospital Nuns, some servants and the chaplain. She was put in the care of Mother Catherine de Saint-Augustin, who suffered painful bruises from struggles with malevolent spirits who attacked her in her cell at night in their attempts to wrest the young girl from her protection. The visionary nun was able to overcome these spirits through the intercessions of the deceased missionary Father Brébeuf. When Barbe Halé returned — supposedly immune to diabolical attack — to her master, Robert Giffard, seigneur of Beauport, the possession returned. Mother Marie de l'Incarnation and Father Paul Ragueneau said that in houses where she stayed ghosts were seen, drums and flutes could be heard playing, stones detached themselves from the walls and flew here and there. The girl said she could see the magician and his companions. It was only after a relic of Father Brébeuf was employed in the service of exorcism that she was liberated from the spell of "the magician who wished to marry her and of the companions he employed to arrive at his goal."[51]

There was a disinclination to proceed with formal charges of witchcraft and sorcery in the courts. In 1666 one of the Hospital Nuns at Quebec reported the theft of some consecrated hosts from their chapel and suggested that it resembled similar thefts which had preceded the appearance of black masses in the Paris region the previous year. The Sovereign Council took no action. In 1671 occurred the trial for "the child strangled by the Galbrun woman and other acts of witchcraft", but the Sovereign Council elected to prosecute only for infanticide and not for witchcraft. In 1682 a Mme. de Folleville, who ran a thriving cabaret in Montreal where such well-known traders as Duluth and Le Gardeur de Repentigny came to drink and play cards in a back room, was accused of furtively keeping a book on black magic. She was banished from Montreal but was able to have the sentence quashed. A few years later a Marie Godet claimed that a Jean Campagnard had tried to bewitch her by giving her a gift. He managed to give a pound of butter to her servant so that she eventually came into possession of this "gift"; when she later fell ill she concluded it was an evil spell. Although witnesses testified that Campagnard caused cattle to die and that he brought illness to several individuals, he was not convicted.[52]

Then in 1676 there were rumours of an outbreak of witchcraft and sorcery at the Sulpician mission and reservation of La Montagne. The *Abbé* Guillaume Bailly, posted there as director and schoolmaster, had become deeply interested in visions and dreams. Other Sulpicians became affected by Bailly's belief in witches to the extent an inquiry had to be launched. The Superior in Paris sent a cautionary note of advice in March, 1680 in dealing with Amerindians who were allegedly "possessed":

> First, do not question at all on this matter those persons who do not accuse themselves thereof.
> Secondly, do not interrogate too scrupulously on certain useless details even those who accuse themselves.
> Thirdly, do not believe too readily what they say unless you are in possession of definite proofs that it is not imagination at all but is reality.
> Fourthly, treat them the same as other sinners in granting them or refusing them the sacraments.[53]

The source of this unusual behaviour appears to have been the priest Bailly, for in 1689 he and two Sulpician companions became involved with a visionary nun who claimed to receive spirit messages from the other world. The three priests were recalled to France for "consultation" and soon Bailly was forced to leave the community of Saint-Sulpice.

In 1742 there was a great scandal in Montreal when a soldier employed a religious book and a crucifix as accessories in an act of prognostication and divination. A shoemaker named Robidoux had asked a soldier of the Montreal garrison named Havard to employ his occult powers by using a mirror to make appear the face of a thief who had robbed him of 120 livres. A large crowd assembled to watch the several hours of dramatic incantations which included smearing a mirror and a crucifix with oils and coloured powders, and lighting and snuffing of candles. Soon gossip had it that Havard was of Jewish origins — for profanation of churches was popularly attributed to Jews, Protestants and dabblers in the occult. Some asserted that he had outraged the crucifix, that he had pierced it with a knife and that blood had spurted from the wound. Havard and Robidoux were arrested and tried; Havard was sentenced to make a public confession and to spend five years in the galley fleets, while Robidoux was to be pilloried and banished from Montreal for three years. An appeal to the Sovereign Council resulted in Havard's sentence being reduced to three years in the galleys, and in Robidoux's being levied a fine of three livres payable to charities for prisoners. Bishop Pontbriand was making his pastoral visitation of Montreal at the time of the trial; he found that the sense of outrage and public indignation was so intense that he issued a *mandement* expressing the town's horror and distress over the incident of the "outraged crucifix". By way of public penance and compensation, a general procession was organized from the parish church to the chapel of Bonsecours where the ceremonies of the adoration of the cross would be observed. Because so many parishes now wished to possess this "outraged crucifix" as a sort of relic, the Bishop decided to give it to the safekeeping of the Hospital Nuns of Quebec.[54]

At least a majority of the colonials, like the common people of the mother country, seem to have practised their religion, more out of social convention and habit than out of any over-zealous conviction or superstitious fear. Most performed their Easter duties and took part in midnight mass at Christmas, although fewer attended mass faithfully each Sunday. Even those who did attend regularly did not always show the respect and attention that one might expect of them. In every decade there were priests who complained to the bishop and to the secular authorities about the laxity of religious practice. Nevertheless, the Canadians seem to have been a generally religious people. Their chief fault was that they performed their religious obligations in much the same way as they performed their social obligations, and in this they followed rather well the example of their Kings. Anyone who refused to conform to the conventional life-style was quickly marked; be that as it may, few entered into the religious observances with either deep and fervent conviction or mystical fanaticism. Peter Kalm observed in mid-eighteenth century that the colonials — even the garrison troops — were faithful in reciting their morning and evening prayers, in saying grace before and after meals, and in saluting various shrines and memorials. He wrote:

> It was both strange and amusing to see and hear how eagerly the women and soldiers said their prayers in Latin and did not themselves understand a word of what they said. When all the prayers were ended the soldiers cried *Vive le Roi*! and that is about all they understood of the prayer proceedings. I have noticed in the papal service that it is directed almost entirely toward the external; the heart representing the internal is seldom touched. It all seems to be a ceremony. In the mean-time the people are very faithful in these observances, be-cause everyone tries by these means to put God under some obligation and intends by it to make himself deserving of some reward.[55]

It would be erroneous to suppose that religion was the chief moti-vational force behind all aspects of everyday living. Such an in-terpretation could only come from an unwarranted association of early seventeenth-century eschatological thought and *dévot* re-vivalism, and the projection back into early times of nineteenth-century ultramontanism, with the general tone of colonial Catholi-cism. While it is true that, during the early missionary period when the religious foundations of the colony were laid, a mystical and even fanatical Catholicism made itself felt, it did not dominate thought and action after 1663. Utopian visions and eschatological dreams faded into the romantic background; and by that standard, religiosity declined as settlement progressed, as more aspects of French life were transferred to the colony, and as the metropolitan sources of ecstatic religiosity dried up. The episcopacy of Saint-Vallier seems to have marked a low point in religious conviction, although Pontbriand was certain that the church in his own day was disorganized and undisciplined beyond comparison. These were far cries from the fervently practised Catholic uniformity that some historians have erroneously seen in New France.

The institution of slavery, for example, was never condemned outright. It was tempered, not so much by humanitarian considerations, as by religious conviction that the blacks and Amerindians had souls to save and numbers to add to the Church Militant. The *Code Noir* (1685), though never registered in Quebec, was observed insofar as it required that children of slaves be baptized, and that adults refrain from labour on Sundays and other days of obligation to attend to their religious duties. Large-scale slavery was not practiced in New France. As Louis XIV observed, the climate was 'too inclement for Negroes', and there were no plantations requiring extensive manpower.

There were, of course, a few extremely religious colonials who formed an elite or sanctimonious minority. Particularly among the church founders in the first half of the seventeenth century were some who practiced self-mortification to the extreme. Bishop Laval would let his meat almost putrify before eating it, and was reported to have sucked the pus from the bandages of patients at the hospitals he visited. One Hospital Nun had so mastered her human impulses that she could impassively pick up a caterpillar from the ground and swallow it. Most of the clergy and nuns practiced mortification by wearing hair-shirts, leather belts, and other penitential devices designed to inflict discomfort and even pain. Father Massé set for himself the rule that if he ever permitted an unbecoming word to issue from his lips he would pick up with his tongue the spittle and phlegm which others had expelled. The men who gathered around François Charon to engage in a ministry of charity and teaching were imbued with the highest spiritual objectives and the severest sense of self-discipline. Jeanne Le Ber was a mystic who aroused much curiosity (and also general admiration and respect), by her rather self-willed type of withdrawal from the world and simultaneous refusal to submit to any of the established forms of cloistered life. It is little wonder that some of the Amerindian neophytes took up the new religion with excessive zeal, imposing on themselves severe fasts and vigils, and even resorting to self-flagellation. At Tadoussac converts were reported to have mingled their blood with their tears during the moving observances of Holy Week.

The cult of the Virgin Mary took firm root in the colony, and that of the Sacred Heart of Jesus was introduced. The cathedral at Quebec was dedicated to the Immaculate Conception. The statue of Mary was often carried in processions, and in the forts military chaplains recited the litanies of the Blessed Virgin. The recitation of the rosary was also introduced into New France, as were devotions to the Holy Family, the guardian angels, and the patron saints of the parish. Especially venerated were St. Joseph, St. Francis-Xavier, St. Louis, St. Flavian and St. Felicity. The *mandements*, correspondence and sermons of the period made only infrequent mention of the direct adoration of Jesus; the people seemed to prefer the intermediary approach through the Virgin Mary and the saints and the adoration of the Blessed Sacrament.

Fast days numbered fifty-nine each year, or the equivalent of two months. No meat or dairy products were to be touched on fast days, and only one meal was served at noon with a very light supper in the evening. To the fast days were added another ninety days of abstinence each year when meat was not to be served. However, the colonists seem to have eaten eggs, butter and cheese throughout Lent despite church rules on fasting. Moreover, they had plenty of fish to substitute for meat, and early in the seventeenth century the Sorbonne had decreed that the beaver, whose flesh was much esteemed, was a fish and not a mammal and therefore could be eaten on meatless days. It would appear that a number of habitants also choose to follow their own interpretations and classified much game as outside the rules of abstinence.

In addition to the fifty-two Sundays of the year, the people observed an additional thirty-three obligatory feasts when attendance at mass and cessation of labour were enjoined. In fact, both Easter and Pentecost were three-day festivals. Maurepas, the Minister of Marine, reminded Bishop Pontbriand that in France this number had been reduced considerably. Pontbriand, accordingly, reduced the number of additional feast days from 33 to 14 by moving the observance of 19 of them to the nearest Sunday. This was to comply with the wish of Louis XV that the inhabitants have more working days available.[56] Actually, the general reaction was unfavourable, and Pontbriand reported that many colonists were disturbed by what they called "the change in religion". They were not reconciled for a number of years. The incident indicated the traditional values which dominated religious perception.

It is perhaps significant that while edicts of 1673 and 1675 concerning regalian rights, and the Four Articles of the Gallican church (1682) were never registered at Quebec, both the edicts of 1666 against blasphemy and of 1679 against duelling were registered by the Sovereign Council. The bishops' fulminations against immodest dress, extreme vanity, fornication and a wide range of immoral and questionable behaviour were not groundless. A study of criminality does not establish norms, but it can indicate the incidence of deviation from generally accepted standards, the areas which aroused the greatest official and/or popular repugnance, and the severity of punishments exacted. Adultery, fornication and drunkenness were greatly deplored by the ecclesiastics but often lightly punished by civil authorities, whereas rape, bestiality and prostitution were taken much more seriously by the civil power. The administration of justice was always closely tied to a moralistic and religious set of values. Thus, in 1673 four men who — under cover of darkness and the influence of liquor — broke into the home of a Montreal notary to steal some wine, brandy, salted eels and tobacco, were sentenced "to be exposed at the door of the parish church, on a feast day or Sunday, following high mass." The locksmith who had furnished them with passkeys to execute this breaking and entering was required to appear barehead, hands bound, bottles and keys chained about his neck along with a placard detailing his crime, and was required to make "honourable amends" at the door of the parish church. These were sentences greatly reduced by the Sovereign Council for the court of first instance at Trois-Rivières had ordered whippings and branding with hot irons.[57] Judicial procedure allowed for trial by ordeal and executions were gruesomely cruel public performances which — although they aroused no apparent sympathy for the tortured criminal — did result in the universal abhorrence of the hangman and the persecution of his family.

Drunkenness, gambling and quarrelling were the failings of the *habitants* most deplored by the clergy and described by a number of them as "universal characteristics of the Canadians." By 1724, Saint-Vallier was so disturbed by the colonists' heavy drinking that he sent a circular letter to the parochial curates instructing them to refuse absolution to all *cabaretiers* who failed to observe the Sunday closing laws and served liquor indiscriminately. This attempt to promote the temperance crusade launched by his predecessor was accompanied by a realization of the weaknesses of his flock, for the Bishop refrained from setting out means of enforcement or providing penalties for infractions. Instead, he reminded his clergy that "it is I who so commands you on God's behalf and you owe me obedience." He concluded with an ineffectual "you will give me the pleasure of reading these few words from the pulpits of your churches."[58]

Immorality was a great social problem, especially in the principal towns and at the military posts. Some of the outstanding army officers, heroes of the colonial frontier warfare, were tried and convicted for such crimes as kidnapping, rape and seduction. The Acadians were described in 1703 by their principal missionaries as "more corrupted in manners than the heretics", and the Ministry of Marine was told that the immorality of the inhabitants of the scattered Atlantic coastal settlements was beyond description. In Louisiana the first official reports told of unequalled debauchery on the part of the soldiers. The Grand Vicar of Quebec said in 1716 that half the town was a bordello; on the other hand, the greatest source of scandal for the Montreal clergy in 1719 was that the men wore only shirts, no breeches or underclothing, to work on hot summer days. Even the brides, the "King's daughters", imported to boost the colonial population and found solid Christian homes and families, were, as one writer said, "a mixed cargo", and there were a number of women of easy virtue and troublesome disposition among the "King's daughters". The nuns who chaperoned them were anxious to have them marry as rapidly as possible to rid them from their convents. There was a marked increase in disorderliness following their arrival at Quebec, and on at least one occasion, so august a body as the Sovereign Council was accused (in anonymous scrawlings on the walls of the city) of engaging in pimping. Nearly all the Intendants, who seemed not to have had any particular attachment to religious austerity, deplored the morals of the colonials. Governor Denonville even wanted to repatriate some of the women sent to Quebec, but Louis XIV advised forced public labour as a better alternative to bring about reformation of their ways. In 1718 the Council of Marine devoted a session to discussing the problem of "little savage slaves" kept by Canadians for immoral purposes. Several of the fur traders and missionaries in the upper country indicated during the eighteenth century that the soldiers and voyageurs in the Western country kept concubines. The *métis* population was considerable, of course, but was never subject to a census in the upper country, making a mockery therefore of so-called statistics of illegitimate births and *métissage*. While the parish registers indicate few illegitimate births, the fact remains that the state officials thought the problem sufficiently important to obtain royal permission to take direct charge of the education of bastard children.

The colonists were far from docile, subservient, downtrodden, inarticulate, priest-ridden peasants. Contemporary documentation shows them to be remarkably independent, aggressive, self-assertive, freedom-loving and outspoken individuals. Saint-Vallier and Pontbriand both deplored their lack of respect for constituted authority, their boldness and brashness, their materialism and independence of mind. The bishops' circulars often lashed out against seditious talk, murmurings against God and King, and discourses "tending to independence" and "encouraging continuous discontentment of the masses." In the parish of Champlain, the seigneur had the priest thrown out of the manor-house when he came to ask alms. At St. Antoine-de-Tilly, the parishioners broke down the rectory fence to hold a noisy demonstration in front of the priest's house, and at Isle-aux-Coudres, the people prevented a priest from crossing the island to take the sacrament to the sick.[59] This was scarcely the behaviour of a priest-ridden and oppressed populace. It may have been blind rebellion against an authoritarian system, but quite evidently the authoritarian system could not exercise the social control necessary to enforce the obedience and compliance it expected. The inhabitants of Montreal started a great tumult against Intendant Bigot and Bishop Pontbriand when they learned of a plan to amalgamate the General Hospital at Montreal with that of Quebec. On the other hand, when it came to public officials defrauding the King's service, the common people seemed to have no strong objections because it was commonly believed that each Easter the King made a gift of all that had been stolen from him.

The growing feeling of Canadianism — of a separate colonial identity — was noted first by the "Belgian" bishop, Dosquet, during his brief visit to the colony. He believed that the colonial-born clergy tended only to accentuate and encourage this colonial "nationalism", and he therefore recommended the sending of more clergy from France to "inspire" the Canadian *habitants* with "the fidelity, love and zeal that subjects owe their King." He also proposed that there should be one French priest for every two Canadian priests, and that in the assignment to parishes the French clergy should be dispersed among the colonial-born.

At the end of the French period, the clergy were becoming concerned about the growing urbanization of the colony. By the end of the reign of Louis XIV, New France was a largely rural society and there was the hope that with a growing population, the filling out of the seigneurial tracts and the development of a parochial system with regular services, resident curates and adequate schooling, a more controlled society would emerge. However, the towns began to grow more rapidly than the rural areas, and soon about one-quarter of all Canadians lived in towns detached from the land. Even more disturbing was the strengthening of a worldly outlook and the development of a courtier society, particularly at Quebec — aping some aspects of court life in France — and also reproducing the worst features of military garrison life, at Montreal, Louisbourg and Detroit. The clergy, from Pontbriand to the lowliest deacon, inveighed with good reason against the drunkenness, sexual laxity, gambling, and the general worldliness and pleasure-madness of a growing segment of colonial society. It was not surprising that some of the clergy speculated that the British Conquest was some kind of Divine retribution, a sort of "Babylonian captivity" to cleanse Israel of her filthy whoredoms.

> High life in spite of the miseries and impending loss of the colony, has been most active in Quebec, there have never been so many balls and so much gambling. . . .[60]

These were the comments, on the very eve of military collapse, of Montcalm. He too perceived the "madness" of which the clergy complained.

Conclusions

Exoticism and utilitarianism were the chief motives of exploration and settlement; New France was a "new world" which aroused the curious, the venturesome and the dedicated. New France was regarded at once as the earthly paradise and as the kingdom of demons. Amerindian patterns of living were seen by some as superior to sophisticated and prententious European customs, and by others as heathen darkness and devil possession. Thus the missionary motive loomed large in the planting of the Catholic faith in the colony; nevertheless, religious inspiration and drive never became the predominant motivation of colonization. In some cases, it was merely a convenient cloak of righteousness for very materialistic pursuits.

Most significant about the Amerindian missions — successful as they were within narrow limits and in comparison with the other European experiences in North America — is the fact that the majority of the Amerindians steadfastly resisted assimilation. On the other hand, the North American environment and the native way of life, which was atuned to that environment, required the French to make major adjustments, to live almost in tribute to the natives in the interior, and to adopt numerous aspects of native folkways. Catholicism, as introduced to the tribesmen, was inextricably interwoven with European culture and civilization. It possessed a value system and moral assumptions that were more Renaissance French than primitive Christian.

The initial missionary hope had been to convert the natives and assimilate them into a French sedentary way of life — some idealists in the early decades went so far as to dream of a fusion of races — but their objectives were soon modified. The fur trader was more successful in attaching the tribesmen to the French economy than was the missionary in attaching them to a French life-style. Nevertheless, the Amerindian missions continued to play an important diplomatic and political role in connecting many tribes to the French cause in North America.

In the relations between church and state, or more properly between the politico-military aspects and the religious aspects of French national undertakings, it was the King as "eldest son of the Church" and anointed monarch who was at the apex of the pyramid of power and authority. The sacerdotal ministry, although conceded to be of divine origin, was not permitted to exercise its autonomous and independent sacred office except within the political and cultural bounds defined by the secular power. Gallican officials (among them a succession of industrious and ambitious Intendants in New France in the service of an equally zealous Ministry of Marine) staunchly defended what they regarded as "the rights and privileges of the Gallican Church as established in this realm" against supposed incursions from, or over-extensions of, the ecclesiastical power. In fact, many of the quarrels between church and state officials were eventually settled by the monarch in person, and these as often as not constituted interventions of the royal prerogative in defence of the national church against overbearing royal officials.

From 1659 forward, the people looked to the bishop at Quebec, which was elevated in 1674 to a bishopric dependent upon Rome but operating within the Gallican sphere, for spiritual leadership. Laval set the tone for episcopal leadership in New France and Saint-Vallier, his successor, was — if anything — even more conscious of his episcopal rights and privileges and asserted them on all occasions. Both these bishops, although commonly regarded as influential and austere, were absent from the colony for long periods of time. Thereafter, until the arrival of Pontbriand in 1740, the colony was usually without the presence of its Ordinary. The religious orders, particularly the Jesuits in the early seventeenth century, played an important role in setting the moral and spiritual tone of colonial life, indeed to the degree that there was tension between the bishops and the religious orders, from time to time. The parish priests were never able to establish themselves as undisputed leaders in the parishes or *seigneuries*. They were consulted, they spoke out on all manner of questions from their pulpits, but they were unable to coerce the colonists into obedient submission when the latter were unconvinced or opposed. In the rural areas, the church often had a small embryonic village growing up about it — usually consisting of the rectory, the school, and a few tradesmen's dwellings — but the great majority of the *censitaires* lived on their strip farms far from the church or the manor-house.

In the towns, the colonists tended to classify the various groups of ecclesiastics according to their traditional principal roles. The Recollets were the King's chaplains, the Jesuits were the principal missionaries and diplomats among the Amerindians, the Sulpicians were the parish clergy of the Montreal area, and the Seminary secular priests served in the parishes about Quebec. Concurrent with this "division of labour", there was also a social gradation; a popular proverb had it that a hatchet was sufficient to cut out a Recollet, that a secular priest could be made with a pair of scissors, but a Jesuit had to be made with a fine paint-brush. The women's communities were also stratified according to their usefulness to the King's service and his subjects. The Ursulines, limited largely to education, sometimes felt themselves under-valued by bureaucratic and popular assessment alike, whereas the two orders of Hospital Nuns enjoyed broad-based favour and approval. Although the two secular communities of women, the Sisters of the Congregation and the Grey Nuns, encountered initial opposition to their organization as religious institutes, their respective vocations in teaching and hospital work eventually earned them support and recognition. The Brothers Hospitallers, despite their zealousness and the significance of their work, were unsuccessful.

The church in New France has often been accused of Jansenist rigourism and puritanical tyranny; a common belief is that the clergy wielded an undue influence in the everyday aspects of colonial life, "prying" — in the words of Baron de Lahontan — into the private affairs of individuals, and — in the words of Count Frontenac — "intervening" in the political and economic life of the royal province. The numerous and repeated fulminations of the clergy (notably the bishops) are cited as evidence of the puritanical restrictions and heavy-handed clerical control which imposed an oppressive conformity on the colonial population and created a subservient and closed society.

A closer examination of colonial life indicates that the so-called "rigourism" was no more than the ideals of reformed Catholicism as defined and experienced in metropolitan France. The zealous practice of the highest ideals of Catholicism was promoted in New France by partisans of the fervent religious renaissance, the *dévots* or sanctimonious clique which included Bishop Laval, many Jesuit missionaries, Marie de l'Incarnation, Jeanne Mance, the pious founders of Montreal, and countless other pioneers. Attempts were made to preserve the initial religious vision and create a New World church of such pristine purity that it not only would emulate the church of the Apostolic Age but also would usher in the church of the Parousia and the imminent end of the world. New France did not have to contend with corruption of monastic and court life, the heterogeneity of population, the cultural diversity and the social stratification and power structures that plagued the church in Old France. If religious life seemed more intensive in the colony, and religion seemed to play a more prominent role, it was partially because of the zeal of the clergy and missionaries in establishing European forms and practices in an alien environment.

Environmental factors cannot be ignored in the evaluation of the official pronouncements and the deliberate acts of the clergy. None of the doctrines, dogmas or practices enjoined by any of the bishops or their grand vicars differed substantially from what was taught in France. Theological positions were identical to those in the "old country", and moral doctrine was the same. Jansenism was never permitted to take root in colonial soil. Even the catechism and *Rituel* of Bishop Saint-Vallier were responses to local need and situation, and were inspired by the mainstream of Catholic theology and moral philosophy. The over-riding impression that emerges from the mass of documentation is of a population that tended to be unruly, boisterous in its expressions of either joy or anger, independent and self-reliant by habit, vainglorious, easily vulnerable to the sins of the flesh and to wordly pleasures (noted by Saint-Vallier and Dosquet with particular reference to excessive drinking and gambling). The catechetical method of instruction provided the inhabitants with basic answers to fundamental questions and, in addition, provided them with a system of reasoned thought which could be applied to non-religious situations. A population which pursued litigation with the particular intensity and relish of the Canadians, or which held obstinately to its views on tithing and the construction of churches and rectories, could scarcely be accused of being docile, inarticulate, and oppressed into servility.

Warnings, whether pronounced from the curate's pulpit or published by the bishop, and prohibiting edicts and ordinances cannot be taken as reliable gauges of social control. They represent the ideals held up to a society which fell far short of the mark — the desired level of collective and personal behaviour befitting a colony which called itself Christian, believed in a Providential mission in the New World, and hoped for conversion of aboriginal pagans under nominal French sovereignty. The gulf between the ideal and objective, on the one hand, and social reality, on the other, appears much wider in the clerical evaluations of the situation than in the secular reports on the same subject. The church was never able to combat successfully the brandy trafficking, to impose standard tithing, or to provide regular religious services to all the inhabitants of the over-extended colony. If the clergy stressed greatly the intemperance, vanity and love of pleasure of the *habitants*, it was because of agreement with civil officials that these were weaknesses cultivated by the colonial environment. While there were a number of notorious sinners in the colony, most of them eventually conformed more or less to the externals of Catholicism and showed some preoccupation with ultimate salvation.

The colonials could not be accused of moroseness. In fact, it was their gaiety and lightness that too often brought down on them the anger and despair of the spiritual directors. Prior to the arrival of a Vicar Apostolic at Quebec, there were balls and boisterous weddings. The Jesuits (accused by some of troubling consciences and imposing particularly narrow interpretations in the assigning of penance) promoted literature and the arts, especially theatre. Drunkenness may have been more widespread than in France — not an altogether surprising situation given the frontier conditions. Blasphemy became another distinguishing mark of the Canadians, who were able to give succeeding generations a unique vocabulary of French-language *jurons* which edicts, ordinances, sermons and formal education failed to eradicate.

In New France religious ignorance does not appear to have been as deplorable as that of the masses in rural France in the seventeenth and eighteenth centuries. Nonetheless, in their reports the bishops and state officials continually expressed misgivings about the spiritual and intellectual level of the common people. The population of New France, to begin with, was more selective and had sprung from a relatively small nucleus of about 10,000 immigrants. While it is true that about one thousand of this number were not of French origin (a fact which modifies the tradition that all present-day French Canadians are descendants of a homogeneous Norman–Breton original group), they were by the requirements of naturalization, adoption, and in numerous cases abjuration of heresy, compelled to submit to religious indoctrination. Moreover, because there was a conscious effort to establish the Catholic Church firmly in the colony to the exclusion of Protestantism, to evangelize the native peoples, and to protect both colonists and Amerindians from the supposed nefarious influence of the foreign Protestants who shared the continent, a sense of strong religious identity was maintained. This fact was not without important consequences for the Conquest in 1713 of Acadia and in 1760 of Canada. New France, or "Quebec" as the British preferred to call it, did not experience the dechristianization which areas of the mother country would experience after 1789. On the contrary, the church became a rallying point for Canadian national feeling, for group solidarity. The institutional church — under British laws and a Protestant monarch — not only survived the Conquest; it lived to enjoy even greater vigour, and maintained a far more important role in Quebec society's cultural and political life than had ever been dreamed possible.

Notes

Chapter I

1 André Thévet, *Les Singularitez de la France Antarctique, autrement nomée Amérique et de plusieurs Terres, et Isles descouvertes de nostre temps* (Paris, 1555), p. 51.

2 Gabriel Sagard-Théodat, *Histoire du Canada et des Voyages que les Frères Mineurs Récollets y ont faicts pour la conversion des Infidelles* (Paris, 1636), pp. 17-21; also *Archives du Séminaire de Québec, (A.S.Q.)*, Polygraphie VII, No. 83.

3 E. Réveillaud (ed.), *Histoire chronologique de la Nouvelle-France ou Canada* (Paris, 1888), pp. 176-178.

4 Chrestien Le Clercq, *Premier Etablissement de la Foy dans la Nouvelle-France* (Paris, 1691), Vol. I, pp. 241-243, 293-294; Réveillaud, *op. cit.*, p. 119.

5 Candide de Nant, *Pages glorieuses de l'épopée canadienne. Une mission capucine en Acadie* (Paris, 1927), p. 113.

6 Nicolas-Claude de Peiresc, *Correspondance de Peiresc avec plusieurs missionaires et religieux de l'ordre des capucins, 1631-1637* (Paris, 1891), p. 125.

7 *Collection de Manuscrits contenant Lettres, Mémoires et autres documents historiques relatifs à la Nouvelle-France* (Québec, 1883-85), Vol. I, pp. 145-149.

8 *Bibliothèque Nationale* (B.N.), Paris, *Collection Clairambault*, Vol. 1016, p. 493.

9 *Le Journal des Jésuites, publié d'après le manuscrit original conservé aux Archives du séminaire du Québec* (Montréal, 1892), p. 357.

10 Ch. de Grandmaison (ed.), *Chronique de l'Abbaye de Beaumont-les-Tours* (Tours, 1877), pp. 139-143.

11 Dom Guy Oury (ed.), *Marie de l'Incarnation, Ursuline (1599-1672): Correspondance* (Solesmes, 1971), p. 157.

12 *Ibid.*, pp. 208, 286-287.

13 Y. Charron, "Itinéraire spirituelle de Marguerite Bourgeoys", *Revue d'Histoire de l'Amérique française*, Vol. II, No. 3 (décembre, 1948), p. 365.

14 Paul Reyss, *Etude sur quelques points de l'histoire de la tolérance au Canada et aux Antilles* (Gèneve, 1907), p. 21; C.H. Laverdière (ed.), *Oeuvres de Champlain* (Québec, 1870), Vol. V, p. 709.

15 Sagard-Théodat, *op. cit.*, p. 8.

16 Lucien Campeau (ed.), *La Première Mission d'Acadie (1602-1616)* (Québec, 1967), Memorandum of March 13, 1605, pp. 11-12.

17 W. L. Grant (ed.), *The History of New France by Marc Lescarbot*, (The Champlain Society, Toronto, 1907) Vol. II, p. 292. Used by permission.

18 *Archives Nationales de la Province de Québec (A.P.Q.), Manuscrits II*, Vol. I, p. 37; *Archives départementales de la Charente-Maritime (A.D.C.M.)*, Rouen Admirauté de la Rochelle, Series B, No. 5894, October 28, 29, 1621; Sagard-Théodat *op. cit.*, Vol. I, p. 72; Robert Le Blant and René Baudry (eds.), *Nouveaux Documents sur Champlain et son époque* (Ottawa, 1967), Vol. I, No. 177, pp. 420-422.

19 James B. Conacher (ed.), *The History of Canada or New France by Father Francois du Creux, S. J.* (Toronto, 1951), Vol. I, p. 34.

20 Dom Albert Jamet, *Marie de l'Incarnation, Ursuline de Tours. Ecrits Spirituels et Historiques* (Paris, 1939), Vol. IV, pp. 265-266.

21 *Ibid.*, Vol. IV, pp. 109-111.

22 *Public Archives of Canada (P.A.C.), Series H., Martin Collection*, June 1651, p. 85.

23 *A.S.Q., Evêques*, No. 184, Letters-patent of March 27, 1659.

Chapter II

[1] Marc Lescarbot, *Relation dernière de ce qui s'est passé au voyage du Sieur Poutrincourt en la Nouvelle-France dupuis 20 mois ença* (Paris, 1612), p. 21.

[2] W. L. Grant (ed.), *Voyages of Samuel de Champlain, 1604-1618* (The Champlain Society, 1917) Vol. I., pp. 264, 323. Used by permission.

[3] R. G. Thwaites (ed.), *The Jesuit Relations and Allied Documents* (Cleveland, 1896-1901), Vol. VIII, p. 9.

[4] George M. Wrong (ed.), *The Long Journey to the Country of the Huron by Father Gabriel Sagard* (Toronto, 1939), pp. 130-135; H. Harrisse, *Notes pour servir à l'histoire, la bibliographie, et à la cartographie de la Nouvelle-France et des Pays adjacents 1545-1700* (Paris, 1872), p. 71.

[5] *Edict du Roy pour l'Establissement de la Compagnie de la Nouvelle-France* (Paris, 1657), Article XVII, p. 13; *A.S.Q. Polygraphie III*, No. 2; André Chevillard, *Les Desseins de S. Em. de Richelieu pour l'Amérique* (Rennes, 1659).

[6] Thwaites, *op. cit.*, Vol. VI, p. 242; Vol. VIII, p. 226; Vol. IX, p. 254; Vol. XII, pp. 44, 48; Vol. XIV, p. 233.

[7] *B. N., Manuscrits français* 15 619; 18 617; fol. 345; 18 112; 15 620; *A.S.Q., Fonds Verreau XIII*, Nos. 8, 28b; *A.S.Q., Polygraphie XIII*, Nos. 18, 22, 27, 47, 52.

[8] *Les Véritables Motifs des Messieurs et Dames de la Société de Notre-Dame de Montréal pour la Conversion des Sauvages* (Paris, 1643), pp. 26-27, 106.

[9] Thwaites, *op. cit.*, Vol. IX, pp. 216-218.

[10] *Journal des Jésuites*, pp. 77-78, 312; *Archivum Romanum Societas Iesu (A.R.S.I.)*, Rome, *Gallia 110*, Vol. III, fols. 356-357; Paul-André Leclerc, *Le Mariage sous le régime français* (Unpublished Lic. ès Lettres thesis, Laval University, 1956), pp. 107-108.

[11] Thwaites, *op. cit.*, Vol. XLV, p. 148; Léonidas Larouche (ed.), *Le Second Régistre de Tadoussac, 1668-1700* (Quebec, 1972), pp. 86, 140-146, 154, 162.

[12] Wrong, *op. cit.*, p. 97. Used by permission of the Champlain Society, Toronto.

[13] Thwaites, *op. cit.*, Vol. XXXIII, p. 233.

[14] Dom Guy Oury (ed.), *Marie de l'Incarnation, Ursuline (1599-1672): Correspondance* (Solesmes, 1971), p. 649.

[15] *A.S.Q., Manuscrits XVII*, Laval to Louis XIV, June 4, 1684, p. 44.

[16] *A.S.Q., Lettres R*, No. 26, St. Cosme to Saint-Vallier, June 2, 1699.

[17] *A.S.Q., Polygraphie XIII*, No. 18, Declaration of November 16, 1651; No. 22, Act of February 6, 1652; No. 27, Ordinance of May 12, 1656; No. 52, Concession to Onondagas, 1656.

[18] *Archives des Colonies (A.C.)*, Paris, Series F3, Vol. III, Souart to Tracy, October 7, 1667, fol. 353; *Bibliothèque de Saint-Sulpice, Paris (B.S.S.P.), Tronson Correspondance*, Vol. I, Nos. 11-18, 73-85; Nos. 129-130, pp. 211-213; No. 98, pp. 168, 173; *Archives de l'Archevêché de Québec (A.A.Q.), Eglise du Canada*, Vol. I, Brevet of June 15, 1718, p. 160.

[19] *Propaganda Fide: Scritture*, Vol. I, Pt. II, Bishop Hubert to Cardinal Antonelli, June 19, 1788, p. 741.

Chapter III

[1] Roland Mousnier, "L'Evolution des institutions monarchiques en France et ses relations avec l'état social", *XVIIe Siècle*, Nos. 58-59 (année 1963), p. 61.

[2] François Dumont, "Loyauté française et monarchie absolue au XVIIe siècle", *XVIIe Siècle*, Nos. 58-59 (année 1963), pp. 5, 6; Marc Bloch, *Les rois thaumaturges. Etude sur le caractère surnaturel attribué à la puissance royale particulièrement en France et en Angleterre* (Paris, 1961), *passim*.

[3] *B.N., Fonds Dupuy*, No. 520, "Recueil journalier de ce qui s'est négotié et arresté en la Chambre du Tiers Estat . . . ès années 1616 et 1615," fol. 164; *Archives Nationales (A.N.)*, Paris, Series G⁸, *Fonds de l'Agence du Clergé*, Registre No. 632a, Procès-verbal imprimé de la Chambre ecclésiastique aux Etats-Généraux de 1614, February 21, 1615; *ibid.*, Registre 633a, Procès-verbal original de l'Assemblée de 1615, July 7, 1615.

[4] P. Blet, *Les Assemblées du clergé et Louis XIV* (1670-1693), (Rome 1972), pp. 553-554.

[5] *A.C., Series F³*, Vol. III, no. 233; also *P.A.C., Series C¹¹A*, Regulation of March 27, 1647, Vol. I, pp. 438ff.

[6] Chrestien LeClercq, *Establissément de la Foy dans la Nouvelle-France* (Paris, 1691), pp. 498-510; *A.D.C.M., Series E*, Minutes Teuleron, Liasse 1650, Order of Council of Quebec to Jean Lalemant, 1650.

[7] *P.A.C., Affaires Etrangères: Amérique*, Vol. IV, Arrêt of March 7, 1657, p. 302.

[8] Camille de Rochemonteix, *Les Jésuites et la Nouvelle-France au XVIIe siècle* (Letouzey et Ané, Paris, 1895-96), Vol. II, p. 527; *Journal des Jésuites*, pp. 302-3; *A.A.Q., Registre A*, No. 236, Brevet of May 24, 1661, p. 180.

[9] *P.A.C., Series B*, Vol. I, Instructions to Gaudais-Dupont, May 1, 1665, pp. 112-13.

[10] *P.A.C., Series B*, Vol. I, Instructions to Talon, March 25, 1665, pp. 50-51.

[11] *Ibid.*, Minister to Courcelles, May 15, 1668, pp. 208-9.

[12] *Collection de Manuscrits*, Vol. I, p. 226.

[13] R.G. Thwaites (ed.), *New Voyages to North America by the Baron de Lahontan* (A.C. McClurg & Co., Chicago, 1905), Vol. I, p. 385.

[14] P. Clément (ed.), *Lettres, instructions et mémoires de Colbert* (Paris, 1865), Vol. III, Pt. 1, Louis XIV to Frontenac, April 22, 1675, p. 586.

[15] *Mémoires de Louis XIV écrits par lui-même* (Paris, 1923), pp. 96-9.

[16] *A.A.Q., Registre A*, October 3, 1690, p. 290.

[17] *A.S.Q., Chapitre IV*, Archbishop of Paris to Saint-Vallier, April 15, 1694.

[18] Dom Albert Jamet (ed.), *Annales de l'Hôtel-Dieu de Québec, 1636-1716* (Quebec, 1939), p. 85.

[19] F. Isambert *et al.*, *Recueil général des anciennes lois français* (Paris, 1822-33), Vol. XVIII, p. 49.

[20] *A.S.Q., Polygraphie II*, Nos. 67, 68, 69, 70; *ibid; Lettres B*, No. 11, Tremblay to Saint-Vallier, March 13, 1706.

[21] *Ibid.*, Glandelet to Saint-Vallier, 1707, p. 4.

[22] *A.C., Series C¹³A*, Vol. 10, Mornay to Paquet, December 8, 1726, fols. 35v.-36.

[23] *A.A.Q., Eglise du Canada*, Vol. I, Memorandum of 1728, p. 93.

[24] *A.P.Q., Ordonnances des Intendants*, January 6, 1728.

[25] H. Têtu and C.O. Gagnon (eds.), *Mandements, lettres pastorales et circulaires des Evêques de Québec* (Québec, 1887), Vol. I, pp. 537-9. Hereafter cited as *Mandements*.

[26] Comte de Quinsonas, *Un Dauphinois Cinquième Evêque de la Nouvelle-France. Monseigneur de Laubervière (1711-1740)* (Paris, 1936), pp. 37-8.

[27] *P.A.C., Series C¹¹A*, Vol. 86, Beauharnois & Hocquart to Minister, November 10, 1746.

[28] *Ibid.*, Vol. 80, Pontbriand to Maurepas, October 8, 1747.

[29] *Mandements*, Vol. II, June 20, 1745, p. 44.

[30] *Mandements*, Vol. II, June 5, 1759, pp. 137-40.

[31] *Quebec Gazette*, July 3, 1766.

[32] John Knox, *An Historical Journal of the Campaigns in North America* (Toronto, 1914), Vol. II, pp. 259-60.

[33] *Ibid.*, pp. 229-30.

[34] *Edits*, Vol. I, Edict of April 27, 1627, p. 7.

[35] *A.S.Q., Polygraphie IV*, No. 31, Louis XIV to De Cange, July 2, 1659.

[36] *A.S.Q., Manuscrits 14*, Memorandum of Laval concerning Protestants, 1670, p. 207.

[37] *A.C., Series B*, Vol. 72, Council of Marine to Beauharnois & Hocquart, April 20, 1741, fol. 316½.

[38] *A.C., Series C¹¹A*, Vol. 93, Bigot to Minister, October 3, 1749, fols. 257-8.

Chapter IV

[1] *P.A.C., Series C¹¹A*, Vol. 22, D'Auteuil to Minister, October 17, 1705, pp. 380-81.

[2] *Edits*, Vol. I, Declaration of November 25, 1743, p. 577.

[3] Richard Colebrook Harris, *The Seigneurial System in Early Canada: A Geographical Study* (Madison, 1966), pp. 42-44.

[4] *Rapport de l'Archiviste de la Province de Québec (R.A.P.Q.), 1938-39* (Quebec 1939), Vaudreuil, Beauharnois & Raudot to Pontchartrain, October 19, 1705, p. 75.

[5] *A.S.Q., Polygraphie XIX*, No. 6, Contract of association of January 20, 1611.

[6] E. Réveillaud, *Histoire chronologique de la Nouvelle-France ou Canada par le Père Sixte le Tac, Récollet* (Paris, 1888), pp. 123-124.

[7] *A.P.Q., Manuscrits II*, Vol. I, January 18, 1622, p. 31.

[8] A. Launay (ed.), *Lettres de Monseigneur Pallu* (Angoulème, 1904), Vol. I, Pallu to Deydier, December 8, 1670, p. 120.

[9] R. G. Thwaites (ed.), *The Jesuit Rela-*

tions and *Allied Documents* (Cleveland, 1896-1901) Vol. IV, pp. 171-173.

10 Léonidas Larouche (ed.), *Le Second Registre de Tadoussac, 1668-1700* (Montreal, 1972), pp. 151-152.

11 Gustave Lanctôt (ed.), *The Oakes Collection: New Documents by Lahontan Concerning Canada and Newfoundland* (Ottawa, 1940), p. 25.

12 *A.S.Q., Documents Faribault,* No. 40a, Ordinance of July 9, 1644.

13 F. Du Creux, *The History of Canada, or New France* (The Champlain Society, Toronto, 1951), Vol. I, p. 90.

14 "Histoire de l'eau-de-vie en Canada", *Collection de Mémoires et de Relations sur l'histoire ancienne du Canada* (Quebec, 1840), p. 25.

15 *A.A.Q., Registre A,* No. 23, Judgment of February 1, 1662, pp. 25-26.

16 Sacra Rituum Congregatio, Sectio Historia, *Quebecen. Beatificationis et Canonizationes Ven. Servi Dei Francisci de Montmorency Laval* (Laval, 1961), Doc. XVII, No. 10, Reply of University of Toulouse, June 28, 1675, pp. 162-64.

17 *Edits,* Vol. I, pp. 235-236; Judgments, Vol. II, p. 320.

18 *P.A.C., Series B,* Vol. 15, King to Denonville & Champigny, May 11, 1689, fol. 51v.

19 *Mandements,* Vol. I, Judgment of April 6, 1696, pp. 353-357.

20 *Edits,* Vol. III, pp. 439, 446-449.

21 *Mandements,* Vol. I, Mandement of November 26, 1730, pp. 535, 537.

22 Jacques Beauroy, "Notes sur les boissons et l'importation de vins du Midi et d'Espagne en Nouvelle France", *Annales du Midi,* Vol. 83, No. 104 (oct.-déc., 1971), pp. 419-429.

23 *P.A.C., Affaires Étrangères: Amérique,* Vol. IV, Louis XIV to Ventadour, November 7, 1647, fol. 783; Dom Guy Oury, *Marie de l'Incarnation, Ursuline (1599-1672). Correspondance* (Solesmes, 1971), p. 214.

24 Lucien Campeau, "Documents Inédits, Un Témoignage de 1651 sur la Nouvelle-France", *Revue d'histoire de l'Amérique français,* Vol. XXIII, No. 4 (mars 1970), p. 610.

25 *A.S.Q., Séminaire II,* No. 36, March 26, 1663.

26 *P.A.C., Series B,* Vol. I, Instructions to Talon, 1665, pp. 71-72; René Bélanger, *La Dîme ecclésiastique* (Ottawa, 1939), p. 53.

27 Ordonnances, Vol. I, p. 72, n. 1; *A.S.Q., Polygraphies V,* No. 6, August 23, 1667.

28 *P.A.C., Series B,* Vol. VIII, Letterspatent of May 1679, p. 130; Judgments, Vol. II, pp. 321-322.

29 *P.A.C., Series F⁵A,* Vol. III, pp. 4-11; *S.R.C.,* Doc. XLIII, No. 11, de Meulles to Seignelay, November 4, 1683, pp. 297-298.

30 *A.A.Q., Eglise du Canada,* Vol. III, pp. 88-99, 164-174.

31 *Mandements,* Vol. I, Ordinance of April 14, 1717, p. 492.

32 *A.S.Q., Manuscrits,* No. 147c, Notice on tithes in Canada, fols. 15-15v; *P.A.C., Series C¹¹A,* Vol. 78, Pontbriand to Minister, September 28, 1742.

33 *A.C., Series C¹¹B,* Vol. 8, fol. 105v; Vol. 11, fol. 22; Vol. 12, fols. 23v-24; Vol. 14, fol. 112.

34 *Edits,* Vol. II, pp. 270, 295, 346, 348, 396, 441, 443, 447, 485, 507, 575, 588; Vol. III, pp. 176, 226, 274, 278, 280, 289, 329, 335, 347, 367, 372, 373, 375, 379, 383, 389.

35 A. Gowans, *Church Architecture in New France* (University of Toronto Press, 1955), pp. 149-154.

36 D. Jousse, *Nouveau Commentaire sur les Ordonnances* (Paris, 1775), pp. 138-140.

37 Harris, *op. cit.,* pp. 76-77.

38 *Mandements,* Vol. II, October 15, 1742, p. 23.

Chapter V

1 P. Clément, *Lettres, Instructions et Mémoires de Colbert* (Paris, 1865), Vol. II, Colbert to de Morangis, October 16, 1682, p. 209.

2 *B.S.S.P., Tronson Correspondence,* Vol. I, No. 100, Tronson to Seguenot, April 12, 1680, p. 184.

3 *A.A.Q., Registre C,* Pontbriand to parish of Saint-Thomas, November 23, 1741, fol. 165.

4 *A.S.Q., Séminaire VII,* No. 72a, Journal of *Curé* Récher.

5 *A.R.S.I.,* Gallia 109 I, fol. 264.

6 Adolph B. Benson (ed.), *Peter Kalm's Travels in North America* (New York, 1966), Vol. II, sp. 448-89. Used by permission of Arthur R. Benson.

7 E. Z. Massicotte, "Fondation d'une communauté de frères instituteurs à Montréal en 1686," *Bulletin de Recherches historiques,* Vol. XXVIII (1922), pp. 37-42; *A.A.Q., Registre A,* Memorandum of May 13, 1694, p. 540.

8 Benson, *op. cit.*, Vol. II, p. 452.
9 *Ibid*, Vol. II, p. 446; *P.A.C.*, Series F., Vol. VII; Letters-patent of February 1718, pp. 963-64.
10 *P.A.C., Series C*11*A*, Vol. 43, Council of Marine to Vaudreuil and Bégon, December 23, 1721, p. 270.
11 *P.A.C., Series B*, Vol. 54 (2), King to Beauharnois and Hocquart, April 11, 730, p. 342.
12 Sr. Marie-Pierre (Fracaud), "L'Education des Filles à Niort au XVIIe siècle," *Bulletin de la Société historique et scientifique des Deux-Sèvres*, Vol. IX, No. 4 (1951), p. 33, 38-40.
13 F. Du Creux, *The History of Canada, or New France* (The Champlain Society, Toronto, 1951), Vol. I, p. 268. Used by permission.
14 *A.A.Q., Eglise du Canada*, Vol. VI, Frontenac & Champigny to Pontchartrain, October 10, 1697, p. 61.
15 *A.S.Q., Documents Faribault*, No. 163, September 20, 1649; No. 164, December 28, 1651.
16 Y. Charron, "Itinéraire spirituel de Marguerite Bourgeoys, *"Revue d'histoire de l'Amérique française*, Vol. II, No. 3 (décembre 1948), p. 365.
17 *P.A.C., Series C*11*A*, Vol. 26, Raudot to Pontchartrain, November 10, 1707, pp. 28-29.
18 *Mandements*, Vol. I, February 20, 1735, pp. 543-545.
19 *Ibid.*, August 20, 1735, pp. 347-549.
20 *A.A.Q., Lettres II*, Regulations for confessors, January 10, 1754, pp. 661-664; Regulations for confessors, January 20, 1758, p. 665.
21 *F. X. de Charlevoix, Journal of a Voyage* (London, 1761), Vol. I, p. 114.
22 G. Panel, *Documents concernant les pauvres de Rouen* (Roeun, 1917), Vol. II, Arret of November 15, 1675, p. 72; Raoul Allier, *La Cabale des Dévots*, (Paris, 1902), pp. 282-284, 410-412.
23 *A.S.Q., Polygraphie III*, No. 22, Obedience of Hospital Nuns, October 2, 1659; No. 23, Contract of March 29, 1659.
24 *Jugements*, Vol. II, p. 871.
25 *Edits*, Vol. II, April 8, 1688, pp. 119-122.
26 *Benson, op. cit.*, Vol. II, pp. 454-455.
27 *Ibid.*, Vol. II, p. 446.
28 *Edits*, Vol. II, August 27, 1747, pp. 391-392, December 14, 1751, p. 406.
29 Oury, *op. cit.*, pp. 802-803.
30 "Etat présent du Canada, 1754," *R.A.P.Q., 1920-21* (Quebec, 1921), p. 42.
31 *R.A.P.Q., 1921-22* (Quebec, 1922),

Collet to Superior Council, January, 1721, pp. 262-362.
32 *A.A.Q., Registre C*, Pontbriand to parishioners of Saint-Thomas, November 8, 1741, fol. 164; *ibid.*, November 23, 1741, fol. 165.

Chapter VI

1 *Journal des Jésuites*, p. 66; *Mandements*, Vol. 1, pp. 496-8.
2 *Journal des Jésuites*, pp. 262.
3 *Mandements*, Vol. I, February 24, 1735, pp. 545-46.
4 *B.S.S.P., Tronson Correspondence*, Vol. 1, Tronson to Montreal Seminary, March 17, 1676.
5 *A.S.Q., Manuscrits 284*, Tronson's rules for self-examination for a Seminary priest, 1679.
6 *A.S.Q., Evêques II*, No. 207, Notes of *Abbé* Petite.
7 *Edits*, Vol. II, Ordinance of November 12, 1706, p. 425.
8 *A.P.Q., Ordonnances des Intendants*, Vol. IV, Ordinance of March 22, 1710, p. 40.
9 *Mandements*, Vol. 1, February 10, 1732, pp. 540-41.
10 P. Clément (ed.), *Lettres, instructions et mémoires de Colbert* (Paris, 1865), Vol. III, Pt. II, Instructions to Bouteroue, April 5, 1668, p. 403.
11 *Mandements*, Vol. 1, pp. 486-87.
12 *A.A.Q., Chapitre de Québec*, November 3, 1730, fol. 79v.
13 Guy Plante, *Le Rigorisme au XVIIe siècle. Mgr de Saint-Vallier et le sacrament de pénitence* (Gembloux, 1971), p. 156.
14 R.G. Thwaites (ed.), *New Voyages to North American by the Baron de Lahontan* (Chicago, 1905, Vol. I, p. 89.
15 *Journal des Jésuites*, pp. 52, 78.
16 *Ibid.*, p. 353.
17 *Mandements*, Vol. I, pp. 169-171.
18 Thwaites, *New Voyages by Lahontan*, Vol. I, p. 89.
19 "Correspondance de Madame Bégon," *RAPQ, 1934-35* (Quebec, 1935), p. 37.
20 "Lettres de Mère Marie Andrée Duplessis de Sainte-Hélène," *Nova Francia* (Montreal, 1967), Vol. IV, October 30, 1753, p. 51.
21 *Mandements*, Vol. II, December 27, 1751, p. 95.
22 *A.S.Q., Séminaire XV*, No. 25, *Mandement* of February 26, 1682.
23 *Mandements*, Vol. I, pp. 171-173.

[24] *A.C., Series F3*, Vol. VI, Circular of 1686, fol. 272.

[25] *Journal des Jésuites*, pp. 92.

[26] Du Creux, *op. cit.*, Vol. I, p. 108. Used by permission of the Champlain Society.

[27] *Journal des Jésuites*, pp. 75, 166, 385.

[28] *A.A.Q., Eglise du Canada*, Vol. VI, Champigny to Pontchartrain, October 27, 1694, p. 50; *Mandements*, Vol. I, January 16, 1694, pp. 302-304.

[29] *P.A.C., Series F3*, Vol. VII, Extracts of procedures of Sovereign Council, 1694, p. 270.

[30] Thwaites, *New Voyages by Lahontan*, Vol. I, pp. 89-90.

[31] Adolph B. Benson (ed.), *Peter Kalm's Travels in North America* (New York, 1966), Vol. II, p. 473.

[32] *Mandements*, Vol. II, Circular of April 20, 1742, pp. 15-17.

[33] *Ibid.*, Vol. I, March 29, 1664, pp. 100-101.

[34] *Ibid.*, Vol. I, pp. 104-105.

[35] *A.S.Q., Manuscrits 147(b)*, Advice to young man contemplating marriage, fols. 4v-5.

[36] *A.S.Q., Manuscrits 147(b)*, Instructions regarding marriage, fols. 7-8v.

[37] *Mandements*, Vol. I, May 24, 1717, pp. 493-494.

[38] Thwaites, *New Voyages by Lahontan*, p. 388.

[39] *Mandements*, Vol. I, pp. 300-301.

[40] Clément, *op. cit.*, Vol. III, Pt. II, Colbert to Duchesneau, May 15, 1678, p. 633.

[41] *A.A.Q., Registre A.*, No. 173, p. 131; also *Mandements*, Vol. I, p. 114.

[42] E. Réveillaud (ed.), *Histoire chronologique de la Nouvelle-France ou Canada* (Paris, 1888), p. 2-3; *A.S.Q., Lettres N*, No. 52, Dudouyt to Laval, March 9, 1681.

[43] *P.A.C., Affaires Etrangères: Amérique*, Vol. V, Frontenac to Minister, November 13, 1673, fols. 324-325.

[44] *A.S.Q., Polygraphie IV*, No. 35, police regulations of May 11, 1676.

[45] *B.S.S.P., Tronson Correspondence*, Vol. I, No. 246, Tronson to Rémy, April 27, 1684.

[46] R. Mandrou, *La France au XVIIe et XVIIIe siècles* (Paris, 1970), p. 162.

[47] *Journal des Jésuites*, pp. 53-54, 89-90, 111, 127, 141-142.

[48] R. Mandrou, *Magistrats et Sorciers en France au XVIIe siècle* (Paris, 1968), pp. 221-226.

[49] *Rituel du diocèse de Québec* (Paris, 1703), pp. 570-572, 589.

[50] *A.J.M., Documents Judiciaires*, Interrogation of René Besnard Bourjoly, November 2, 1658.

[51] *S.R.C., Joannis de Brébeuf*, pp. 669-671; P. Ragueneau, *La Vie de la Mère Catherine de St. Augustin* (Paris, 1671), p. 291.

[52] *A.P.Q., Procédures Judiciaires*, Vol. I, Case of Jean Campagnard, February 20, 1685.

[53] *B.S.S.P., Tronson Correspondence*, Vol. I, No. 97, Tronson to Dollier de Casson, March 20, 1680, pp. 166-167.

[54] *A.S.Q., Polygraphie XIII*, Nos. 5-10; *A.J.M., Procès Fameux, 1734-1756.* Case of Havard, June 30, 1742; *Mandements*, Vol. II, pp. 19-21.

[55] Benson, *op. cit.*, Vol. II, p. 422.

[56] *Mandements*, Vol. II, November 24, 1744, pp. 40-43.

[57] *Jugements*, Vol. I, pp. 718, 725-727.

[58] *Mandements*, Vol. I, pp. 511-512.

[59] E. Hamelin, *La Paroisse de Champlain* (Trois-Rivières, 1933), p. 32; *A.A.Q., Registre C.*, Pontbriand to parishioners of St. Antoine de Tilly, October 23, 1749, fol. 200; A. Mailloux, *Histoire de L'Isle-aux-Coudres depuis son établissement* (Montreal, 1879), p. 57.

[60] H.R. Casgrain (ed.), *Collection de Manuscrits du Maréchal de Lévis* (Québec 1895), Vol. VII, p. 495.

Bibliographical Note

This is meant as a guide to the principal works and must not be construed as an exhaustive bibliography.

The MANUSCRIPT SOURCES are abundant. They can be summarized under three principal headings: national or state archives; regional or municipal archives and libraries; and archives of religious institutes and communities. The chief national or state archives of interest for the church in New France are the Public Archives of Canada in Ottawa, the Archives Nationales in Quebec, the Archives des Colonies, Archives de la Marine and Archives Nationales in Paris, the National Library in Ottawa, the Bibliothèque Nationale in Paris and the Newberry Library in Chicago. The Sulpician Archives in Paris and in Montreal are a valuable source of information, as are the archives of the Seminary of Quebec, and the Jesuit archives at St. Jérôme, Chantilly and St. Louis. The Ursulines, Hospital Nuns, Grey Nuns and Sisters of the Congregation all have their archives and libraries. Relevant information was gleaned in the departmental libraries at La Rochelle, Nantes, Rouen and Tours, also at the municipal libraries at Montreal, La Rochelle and Rouen, and at the Archdiocesan Archives in Quebec.

The most useful and accessible repository for Canadian researchers is obviously the Public Archives in Ottawa. Particularly rich in church history are the series MG-17 A — Ecclesiastical archives — Catholic Church; MG-18 E — Religious records; MG-1, Series $C^{11}A$, $C^{11}D$, F^3, F^5A; MG-3, Series K, Monuments historiques; MG-5, Foreign Affairs, Mémoires et Documents, Amérique. The parish records are found in MG-8, section G.

The principal PRINTED COLLECTIONS OF SOURCE MATERIALS are the Champlain Society publications which include Le Clercq's *New Relation of Gaspesia*, Du Creux's *The History of Canada or New France*, and Sagard's *The Long Journey to the Country of the Huron*; the Literary and Historical Society of Quebec publications of François Dollier de Casson, *Histoire du Montréal, 1640–1672* (1871) and François Vachon de Belmont, *Histoire du Canada* (1840); the Société Historique de Montréal editions of the *Voyage de MM. Dollier et Galinée* (1875), J.J. Olier's *Les Véritables Motifs* (1880), and Marie Morin's *Annales de l'Hôtel-Dieu de Montréal* (1921); and the Sacred Congregation of Rites (Vatican) publications of *Positio causae*. . . for the beatification and canonization of Bishop Laval, Catherine Tekakwitha, Brébeuf, Lalemant, Daniel, Garmier, Chabanel, Jogues, Goupil, and Lalande which contain a mass of important documents. We are also indebted to several editors and compilers: J.G. Shea has given us P.-F.-X. de Charlevoix's *History and General Description of New France*, 6 vols. (1866–72), Chrestien Le Clercq's *The First Establishment of the Faith in New France*, 2 vols. (1881), and 26 volumes of Jesuit *Relations*; R.G. Thwaites has contributed Louis Hennepin's *A New Discovery of a Vast Country*, 2 vols. (1903), and the monumental *Jesuit Relations and Allied Documents*, 73 vols. (1896–1901).

Other major documentary collections include: L. Campeau, *La première Mission d'Acadie, 1602–1616* (Les Presses de l'Université Laval, Quebec, 1967); Louis de Héricourt, *Les Lois ecclésiastiques de France* (Paris, 1756); Mère Juchereau de Saint-Ignace, *Les Annales de l'Hôtel-Dieu de Québec, 1636-1716* (Quebec, 1939); Dom Guy Oury, *Marie de l'Incarnation (1599-1672): Correspondance* (Solesmes, 1971); E. Réveillaud, *Sixte Le Tac: Histoire chronologique de la Nouvelle-France ou Canada* (Paris, 1888); Henri Têtu & C.-O. Gagnon, *Mandements, lettres pastorales et circulaires des évêques de Québec* (Quebec, 1887), Vols. I, II; C.-F. Baillargeon, *Recueil d'ordonnances synodales et épiscopales du diocèse de Québec* (Quebec, 1859).

Bishop Saint-Vallier's *Catéchisme du diocèse de Québec* (Paris, 1702) was reprinted in Montreal in 1958, but not his *Rituel du diocèse de Québec* (Paris, 1703).

In the area of SECONDARY SOURCES the reader is directed to the following publications relating to religious life and institutions in New France:

Bellanger, G.	*La bonne Sainte Anne au Canada et à Beaupré* (Quebec, 1923)
Bertrand, C.	*Monsieur de la Dauversière* (Montreal, 1947)
Bonneau-Avenant, C.	*La duchesse d'Aiguillon, 1604–1675* (Paris, 1882)

Campbell, T.J.	*Pioneer Priests of North America, 1640–1710* (New York, 1908–1910), 2 vols.
Casgrain, H.-R.	*Les Sulpiciens et les prêtres des Missions Etrangères en Acadie, 1676–1762* (Quebec, 1897)
Chinard, Gilbert	*Les Réfugiés huguenots en Amérique* (Paris, 1925)
Couanier de Launay, E.L.	*Histoire des religieuses hospitalières de Saint-Joseph, France et Canada* (Paris, 1887)
D'Allaire, Micheline	*L'Hôpital-Général de Québec, 1692-1764* Editions fides, Montreal, 1971)
David, Albert	*Les Missionaires du Séminaire du Saint-Esprit à Québec et en Acadie au XVIIIe siècle* (Paris, 1926)
Daveluy, M.-Cl.	*La Société Notre-Dame de Montréal, 1639–1663* (Editions Fides, Montreal, 1965)
Donohoe, T.	*The Iroquois and the Jesuits* (Buffalo, 1895)
Doyle, Sr. I.	*Marguerite Bourgeoys and her Congregation* (Gardenvale, 1940)
Duclos, R.-P.	*Histoire du Protestantisme français au Canada et aux Etats-Unis* (Lausanne, 1913), Vol. I.
Duffin, Mary	*A Heroine of Charity: Venerable Mother d'Youville, Foundress of the Sisters of Charity, Grey Nuns, Montreal, 1701-1777* (New York, 1938)
Eastman, Mack	*Church and State in Early Canada* (Edinburgh, 1915)
Faillon, E.-M.	*Histoire de la colonie française en Canada* (Montreal, 1865–66) 3 vols.
Faillon, E.-M.	*Vie de Mademoiselle Mance et histoire de l'Hôtel-Dieu de Villemarie en Canada* (Paris, 1854), 2 vols.
Faillon, E.-M.	*Vie de Soeur Bourgeoys, Fondatrice de la Congrégation de Notre-Dame de Villemarie* (Montreal, 1953), 2 vols.

Gosselin, Auguste	*L'Eglise du Canada depuis Monseigneur de Laval jusqu'à la Conquête* (Quebec, 1911–1914), 3 vols.
Gosselin, Auguste	*La Mission du Canada avant Mgr. de Laval, 1615–1659* (Evreux, 1909)
Gowans, Alan	*Church Architecture in New France* (University of Toronto Press, Toronto, 1955)
Goyau, Georges	*Une Epopée mystique: Les Origines religieuses du Canada* (Paris, 1934)
Gueudré, M. de Chantal	*Les monastères d'Ursulines sous l'ancien régime, 1612–1788* (Paris, 1960)
Hudon, L.	*Vie de la Mère Catherine de Saint-Augustin* (Paris, 1925)
Janin, Joseph	*La Religion aux colonies françaises sous l'ancien régime* (Paris, 1942)
Jouve, O.-M.	*Les Franciscains et le Canada: l'établissement de la foi, 1615–1629* (Quebec, 1915)
Kennedy, J.H.	*Jesuit and Savage in New France* (New Haven, 1950)
Lévesque, E.	*L'Oeuvre de la Compagnie de Saint-Sulpice dans l'Amérique du Nord* (Paris, 1929)
Moir, John & Grant J.W.	*The Cross in Canada: Vignettes of the Churches across Four Centuries* (Ryerson Press, Toronto 1966)
Moir, John S.	*Church and State in Canada, 1627–1867* (McClelland & Stewart, Toronto, 1968)
Nant, Candide de	*Pages glorieuses de l'épopée canadienne, Une mission capucine en Acadie* (Montreal, 1927)
O'Neill, Charles	*Church and State in French Colonial Louisiana; Policy and Politics to 1732* (Yale University Press, New Haven, 1966)
Palm, Mary B.	*The Jesuit Missions of the Illinois Country, 1673–1763* (Cleveland, 1933)
Plante, H.	*L'Eglise catholique au Canada de 1604 à 1886* (Editions Bien Public, Trois-Rivières, 1970)

Pontbriand, V. de	*Le dernier évêque du régime français, Monseigneur de Pontbriand, 1740–1760* (Paris, 1910)
Porter, Fernand	*L'Instruction catéchistique au Canada, 1663–1873* (Montreal, 1949)
Quinsonas, Comte de	*Une Dauphinois, cinquième évêque de la Nouvelle-France, Monseigneur de Lauberivière (1711–1740)* (Paris, 1936)
Reyss, Paul	*Etude sur quelques points de l'histoire de la tolérance au Canada et aux Antilles* (Geneva, 1907)
Rochemonteix, C. de	*Les Jésuites et la Nouvelle-France au XVIIe siècle* (Paris 1895–96), 3 vols.
Rochemonteix, C. de	*Les Jésuites et la Nouvelle-France au XVIIIe siècle* (Paris 1906), 2 vols.
Rousseau, Pierre	*Saint-Sulpice et les missions catholiques* (Montreal, 1930)
Shae, J.G.	*The Catholic Church in Colonial Days (1521–1763)* (New York, 1886)
Têtu, Henri	*Les Evêques de Québec* (Quebec, 1889)
Trudel, Marcel	*L'Eglise canadienne sous le Régime militaire, 1759–1764* (Les Presses de l'Université Laval, Quebec, 1957), 2 vols.
Walsh, H.H.	*The Church in the French Era: From Colonization to the British Conquest* (Ryerson Press, Toronto, 1967)

INDEX